C000143017

Music making

in the west riding of yorkshire

Edited by Adrian Smith

Foreword by Arthur Butterworth MBE

Published by

R H Wood

51 The Village

Farnley Tyas

Huddersfield

HD4 6UQ

Copyright © R H WOOD, A A SMITH, 2000

ISBN 0-9539885-0-3

Logos, photographs and illustrations in this book are reproduced by kind permission of the contributors concerned and cannot be reproduced in any form without their express permission.

Whilst the publisher has made every effort to give credit for images used in this book, and, when necessary, to trace copyright for reproduction, he apologises in advance for any omissions. Anyone who feels that inadequate acknowledgement has been given should contact the publisher at the above address and he will endeavour to make appropriate amends in any future edition.

Main text typeset in Galliard

Main cover photo courtesy of Bradford Central Library. Insets: Black Dyke Band, York Waits, Worrall Male Voice Choir, Opera North (Photo: DONALD COOPER)

Title page photo: Maurice Sykes and his orchestra at Slaithwaite Carnival (c 1930)

Main Foreword photo by C H WOOD

Cover design by PHIL HANSEN

Designed and typeset by BARBARA ALLEN

Printed by AMADEUS PRESS, Cleckheaton, West Yorkshire

CONTENTS

FOREWORD

by Arthur Butterworth MBE

When Adrian Smith's book, *An Improbable Centenary*, first appeared ten years ago, it outlined the quite remarkable saga of just one amateur musical organisation's long and eventful history. Quite apart from all that it revealed, it established the author (a musician whose influence and enterprise completely turned round the ailing fortunes of the Slaithwaite Philharmonic) as an historian of flair and imagination, able to bring to life what otherwise could have remained dull and prosaic facts.

This new account of music-making, in a part of the country long acknowledged for the vitality of its people in pursuing a wide variety of interests in every kind of musical performance, casts the net even further afield. Over the decades there have been a number of articles and modest accounts about the region's music-making. For the most part, however, these have been limited to the narrow horizons of individual organisations and their role in their communities; what has been lacking is a comprehensive survey of music-making, amateur and professional, in Yorkshire today.

Although a Lancastrian, I have had the good fortune to have lived in Yorkshire and to have been involved in its music-making, at all levels, both professional and amateur, for nearly forty years, so

that it is now possible to view the subject from a long perspective. Like all such surveys, this book salutes continuity but also chronicles change; and it poses the obvious question: have things changed for the better in that time? This is impossible to answer. Some might regret the demise of a kind of music-making they once enjoyed – the indigenous church choirs in every town and village, or the local brass band that played in the park on fine summer afternoons.

Sixty or seventy years ago, there were orchestral concerts, professional and amateur, that were well patronised. Today there are more than in earlier times; but they are – depending on your taste – more sophisticated in the way in which they are presented and particularly in the repertoire offered. Professional performance has been complemented, and technically challenged, by the staggering increase in amateur capability and enterprise, as this book amply demonstrates.

INTRODUCTION

This book sprang from modest beginnings. Like all bright ideas – in this case, the publication of a comprehensive survey of music-making in our native West Riding – its inception stemmed from a naïve belief that the subject did not appear to have been sufficiently explored or documented: only a handful of substantial monographs had been published, and the sole general survey (J Sutcliffe Smith's *A Musical Pilgrimage in Yorkshire*) dated from as long ago as 1928. How right I was – but how enormous the task I had inadvertently taken on – quickly became apparent. The more I explored, the more fascinating the subject became, the more cross-referencing between topics I found, and the more people I met with an in-depth knowledge of their chosen field who were willing to participate.

The book that has emerged contains a rich diversity of articles of varying lengths by a host of well-qualified contributors, each shedding light on or compounding the mystery – just why is music so inherent in the people, the towns and the valleys of the West Riding? And why, more particularly, should the Huddersfield district have been so prodigiously active in this field?

Special thanks must go to Adrian Smith, who bravely took on the task of general editorship. Adrian has also produced by far the greater part of the writing, and from his unique background of historian, musician and writer, has managed to steer a coherent route between all our contributors as well as filling a good many potential gaps himself. I am hugely indebted to him for his input and guidance throughout the project. I must also thank John Hansen for his tireless work as my right-hand man, particularly for his persistence in chasing up contributors, real or imagined.

Only as we neared the end of our task have we realised that because of pressure of time and other factors many worthy subjects have had to be overlooked. We make no mention of music clubs, for instance, of jazz or folk music, with their festivals in Marsden and Holmfirth, nor is there coverage of the many Gilbert and Sullivan societies in the region; and youth choirs and orchestras receive only occasional and passing mention.

The list for possible inclusion in what will inevitably become a second edition grows. We simply invite comment and suggestion to help us make future editions more comprehensive.

RICHARD WOOD

Choral Music

INTRODUCTION

One of the most important features of music-making in Victorian Britain was the rise in the number of choirs, their levels of expertise, and the quantity of music available to widen their repertory. There were many reasons why this upsurge in choral singing happened throughout the country and especially in Yorkshire where choral singing formed – and continues to form, if less prominently – an important part of the cultural and social fabric.

A visit to the nearest large municipal library, particularly in a northern city, is perhaps the best first step in trying to find out more about this musical phenomenon. The building itself (or its predecessor) may well date from the mid-nineteenth century, standing as an enduring monument to the civic pride and zeal for progress, learning and self-improvement that characterised that period. Even small towns had fairly lavishly-endowed library or Mechanics' Institute buildings in conspicuous locations. Today, though a library's music section may be increasingly dominated by CDs and videos, the choral music enthusiast will still find much to interest him, especially if the town has enjoyed a long choral tradition. There will be a section devoted to oratorio, almost certainly including Bach's two great Passion settings, Elgar's *The Dream of Gerontius*, Mendelssohn's *Elijah*, Haydn's *Creation*, and of course the ubiquitous Handel's *Messiah*, perhaps in more than one edition. Nearby, there could well be a section devoted to cantatas; other classifications might point the way to smaller pieces such as anthems and partsongs.

So far, so good. All the items mentioned above are standard works, accessible on radio, CD, in score or at live performances. But further delving is likely to reveal another significant feature of the library's choral collection. Interspersed among the well-known choral works, there will probably be copies of numerous unfamiliar pieces, many by English nineteenth-century composers whose music is almost totally forgotten nowadays. These pieces, of which many hundreds of examples were published in every vocal category, reflect a wealth of choral activity which gave unprecedented commercial opportunities to music publishers and retailers, professional performers and music teachers, particularly in the decades leading up to World War I.

In many libraries, however, what is to be seen on the shelves may represent only a fraction of the full collection. Elsewhere will be stored multiple copies of choral pieces, languishing victims of the 'Oh, nobody wants to borrow/sing/listen to that stuff nowadays' attitude. Some libraries have dealt such music a worse fate – 'de-accessioning', the euphemism favoured in library circles for 'throwing out'. I shall never forget the experience, a few years ago, of witnessing one such exercise. A large municipal library telephoned me to say that the 'de-accessioning' of its music stack was in progress, and that immediate attendance was required if I wished to save anything at all. Arriving by train with one helper I found trolley-loads of choral music being thrown into a skip outside the building. There was far more than we could possibly have saved. and our only recourse, a painfully inadequate one, was simply to grab whatever we could. It was like looting. Given a proper chance, we could have rescued one copy from each set, so that all the music could have been further scrutinised. Indiscriminate clearouts like this are an inestimable hindrance to the pursuit of a balanced view of what nineteenth-century choral music-making was like to the people who took part in it.

What lay behind this growing enthusiasm for choral music in the nineteenth century? Many factors contributed, and it is always difficult to determine cause and effect. One factor was the modest increase in leisure time and disposable income that was being made available to factory workers, so that they had more time to practise and could afford to purchase music or maybe even a musical instrument. Another was the growth of public transport, which facilitated gatherings for musical and other social occasions. As the technology of music printing became more advanced and publishing and sales more efficient, prices fell, meaning that more music could be bought by individuals who consequently became acquainted with a wider repertory. As an adjunct to this, the spread of musical literacy was aided by the sight-singing movement, for which the tonic sol-fa system was devised. The rise of Nonconformism, particularly in the towns and cities of northern England, and of the Sunday School and Temperance movements, resulted in the formation of corporate bodies ideal for the promotion of choirs. These movements also encouraged the participation of women in choral singing (which was seen as a respectable pursuit, unlike opera) – nonconformist chapels in particular had mixed-voice choirs, whereas Anglican churches had traditionally had only male-voice ones, especially if they followed cathedral or Tractarian persuasions and conduct.

Local civic dignitaries and factory-owners were often very keen to promote and support the musical efforts of those they may have perceived as their social inferiors. Broadly speaking, this reflected the spirit of an age in which personal betterment and the assertion of civic pride were important aspirations. Such aspirations were often consciously promoted to prevent dissent and rebellion among workers dissatisfied with their harsh social conditions. Mechanics' Institutes, libraries, town halls, museums and concert halls were built in abundance, as spectacular manifestations of civic and corporate pride. It is perhaps hard today to appreciate the excitement and sense of achievement which they engendered when they were new, or to understand their significance to local communities which in the past had lacked

even a cathedral or castle in which to glory. Chapels, too, as symbols of Nonconformism, began to proliferate. Although many of these buildings are now lost, enough remain to provide a fascinating glimpse of local history in Victorian times, and (in some cases) of the history of choral music in particular.

All these social and cultural strands were reflected in the music festival, an institution which had long been a feature of the life of many cities, including Leeds, York and Sheffield. The opening of St George's Hall in Bradford, for instance, was the occasion in 1853 for the first in what was intended to be a series of triennial festivals (in fact only two more – in 1856 and 1859 – took place). To celebrate the opening, a special choir had been assembled: over three days works performed included the first performance of an unpublished *Credo* by Mendelssohn and his *St Paul*, Handel's *Messiah* and extracts from *Israel in Egypt*, Haydn's *Creation*, Beethoven's *The Mount of Olives* and anthems by Sir Michael Costa (the Festival's conductor). The array of soloists, locally and nationally renowned, included Clara Novello, whose celebrated rendition of the National Anthem was virtually an obligatory feature of any self-respecting music festival.

The demands of festival participation undoubtedly fostered an improvement in the standard of Yorkshire choralists: they became famous nationally and internationally for their musicianship, discipline and strength. Contingents from northern choirs were called upon to participate in the gigantic 'Handel festivals' that took place in the Crystal Palace, London, and on a more modest scale elsewhere. Meanwhile, new civic festivals were being established.

For the inauguration of Leeds Town Hall in 1858, the Yorkshire composer William Sterndale Bennett was commissioned to write a new cantata, *The May Queen*. Queen Victoria performed the opening ceremony, and Bennett himself conducted many of the concerts that followed in the four-day festival. The Queen was regaled by the sound and spectacle of 27,000 charity children singing the National Anthem on Woodhouse Moor: assembling such large numbers must have been a nightmare of organisation but perhaps it was a cheaper option than engaging Clara Novello...

Not to be outdone, Huddersfield promoted a festival in 1881 to inaugurate its recently-built

Town Hall, at last giving its inhabitants a suitable location for large-scale concerts. The Hallé Orchestra was engaged, Charles Hallé conducted the concerts, and an array of distinguished soloists performed in works such as Mendelssohn's *Elijah*, Spohr's *The Last Judgement*, Berlioz's *The Damnation of Faust* and Rossini's *Stabat Mater*. At the end of the festival Hallé commented that the specially assembled choir of 277 voices was the finest he had ever conducted. Despite the enthusiasm generated by the 1881 festival, however, the original idea of a triennial festival was not fulfilled.

Much less well documented than the activities of the large festivals and the major choral societies, but no less significant, were those of a host of small choral societies (in the Huddersfield area, for instance, there were choral societies in Marsden, Slaithwaite, Lindley and Holmfirth), not to mention those of innumerable church and chapel choirs. It was particularly to cater for their aspirations that the competitive festival movement emerged in the last quarter of the century: by 1914, such competitions numbered 75. It is clear that local communities took great pride in their choirs. The following is an account in the then principal national musical monthly periodical, *The Musical Times*, of June 1896, concerning the triumph of a Saltaire choir at the Morecambe Festival:

A Choral Competition took place at Morecambe on April 25, and the singers of the Wesleyan Chapel, Saltaire, took part. It is a local usage, under such circumstances, for the population to await the return of their champions, and to rejoice in their victory or lament their defeat. The custom was observed at Saltaire, some hundreds of persons gathering at the railway station, passing the time of waiting by singing glees and anthems, or discussing the chances of the fight waged in the town by the sea. At 1 30 am the belated train arrived, bringing news of victory, and, says a report, 'despite the fact that rain had commenced to fall, time-honoured custom demanded a short concert "on the bridge". Here the vigorous songsters took their stand, and, somewhat sleepy and travel-weary, sang Pinsuti's emotional part-song, *The sea hath its pearls*, and, considering the state of the weather, expected that this would suffice. But no! The audience would hear all, and *Great God of love* (Pearsall) was sung splendidly – without copies, and under

the umbrella's canopy, for now rain was coming down in torrents. Enthusiasm being somewhat quenched and curiosity satisfied, singers and audiences dispersed, and the little town resumed its normal respectability of demeanour.

The Huddersfield Choral Society

Nº 297. GLORIA *From the "Twelfth Mass"* .. .. .. " MOZART 3ᵈ

WOOD'S COLLECTION
OF
GLEES, ANTHEMS, TUNES, PART SONGS & C.

Nº 263.	O TELL ME HOW TO WOO THEE	A. T. T. B.	A. PEARSON	3ᵈ
Nº 264.	NEARER MY GOD TO THEE	*Anthem*	A. BERRIDGE	3ᵈ
Nº 265.	HEAR THOU IN HEAVEN	*Anthem*	F. COOPE	3ᵈ
Nº 266.	BRIGHT AND JOYFUL	*Anthem*	J. B. BIRKBECK	3ᵈ
Nº 267.	HARK ! THE ROBIN	*Carol for A. T. T. B.*	J. H. PEARSON	2ᵈ
Nº 268.	BLESS THE LORD	*Anthem*	F. ROEBUCK	4ᵈ
Nº 269.	WELCOME, WELCOME	*Glee A. T. T. B.*	J. YARWOOD	3ᵈ
Nº 270.	OF A' THE AIRTS	*Glee A. T. T. B.*	W. SHORE	1½ᵈ
Nº 271.	IN THAT DAY	*Anthem*	F. MARSHALL WARD	3ᵈ
Nº 272.	PHILLIS THE FAIR	*Part Song S. A. T. B.*	F. COOPE	2ᵈ
Nº 273.	GOD IS LOVE	*Chorus*	A. PEARSON	1½ᵈ
Nº 274.	THE SKYLARK	*Part Song S. A. T. B*	HENRY KNIGHT	2ᵈ
Nº 275.	A JOLLY FULL BOTTLE	*Glee A. T. B.*	arr. by H. STATHER	2ᵈ
Nº 276.	PIE-OUS JOHNNY HORNER	*Humorous Part Song S. A. T. B.*	F. COOPE	3ᵈ
Nº 277.	PRAISE THE LORD	*Anthem*	F. COOPE	3ᵈ
Nº 278.	MY OLD WIFE	*Song and Chorus* adapted by J. E. IBESON		3ᵈ
Nº 279.	THE ARROW AND THE SONG	*Part Song T. A. T. B.*	F. W. SYKES	2ᵈ
Nº 280.	ALL THY WORKS PRAISE THEE	*Anthem*	I. DEARNALEY	3ᵈ
Nº 281.	OLWEN DEAREST	*Part Song (A) or T.T.B.B.*	J. HENRY	2ᵈ
Nº 282.	HAIL SMILING MORN	*Glee T. A. T. B.*	SPOFFORTH	1½ᵈ
Nº 283.	ABIDE WITH ME	*Hymn Anthem*	SHELLEY	2ᵈ
Nº 284.	THE LORD IS RIGHTEOUS	*Anthem*	F MARSHALL WARD	2ᵈ
Nº 285.	GO BEAR THE JOYFUL TIDINGS	*Choral March*	H. STATHER	4ᵈ
Nº 286.	O LORD MY GOD	*(Solomon's Prayer) Men's Voices*	ROLAND ROGERS	2ᵈ
Nº 287.	O GIVE THANKS	*Anthem*	HENRI LAMARQUÉ	3ᵈ
Nº 288.	GREAT AND MARVELLOUS	*Anthem*	F. MARSHALL WARD	3ᵈ
Nº 289.	ALL THE YEAR IS CROWNED	*Anthem*	A. BERRIDGE	3ᵈ
Nº 290.	COME, LET US JOIN	*Anthem*	F. COOPE	3ᵈ
Nº 291.	THE LORD IS MY STRENGTH	*Anthem*	W. PATTEN	3ᵈ
Nº 292.	THOU'RT PASSING HENCE	*Sacred Part Song S. A. T. B.*	H. STATHER	3ᵈ
Nº 293.	HEAR MY PRAYER	*Soprano Solo and Chorus*	MENDELSSOHN	6ᵈ
Nº 294.	JESU, MY LORD	*Anthem*	EDGAR HADDOCK	3ᵈ
Nº 295.	I WILL GIVE THANKS	*Anthem*	F. MARSHALL WARD	4ᵈ
Nº 296.	SIX RESPONSES TO THE COMMANDMENTS		FREDERIC JAMES	2ᵈ
Nº 297.	GLORIA *From the "Twelfth Mass"*		MOZART	3ᵈ
Nº 298.	AND THE GLORY OF THE LORD	*Chorus*	HANDEL	1ᵈ
Nº 299.	ROCK OF AGES	*Soprano Solo and Chorus*	DUDLEY BUCK	1ᵈ
Nº 300.	LORD OF OUR LIFE	*Hymn-Anthem*	E. G. BINGHAM	2ᵈ
Nº 301.	SING UNTO GOD	*Anthem*	W. PATTEN	3ᵈ
Nº 302.	THE EARTH IS THE LORD'S	*Anthem*	F. ROEBUCK	4ᵈ

67, New Street, HUDDERSFIELD. J. WOOD & SONS LIMITED 9, New Ivegate, BRADFORD

All this musical activity raises a further question: what did choirs, large and small, actually sing – and who provided the music? This is the point at which a visit to a library stack may well prove its worth, because there are likely to be found the richly varied items that filled out the choral societies' repertory. Although much of this material is not what a music historian might regard as important, it nevertheless offers a glimpse of what nineteenth-century choral singers routinely experienced, in addition to the 'landmark' works by Handel, Haydn and Mendelssohn.

As far as availability of music was concerned, probably the most significant event was the instigation by the publishing house of Novello in London of its inexpensive series of choral works in 1847. Although at first only oratorios and other large-scale composite pieces were issued, the list of publications diversified and grew rapidly. This was both a reflection of, and stimulus to, demand. Even so, the pre-eminence of Novello can be exaggerated. Throughout the nineteenth century there were numerous other music publishers in London and elsewhere. Some were highly specialised; others acted as benefactors, promoting concerts, supplying pianos for use in them, and engaging professional performers to raise the profile of their publications. Developments in printing technology, such as the use of offset lithography, led to greater efficiency and economy of production, and in the 1860s the duty on paper and printing was abolished. It is hardly surprising that music publishers did well.

But commercial success was not the only favourable result. From evidence such as multiple arrangements, for instance (for what ensemble or individual instrument was Sullivan's *The Lost Chord* not arranged?), it is clear that the music often meant a great deal to singers and their listeners. The market for choral music was avid but not indiscriminate. Targeting the same markets, provincial publishers, often using material by composers not nationally known, evidently filled gaps left by the larger London firms. These firms came and went: some still survive, though only Banks of York is still a music publisher. Past lists of choral music are otherwise difficult to find – the catalogues of the firm of John Blackburn in Leeds (once a substantial publisher of choral music), for instance, no longer exist. Some are to be found, however, in *The Catalogue of Printed Music in the British Library to 1980*, one being the choral music collection published by Joseph Wood & Sons of Huddersfield and Bradford. Founded in 1850, the firm published a series of nearly two hundred mostly small-scale choral pieces, nearly all for mixed voices, between about 1880 and about 1914. This publishing operation ceased rather than being taken over by another firm, but the music business itself continues to operate, chiefly in Bradford, in music retail, organ-building and early music.

The Wood collection has several remarkable features, judging from some trends in other companies' outputs. It did not use ornate covers, nor did it subsist on royalty ballads. It had a large list, it survived for several decades, and it was not swamped by Novello. Nor did it cater only for Yorkshire tastes, although there were choral arrangements of tunes with Yorkshire associations, such as *On Ilkla' Moor baht 'At*, the tune Old Foster (as distinct from the most usual tune Winchester Old) commonly sung to *While Shepherds Watched their Flocks by Night*, and *Pratty Flowers*, the so-called 'Holmfirth anthem'. There were pieces by composers with Yorkshire connections, for example *Sweet and Low* by Joseph Barnby, and *God is a Spirit* from *The Woman of Samaria*, an oratorio by William Sterndale Bennett. Several other composers, prominent in Yorkshire musical life but not famous nationally, were connected with the Huddersfield Choral Society: they included Joseph Edgar Ibeson, its accompanist and deputy conductor between 1884 and 1915, and earlier conductors John North and James Battye.

The music covered a wide range of vocal genres, both sacred and secular. Some include dedications, such as the following at the head of a grandiose but fairly easy anthem for organ and mixed voices: *Prepare Ye the Way of the Lord* Anthem composed for the Centenary Celebration (January 1895) of Lockwood Baptist Chapel. H[erbert] Stather.

Herbert Stather, an industrious and accomplished composer, seems not to have been part of the Huddersfield Choral Society circle, although he may have run his own small publishing company near Huddersfield. Another, more picturesque, example of Stather's work in the Wood collection is the following piece for mixed choir and piano, dating from 1902: *The Battle of the Baltic*. Words by Thomas Campbell. Choral Ballad. Dedicated to the Members of the Huddersfield Co-operative Prize Choir and their esteemed conductor D W Evans Esq.

This dedication suggests that the choir enjoyed

high local prestige. The music, although entirely forgotten now, was clearly important to those who, in 1902, performed and listened to it.

In terms of musical style, there are pieces in the Wood collection considered repugnantly sentimental by post-Victorian generations, but the styles were in fact highly varied. There are also some striking absences – few pieces with tonic sol-fa notation, and few composite works such as cantatas. There is nothing in the collection by Sir Walter Parratt, one of Huddersfield's most famous native musicians, and nothing showing the influence of the burgeoning 'English renaissance' movement led by Vaughan Williams.

DR JUDITH BLEZZARD
(Senior Lecturer in Music at
the University of Liverpool)

Footnote: 1900 and beyond

By the start of the 20th century, choral singing had reached its zenith and nowhere more so than in Yorkshire, where the achievements of the Victorian era were sustained and indeed personified by the towering figure of Sir Henry Coward, especially in Sheffield, Leeds and Huddersfield. Two World Wars, however, and the seismic shifts in the century's social, political, cultural and above all technological evolution, proceeded to change many aspects of life almost beyond recognition. How did choral music fare?

The answer must be, 'Better than might have been expected'. One reason for the late nineteenth century explosion in music-making as a leisure activity was that there were relatively few com-

peting alternatives. As the twentieth century progressed, however, most sections of society came to have more leisure time, and compelling attractions multiplied with dizzying speed.. The cinema, the wireless, gramophone records, television and, most recently, computer-related activities – these and other developments have profoundly affected the way we spend our leisure time.

As for music itself, many, probably the majority, have come to look no further than the world of pop and rock. With the decline of organised religion a good church choir – once the seedbed for the great choral societies – is now very much the exception rather than the rule (though the Anglican cathedral tradition remains as vibrant as ever). Those great choral binges – the triennial festivals – have gone.

These – and other – factors have posed a considerable threat to choral societies which on the whole they have managed to withstand. True, most smaller choral societies have disappeared and a large choral society once numbering 300 voices must settle for half that number today (and often be hard-pressed to find enough male voices, especially tenors).

Nevertheless, all the big Yorkshire choral societies continue to flourish; and their repertoire has been much enriched by a steady infusion of twentieth century masterpieces by English composers – Elgar's *The Dream of Gerontius*, Vaughan Williams' *A Sea Symphony*, Walton's *Belshazzar's Feast*, Britten's *War Requiem* and Tippett's *A Child of Our Time* are those which immediately spring to mind. *Messiah* still rules, and *Elijah* is back in favour, while Orff's *Carmina Burana* has achieved cult status.

To concentrate on choral societies, however, is to distort the picture, for in many other forms, choral music has actually expanded both in range and quality. Yorkshire is still a bastion of male voice choirs (three of today's leaders in this field come from the Huddersfield district alone); and the last quarter of the 20th century has seen the arrival of many newcomers to the choral field – ladies' choirs, chamber choirs, youth choirs, 'early music' choirs. Nor must the thriving amateur operatic societies be overlooked (again in Huddersfield and district alone, a dozen or so such societies exist).

In short, at the start of the 21st century, the choral scene shows no sign of diminishing vitality, or, for that matter, audience appeal.

ADRIAN SMITH

Bradford Festival Choral Society

In 1849 Mr Samuel Smith (later to become Mayor of Bradford) proposed that the city's lack of a suitable concert hall should be addressed. A private company was set up to remedy this, and in 1853 the opening of the new St George's Hall (with a seating capacity then well in excess of 2,000) was celebrated with a three-day music festival.

Although choral bodies already existed in the city – the Bradford Musical Friendly Society, for instance, founded in 1821, and in 1867 renamed the Bradford Old Choral Society, was destined to remain active until 1980 – a new chorus of 220 voices drawn from many parts of the West Riding was formed specifically for the occasion. For a second festival in 1856, this chorus was reassembled; afterwards it was decided that the chorus should be placed on a permanent footing.

Such were the origins of the Bradford Festival Choral Society. Many of the members travelled considerable distances for the rehearsals and if they arrived before 7 30 pm, they were to be given a

cup of coffee and a bun (otherwise the members would visit local pubs 'where they stayed too long'): the Society was accordingly nicknamed 'the coffee and bun society'. This practice continued for many years, but became a serious drain on finances and was abandoned in 1875.

Another – to us curious – feature of the early society was that it had two classes of members: those 'competent to sustain their part in choruses of moderate difficulty' paid an annual subscription of 1/-; but those 'not so far advanced' had to pay 1/- a quarter. (How, one wonders, was the dividing line determined?). A further sharp contrast with today's situation – no more tenors and basses could be accepted, but there was a scarcity of sopranos.

Under William Jackson (then recognised as one of the county's foremost choral conductors), the new society gave a performance of *Messiah* in December, 1856, and in May 1857 a 'miscellaneous' programme (part-songs interspersed with well-known choruses from operas and oratorios

Chorus at St George's Hall, 1953. Photo YORKSHIRE POST

and vocal solos) of the type greatly favoured in Victorian times (and favoured even today, though not by choral societies!). Within two years the BFCS had already gained the ultimate accolade – that of being summoned to Buckingham Palace to sing for Queen Victoria. Another notable occasion in the early days was a concert given in 1861 when Jenny Lind, who was on one of her many 'farewell' tours, appeared as soloist. The critic of the *Bradford Observer* suggested that she was long past her best and that her retirement was clearly a necessity:

'...May happiness and domestic comfort now be her lot.' In 1865 'Charles Hallé's Band' began what has proved to be the Hallé Orchestra's long and fruitful association with both Bradford and the BFCS. In 1870 a concert to celebrate the centenary of the birth of Beethoven included a performance of the *Missa Solemnis*. Arthur Sullivan came to conduct his *The Light of the World* in 1875 – the first of many prominent English composers to conduct their own works with the chorus, including Stanford, Parry, Elgar and Edward German.

William Jackson had remained conductor until his death in 1866. This remarkable man was widely loved and respected – not least because as a musician he was almost entirely self-made (he was originally a cornmiller by trade). Among the mourners at his funeral was a Mr Wilson, his first piano teacher, then a very old man, who walked all the way from Pateley Bridge to Bradford for the occasion. Jackson's more immediate successors included Robert Burton (1878-1887), by all accounts a gifted but difficult man who at one time or another conducted – and fell out with – most of

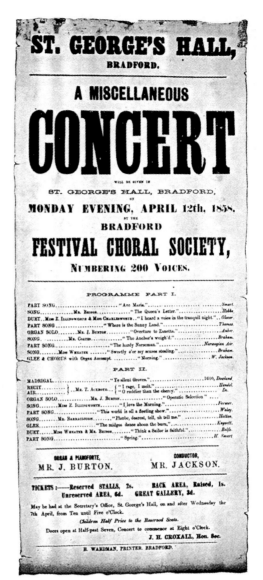

the great choral societies in the West Riding.

It was under Sir Frederick Cowen (conductor, 1897-1918) that the Chorus firmly established itself as one of the leading choral societies in the land, despite recurring financial difficulties (the 1899 AGM, for instance, was told that 'the Society cannot afford to go on losing £40.00 a year'. If expenses were reduced, that 'would lower the tone and character of the concerts'. The members were also informed that the subscriptions levied by other societies were considerably higher than theirs). In 1904 Elgar's *The Dream of Gerontius* was heard in Bradford for the first time. The 1906 Golden Jubilee was marked by an invitation from the Royal Philharmonic Society to join the 'Philharmonic' Orchestra in a performance of Beethoven's Choral Symphony in the Queen's Hall, London. (A special train was chartered for the occasion: carrying 323 passengers, who were served with breakfast on the outward journey, and supper on the journey home, it was probably the longest train – 'vestibuled from end to end' and over 250 yards in extent – ever to run out of Bradford).

Cowen was to be followed as conductor by Sir Edward Bairstow (1918-25) and Sir Malcolm Sargent (1925-51). After Maurice Miles' brief two-year spell (1951-53) no permanent conductor was appointed until Sir David Willcocks, who held the post from 1957-1974 (at his last concert he was praised for 'getting results by friendship'; he was to return in 1999 to conduct *Messiah* on the occasion of his 80th birthday). From 1974 to 1978 Sir Charles Groves directed the choir (a performance of *Bach's Mass* in B Minor was hailed as being 'on the side of the angels – one of the most gripping readings ever given').

Later conductors – Richard Hickox (1978-89), David Lloyd Jones (1989-97) and, since 1997, Brian Kay – have continued to sustain both the quality and variety of the choir's achievements. None of these achievements would have been possible, of course, without the dedication of members and officials. Of many chorusmasters in this period, particular mention must be made of the greatly-respected George Stead (1948-69).

From its earliest days, the Society, while not neglecting the standard choral classics (by 1956 it had clocked up no fewer than 101 performances of *Messiah*) has always promoted the new music of the day. In 1889, for instance, it performed Parry's *Judith*, a work then highly thought of, but now totally forgotten; on the other hand, his *Blest Pair of Sirens*, which he conducted for the Society in 1895, is still regularly performed. In recent years the BFCS has pursued a pioneering repertoire. In 1953 it gave the first performance in England (other than via BBC studio broadcasts) of Janacek's *Glagolitic Mass*; in 1964, the first northern performance of Britten's *War Requiem* (the soloists were Heather Harper, Gerald English and John Shirley Quirk: the performance was hailed as 'a triumph'). Other notable landmark performances have included Bloch's *Sacred Service* (1962), Bliss's *The Beatitudes* (1962), Tippett's *A Child of Our Time* (1975) and William Matthias's *This World's Joie* (1978).

Two other occasions were of special significance. One was the Delius Festival, held in 1962 to commemorate the centenary of Bradford's most famous musical son, at which the choir sang his *Appalachia*, *Songs of Sunset* and *Songs of Farewell*. The other occurred in May, 1965, when the 100th anniversary of the Bradford Subscription Concerts (initiated by the Halle Orchestra in 1865) was marked by a wonderful performance of Verdi's *Requiem* conducted by Sir John Barbirolli (by a strange coincidence, the present writer was there, and has particular memories of the concert).

Indeed, as one studies the list of works performed in the first 100 years and add to it the complete collection of programmes kept by Enid McKelvie since 1948, it is clear that there is virtually no major work in the choral repertoire that has

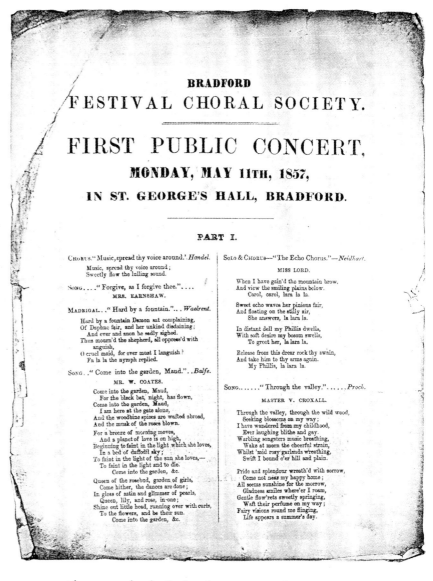

not been sung by the Society (on a cursory glance, Bruckner, Monteverdi's *Vespers* and Franz Schmidt's *The Book with Seven Seals* are notable absentees). There are obvious favourites (and not only *Messiah*): more interesting, perhaps, is the large number of works whose first performance by the Society appears also to have been their last! What would we make of Macfarren's *John the Baptist*, Cowen's *The Veil* or Romberg's *Transient and the Eternal* – to name just three such works – were they to be exhumed?

As befits a chorus of its stature, the finest soloists in the land have always been engaged and it has been accompanied by the best orchestras in the north: though such a policy has at times posed financial problems, it is one to which the Society resolutely adheres. On a more 'popular' front it has enjoyed a long association with the Black Dyke Mills Band – the joint Carol Concerts which they present are always a highlight of the Christmas season. The first of these was held in 1961 and the collaboration later led to three commercial recordings being issued in 1968 and 1970.

In 1956, when the BFCS celebrated its centenary, Percy Holt, its then President, wrote:

'The Society has gone through hard times in the past, nor is it easy today to finance our concerts. But come what may we shall in the years that follow continue to sing – because we have a pride of achievement in doing something ourselves and because, like our forebears of 100 years ago, we love to make music'.

Almost 50 years later, problems notwithstanding (in recent years, the Bradford concert-going public has become somewhat fickle in its ways), that resolve remains unshaken.

Halifax Choral Society

The founder of the Halifax Choral Society was William Priestley, born in 1779. He was an eminent musician and literary gentleman who at his Lightcliffe home in 1817 held a momentous dinner party at which the broad idea of the Halifax Choral Society was born. Rehearsals started soon afterwards leading to the first concert in 1818 at which Haydn's *Creation* was performed. Thus the Halifax Choral Society having been born in 1817 becomes reputedly the oldest Choral Society in the country, some say the world.

William Priestley was also responsible for the provision of the hand-written scores, some of which exist today in his own handwriting, in the Society's archive. The first conductor of the Choral Society was a Mr Joseph Bottomley. Some of the founders and earlier members of the Society are recorded as Messrs Emmott and Turney, and amongst others were Mr Daniel Sugden, Mr William Greenwood and none other than Miss Susan Sykes who was later to become Mrs Sunderland, Yorkshire's 'Queen of Song'.

The Society's records plot the progress of its development over the next century and a half, noting the efforts the Society made to contribute to the musical life of Halifax. It raised funds for the new Victoria Hall and was very much in evidence at its opening in 1901. The choir membership at this time is recorded as being 228 including 40 tenors and 46 basses. Music costing around 1/6d per copy was hired from no fewer than 13 hire companies which certainly kept the librarian busy.

The Society elected to keep going through the two world wars, both to keep spirits up and to raise funds for wartime causes. Many well-known soloists appeared during these years: Heddle Nash, Webster Booth and Isobel Baillie sang for the Society on many occasions between the years 1928 and 1948, and commanded sizeable fees.

In 1948 Dr Melville Cook, Organist of Leeds Parish Church, succeeded Shackleton Pollard as conductor and the perilously low level of the society's funding led him to give piano recitals and lectures to supplement its income. Dr Cook left to become organist of Hereford Cathedral in 1956 but not without leaving his mark. He had set high standards and taught the society a great deal. The poor state of the Society's finances and low choir numbers remained nevertheless two serious problems, and by 1958 there weren't enough tenors

and basses to do justice to the annual performance of *Messiah*. The Society was reduced to advertising for members both in the press and amongst local churches.

The choir took a turn for the better following the appointment of Dr Donald Hunt, again organist from Leeds Parish Church. The Society's first performance with the Royal Liverpool Philharmonic Orchestra was on Boxing Day 1958 in a televised broadcast. Herbert Howells conducted the choir in his own work *Hymnus Paradisi*, an extremely challenging piece. These were busy times for the choir; the names of the soloists make impressive reading, including Owen Brannigan, Peter Pears, Norma Procter, Ada Alsop and Dame Janet Baker.

The next few years leading up to the Society's 150th birthday were momentous ones. Isobel Baillie and Owen Brannigan assisted in the cele-

John Pryce-Jones and the Halifax Choral Society

brations and the Earl & Countess of Harewood became the Society's Patrons. The choir numbers swelled to over 200 and the funds regained some strength.

In 1988 Dr Hunt's chosen work for his final concert with the Society was *The Dream of Gerontius* and the soloists were Dame Janet Baker, Robert Tear and Brian Rayner Cook who, with the Royal Liverpool Philharmonic Orchestra, contributed to a marvellous farewell concert. Donald Hunt had been with the Society for 30 years. At the same concert, the Society also said goodbye to Simon Lindley who had been its chorusmaster for some time.

John Pryce-Jones was appointed musical director in 1988. His enthusiasm and concentration on vocal techniques have contributed to improving standards which inevitably have led to increased audience figures and important engagements. The choir appeared at the Bridgewater Hall in Manchester in 1998 and at the Royal Albert Hall for a 'Best of the Last Night of the Proms' in March 2000.

The choir now performs with the best professional orchestras and with major soloists from the UK and abroad and joins with other choirs and brass bands to perform large-scale works. It has several recordings to its credit. The Victoria Theatre, Halifax, remains its ancestral home.

Holmfirth Choral Society

The town of Holmfirth has become widely known in recent years because of its association with the TV show *Last of the Summer Wine*. It has however been a centre of local performance arts for many years.

There has been a long line of brass bands within a five mile radius of its centre; it has had more than one active amateur dramatic society, and at least one amateur operatic society. But possibly the longest-running tradition is that of choral singing. Currently in addition to its school-based choirs and church/chapel choirs, there are two mixed groups – the Holme Valley Singers and the Holmfirth Choral Society. There are also male voice and ladies' choirs, and, in nearby Honley, a Gilbert and Sullivan Society.

There has been a Choral Society in Holmfirth for at least 150 years, although the present group is not descended from that of the mid-nineteenth century. One reads in the *Huddersfield Chronicle,*

Holmfirth Parish Church

for instance, that 'in December 1857, the Holmfirth Choral Society gave its fourth quarterly concert at the (Holmfirth) Town Hall – a selection from *Judas Maccabaeus*. Conducted by Mr J Perkin, it was the best that had taken place.' There are other reports from that period which indicate a choir active in oratorio performance, with 'band' (orchestral) accompaniment. Also in 1857, the society performed Handel's *Joshua* and *Messiah* (Handel was apparently no less popular then than now!), all conducted by J Perkin.

One report (*Huddersfield Chronicle,* 10 January 1857) mentions a 70-strong choir, Miss Oldfield who sang *If God be for us*, and instruments which included strings and flutes, cornet-à-piston and ophicleide. Huddersfield Library currently holds a number of orchestral sets of the common oratorios, many of which were donated to the library by local societies including Holmfirth Choral Society, on disbanding. It is interesting that some of these include cornet parts which were not written by the composer, but were published as transposed trumpet parts for the more common cornet.

The conductor mentioned above – Joe Perkin – is still remembered locally as the composer of the Holmfirth Anthem *Pratty Flowers*. This consists of three verses written at the time of the Spanish Armada which Perkin set to the music of 'An Ancient Ballad' around 1857. It has been passed down, with reharmonisations, and is still in print (Wood's Collection no 10) and is performed regularly by various local organisations including the current Holmfirth Choral Society. Indeed the

Society's logo includes its first six notes. (The present writer has in his collection four different printed versions of *Pratty Flowers* – that from the original plates, published by Eli Collins, Holmfirth; a version arranged and published by Joshua Marshall; a version published by Beal, Stuttard & Co Ltd of London, plus that published by J Wood & Sons Ltd). There is yet another connection of this music with Holmfirth Choral Society, because it was respectfully dedicated to C S Floyd, of Sands House, Holmfirth, who inter alia was the president of the old Holmfirth Choral Society in 1857.

During the 1880s, the society's conductor was Mr J North (also the then conductor of both Huddersfield Choral Society and Huddersfield Glee & Madrigal Society). The *Chronicle* of March 16th 1894 reports a performance of Mendelssohn's *St Paul* with J E Ibeson as chorusmaster. This performance was apparently curtailed by omitting three or four numbers because of its length.

Concert programmes from the early part of the twentieth century refer to the Holmfirth District Choral Society, but the present writer knows little about whether or not it evolved from the older group. It was conducted by Arthur Pearson (also Huddersfield Borough Organist, organist of St Paul's Huddersfield and conductor of Skipton Choral Society), and its accompanist was Edred Booth.

Between 1906 and 1913, this choir of around 80 singers performed Handel's *Jephtha*, Prout's *Hereward*, Sullivan's *Martyr of Antioch*, Mendelssohn's *Hymn of Praise*, and other works. The society had its own orchestra of over 30 players. Concerts were given in the Drill Hall, Holmfirth, but also, as in December 1910, in Huddersfield Town Hall (a Huddersfield Corporation concert) where it gave the first Huddersfield performance of Stanford's Irish ballad *Phaudrig Crohoore*.

Some years after this period, Edred Booth became the conductor, and Albert Heeley (organist at Holmfirth Parish Church) the accompanist. In the 1928/29 season, the programme included Bizet's *Carmen*. During the next few years, however, support diminished, finances reached crisis level, and the society disbanded.

The current Holmfirth Choral Society was formed as a result of the efforts of local singers to raise fuds for the relief of many people who suffered loss in a severe flood of the Holme Valley on May 29th 1944, when the Bilberry Reservoir overflowed, sending water down the valley, washing away roads and damaging mills, houses and shops.

The Holmfirth Parish Church choir, augmented by members of other choirs in the district, gave a performance of Haydn's *Creation*. Arthur Coates conducted, with Albert Heeley at the organ. It was a success, and was followed by a performance of *Messiah*, then *Elijah*. During the rehearsals for *Elijah*, a decision was taken to give permanency to the choir, and the named Holmfirth Parish Church Choral Society was born.

This first performance of *Elijah* was interesting in that the entire oratorio was presented – a long programme, so it was split into two parts at 2 30 pm and 6 30 pm. Following this performance, Albert Heeley moved to Scotland (where eventually he achieved a cathedral appointment), and Derick Lockwood became accompanist. The society was renamed Holmfirth Choral Society in 1948, when the work presented was Wallace's *Maritana*.

Arthur Coates remained conductor until 1968, Derick Lockwood accompanist until 1981. The society has had three further conductors – William Booth, Kenneth Glaves, and since 1981, Kenneth Rothery. Two further accompanists have been Frank Wardle, and since 1986, Geoffrey Lockwood.

The society continues enthusiastically today. Over the years, its size has fluctuated; the tenor section in particular has often been undersubscribed. Currently there are just under 100 singers, performing a mix of oratorio, masses, operatic concert versions, miscellaneous short items, and, of course, an annual *Messiah*. Many concerts over the years have been orchestrally accompanied, using local amateur players (the Semneth Orchestra; the Tom Holroyd Orchestra and other ad hoc groups), and more recently the Valley Sinfonia – a group of semi-professional players formed originally to accompany the society, but who now operate also as an independent orchestra.

The Huddersfield Choral Society

The Huddersfield Choral Society was born just before Queen Victoria came to the throne, and over thirty years before the town became a municipal borough. Ever since, the Society has been performing concerts for its subscribers on a regular basis and, increasingly as time has passed, for the general public. Nowadays, the first of the season's three subscribers' concerts is held in the late autumn, the second just before Christmas and the third in the spring of the following year. Both before and after 1881, when the Town Hall was opened and became the Society's concert venue, the second concert has been devoted to Handel's *Messiah* – indeed it is highly likely, though by no means certain, that this work has been performed in full or in part at least once each season since the Society's foundation in 1836.

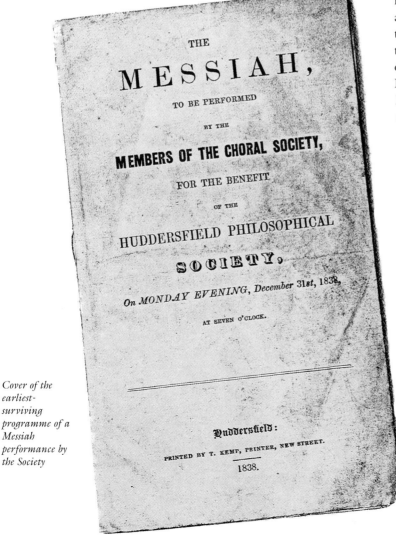

Cover of the earliest-surviving programme of a Messiah performance by the Society

These *Messiah* performances, for which the Society is justly famed, have perhaps overshadowed its equal mastery of many another great musical work. Nevertheless, this is the work that members of the general public have for many years an opportunity of hearing within a day or two of the subscribers' concert each Christmas. At one time tickets for this public concert were to be had on a 'first come, first served' basis at the Town Hall: such was the demand that people were known to queue all night and in all weathers to be sure of obtaining tickets, which were not restricted to a fixed number per applicant. Nowadays, applications are made in advance, and tickets are allocated by ballot – a much fairer system.

Another long-observed tradition is the communal singing of *Christians Awake* – the Christmas Hymn – before both *Messiah* concerts. The assembled company invariably appears thoroughly to enjoy the experience, although it must be said that each new conductor of the choir has had, or so it would seem, to accustom himself, or herself, to this practice which is fulfilled, apparently, with differing degrees of enthusiasm – or, perhaps, of distaste. When Malcolm Sargent began conducting the choir in 1932 it is reported that he refused to conduct 'that jingle' and gave the job to his chorusmaster, Herbert Bardgett: from the Society's point of view, there was clearly no question of abandoning the hallowed tradition! (Sargent, incidentally, was the first of the choir's conductors to delegate the task of rehearsing the choir to a chorusmaster, who was , however, also allowed to conduct the 'public' *Messiah* concert: there is surely no better 'sweetener' than this for a chorusmaster – provided it also comes with an acceptable fee! Wyn Morris, Sargent's short-lived successor, reverted to former practice by taking all the rehearsals himself, but after his departure in 1972 the post of chorusmaster was restored.

After Sargent's death in 1967 the Society introduced another 'public' Christmas concert – consisting of miscellaneous Christmas pieces for which a brass band has frequently either been engaged by the Society or else acted as hosts to it. Often too, on these occasions, the choir's chorusmaster has acted as presenter, a role which has been taken with particular success by Brian Kay both before and after his time as the Society's chorusmaster during the 1980s. His position as a music programme-presenter with the BBC has proved particularly appropriate when the Christmas concert has been recorded for broadcast on radio, as it was most recently in December 1999. (Here, however, it was disappointing to discover that some of his wittiest verbal contributions to the proceedings from the rostrum were not included in the broadcast version of the concert).

Of course the Society does much more than perform three concerts for subscribers each season and a couple of public concerts in Huddersfield at Christmas. Nowadays it may be involved in up to a dozen or so major engagements in any one season, having, moreover, had to turn down other invitations either because of previous commitment or because of the need to limit the work-load of what is after all, one must not forget, an amateur society. There may be one or more additional public concerts in Huddersfield, concerts in London or in other major cities either at home or abroad, recording sessions, either commercial or else for future broadcasting on radio or television, live television appearances – and all these in addition to other less prestigious engagements of a more parochial nature.

The story of how the Society has come to enjoy its present leading position in the world of choral music, from somewhat humble beginnings,

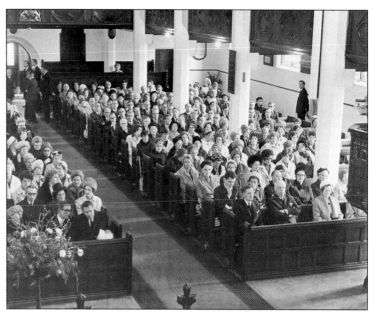

is part of the story of English choral music in particular and of English social history in general. The reason for the Huddersfield choir's rise to such pre-eminence among amateur choral societies, must, like that behind all success stories, be seen as a mixture of the blessings of natural endowment, happy circumstance and good fortune – of nature and of nurture – blessings much evident in Huddersfield from an early date.

BELOW Sir Malcolm Sargent and ABOVE the congregation assembled in Huddersfield Parish Church for Sir Malcolm's memorial service, 14 October, 1967. Photo THE HUDDERSFIELD DAILY EXAMINER.

FAR LEFT Herbert Bardgett

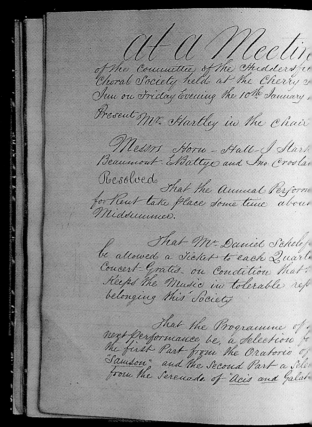

The beginnings were humble enough, but the initial material was not without natural endowment. Sixteen men meeting in a Huddersfield pub – The Plough in Westgate – began it all in June, 1836. For a body which has spent a considerable amount of time and effort since then in performing sacred music, a pub might appear as an unsuitable choice of birthplace. Public houses were, however, frequently used as meeting places in those days. Indeed, the original Committee of Management of the Society regularly held its meetings in public houses of which Huddersfield, perhaps, had then more than its fair share. The Cherry Tree, also in Westgate, was a favourite for several years for such meetings and Thomas Hartley, one of the original sixteen founder-members was himself, aside from being a local singer, the landlord of the Woolpack Inn in Buxton Road. The

ABOVE *James Battye.* CENTRE *entries in the earliest-surviving minute book of the Society's Management Committee, of meetings.* BELOW *Mrs Sunderland*

Society's inaugural rules decreed that each rehearsal should be held in the early days 'on the Friday on or before the full moon in every month', and that each member was entitled to be provided with 'three gills of ale together with bread and cheese'. All sixteen of the founder-members had, as far as one can tell, some claim to musicianship. The number included a church organist who was elected the Society's first conductor, a parish clerk who became its second conductor and who was a prize-winning composer, teachers of music as well as instrumentalists and singers.

A strict code of conduct and system of management was instituted: there was to be no abusive or unseemly language or conduct, and fines were to be imposed for lateness or absence at rehearsals for less than good reason, or for failure to return loaned music on time. The Society did not welcome members who held radical opinions (at the time of its foundation, there was much political unrest which was to lead to the Chartist movement in the 1840s): a new rule introduced in 1842 insisted that

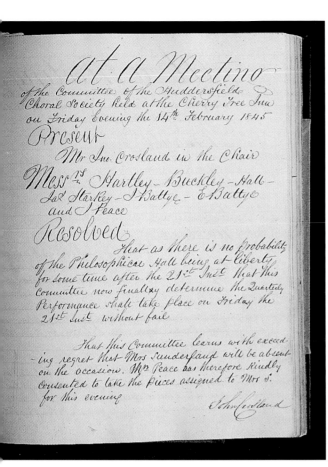

John North

figure, but recruitment now is by no means as easy as it has been in the past. The decline in church and chapel attendance, and thus of the tradition of the singing of sacred music, together with a possibly consequential decline in the public interest in choral music, are undoubtedly partly responsible for this. Moreover, applicants for membership must now submit to a modestly demanding audition – a deterrent, no doubt, to many of those aspiring to become members, who fear that it might in fact prove to be too demanding! It is evident, however, that formal auditions have not always been the rule. In October 1842 a committee resolution declared simply 'that Messrs Lister Peace and John Sykes be admitted members of this Society' which stands in contrast to another resolution made earlier the same year 'that Mr George Greenwood be invited to attend the next rehearsal and that Messrs Hall and I Starkey station themselves on each side of him in order to ascertain whether he can take his part as a Bass vocalist in a creditable manner'. It is not revealed whether Messrs Lister Peace and John Sykes had been similarly vetted. Lister Peace, incidentally, was father to the famous organist Dr A L Peace.

John Bowling

'...no person shall be a member of this Society who frequents the "Hall of Science" or any of the "Socialist Meetings" nor shall the Librarian be allowed to lend any copies of music (knowingly) belonging to this Society to any socialist upon pain of expulsion...'

It was at the 'Hall of Science', which stood – and indeed still stands in Bath Street – that radical politics and philosophies were apt to be expounded at public meetings by the likes of Robert Owen and the Chartists. The new rule was in fact invoked, though not fully enforced, in 1843 when one William Littlewood was 'sent for in this committee room to state his reasons why he attended to perform at the Socialist Hall a few weeks ago, having signed the rule against attending the above place'. He got off with a reprimand.

In the earliest days the Society consisted of no more than about sixty or so members, both vocal and instrumental. Today the 200 or so members are all singers – for many years now, professional orchestras have been engaged for its concerts. At the end of the 19th century the membership had grown to something approaching twice its present

The association of the Society with the musically notable has always been evident. One of the earliest members of the Society, Thomas Parratt, organist at Huddersfield Parish Church (which was rebuilt in the same year, 1836, as the founding of the Society) was father to the organists Henry and Walter Parratt. The former became the Society's first officially appointed organist after the building of the Town Hall in 1881, and the latter was appointed organist at St George's Chapel, Windsor and later Master of the Queen's Music, as well as being honoured with a knighthood. It was at the Parish Church that James Battye, one of the sixteen founder-members of the Society was clerk and who was the choir's conductor from 1852

Thomas Parratt

RIGHT *Robert Senior Burton.*

CENTRE *entries in an autograph album used to register receipt of fees by soloists and conductor during the period of Henry Coward's conductorship*

BOTTOM LEFT AND RIGHT OPPOSITE *sketches by an unnamed artist made at the 1881 Music Festival in the newly-opened Huddersfield Town Hall (far right).*

INSET OPPOSITE *Joshua Marshall*

until 1858. He was awarded the Gresham Prize for the composition of an anthem, having earlier been awarded a prize for a glee by the then Huddersfield Glee Society (described by William Cudworth in his *Musical Reminiscences of Bradford* as the most celebrated in Yorkshire). In this Battye was in company with William Jackson of Masham (celebrated for his composition of the oratorio *The Deliverance of Israel from Babylon*) who also, the year after Battye, received an award for a glee from the same society. Battye, it must be said, was not the only conduc-

tor of the Society to publish his own compositions.

Another notable early member, and close associate of the Society throughout her life, was the nationally-renowned soprano, Mrs Sunderland. As the 17 year-old Susan Sykes, before her marriage at the age of 19 to a local butcher, she first sang with the Society and was later to become its celebrated, professionally-engaged soprano soloist until her retirement in 1864. Most of the early members lived locally, and Susan was no exception. Her home was in Brighouse, where she lived for the rest of her life. In those days before the coming of the railway, most people in the choir would walk to rehearsals from far and near, with or without the guiding light of a full moon. 'Far' would possibly have amounted to a few miles only: one member's resignation is reported to have been caused by his having 'removed to Elland', scarcely five or six miles distant from Huddersfield. Not so far, however, for Mrs Sunderland who, in her young days, would regularly walk from Brighouse to Huddersfield and back twice each Sunday to St Paul's Church where she sang principal treble for many years and where Henry Horn, the Society's first conductor, played the organ. She also thought little of walking to Leeds to sing in a morning concert, doing some window-shopping, then singing at another concert before returning home on foot. She was feted wherever she sang, whether in Yorkshire, London, Edinburgh or Dublin. She sang at Buckingham Palace before Queen Victoria and Prince Albert in 1860 when some forty to fifty Choral Society members were included in a choir of about 200 voices under the Society's conductor at that date, Robert S Burton. The Queen was delighted with her singing, according to reports, and Mrs Sunderland became known as the 'Yorkshire Queen of Song'. Her name, and fame, live on by the inauguration of the Mrs Sunderland Musical Competition in 1888 on the occasion of her Golden Wedding celebrations. A concert to celebrate the occasion was held in Brighouse, the

a top note   a distinguished critic

An interested listener   A Critical Couple.

ALFRED JUBB, LITHO.

choir in attendance including a large contingent from the Huddersfield Choral Society and being conducted by the Society's own conductor, John North. The orchestra was led by John Bowling, who was to succeed North as conductor after the latter's death from typhoid, aged 39, in 1891. Mrs Sunderland died on May 7th, 1905, aged 86.

Since those days the Society has worked with some of the most distinguished musicians in British musical history. For the first 30 years of the 20th century until he was over 80 years old, Henry (later Sir Henry) Coward acted as both chorusmaster and conductor before Malcolm (later Sir Malcolm) Sargent took over for the next 35 years. Subsequent conductors – Wyn Morris, John (later Sir John) Pritchard, Owain Arwel Hughes and Jane Glover – have sustained and developed the choir's musical accomplishments and its connections with the best and brightest of talents in the world of classical vocal music. A list of the soloists who have sung with the choir since mid-Victorian times reads like an extract from Who's Who among British vocal artists and includes many of international renown. Similarly, a list of orchestras which have performed with the choir provides a no less impressive catalogue of the great and famous, as does also a list of the conductors under whose direction the choir has sung. The names of the composers who have written works for the choir, or else conducted it performing their works, or both, are to be found recorded too in the Hall of Fame. Prout began it in 1887 with his *The Red Cross Knight* written to commemorate the choir's golden jubilee (or was it the Queen's? – there is some uncertainty, especially in view of the date!). In 1901 Coleridge-Taylor came to Huddersfield to conduct his *Hiawatha*, Walford Davies in 1909 to conduct his *Everyman*, Parry in 1910 to conduct his *King Saul* and Elgar in 1917 to conduct *The Dream of Gerontius*. In 1926 Vaughan Williams conducted the choir in his *Sea Symphony* with the Hallé Orchestra and was commissioned to write *Dona Nobis Pacem* to celebrate the Society's centenary

Letter from Charles Hallé to Mr Gladney, the 'bandmaster' regarding press comments on the 1881 Music Festival

in 1936. 1943 saw some of the choir in Manchester to sing George Dyson's *The Canterbury Pilgrims* conducted by the composer and in the same year William Walton conducted the choir when it recorded his *Belshazzar's Feast* in Liverpool. Walton wrote his *Gloria* for the choir, to celebrate its 125th anniversary in 1961, and would have written another piece for its 150th anniversary had he lived. This task then fell to Paul Patterson who wrote a setting of the *Stabat Mater* for 1986. In 1980 David Fanshawe participated in a performance by the choir of his *African Sanctus* and in 1982 the choir sang *The Temple of Solomon* commissioned from Anthony Hedges. David Matthews wrote his *Vespers* for the Society to sing at a concert celebrating the centenary of Sargent's birth in 1995, and to mark the Millennium, Colin Matthews composed *Aftertones*.

From early days, the choir was to be heard in other parts of the country. When Robert Senior Burton from Leeds, who succeeded Battye as conductor following the latter's death in 1858, went to Buckingham Palace in 1860 with his Yorkshire Choral Union which included Huddersfield Choral Society members, as previously mentioned, he took it the following day to sing at the Crystal Palace. Sterndale Bennett was there and expressed, not for the first time, his admiration for Yorkshire choristers. 1862 saw members of the Society performing *Israel in Egypt* and *Messiah* at the Handel Festival in London and a specially-written setting by Sterndale Bennett of an Ode by Tennyson at the Great Exhibition at the Crystal Palace.

R S Burton did much to develop the Society musically but was evidently not an easy man to get on with, although highly regarded as a musician. He was the Society's first importation of 'foreign talent'. By the time of Battye's death the railway had arrived, making it possible for him to travel with ease to and from Leeds, where he played the organ at the Parish Church. He was himself soon accused, in turn, of importing foreign talent and thereby disregarding the purpose and intent of the Society's founders to foster local talent. Some of these 'foreigners' were instrumentalists who required payment, as did he, being the first conductor of the choir to receive a fee. Dissatisfaction with the size of that fee prompted him to resign in 1874, an event which seems to have been accompanied by scant regard on the Society's part for his services to it, considerable though they undoubtedly had been. One of its orchestral members, Luke Liversidge, who in 1858 had been in the first place 'required to wait upon Mr Burton' to ascertain on what terms he would 'attend as conductor of the choir', crossed swords with him more than once. The *Huddersfield Chronicle*, reporting somewhat unfavourably on a performance of

If this very sincerely express-
ed opinion can be of any
service to your friend, the
writer, I shall be very glad.

Yours very truly

Charles Hallé

Mr J Gladney

the Society's career came with the building of the Huddersfield Town Hall in 1881. The whole Town Hall undertaking, including the erection of its splendid concert hall, was eventually started following strong pressure from the Society. Ben Stocks, architect, bass singer with the choir, a member of its committee, driving force behind the foundation of the Huddersfield Glee and Madrigal Society in 1875 and later to be elected Choral Society President was, by the time of the near-completion of the Hall, consulting architect for the project. A Grand Festival of concerts was held when the Hall was completed. This included a performance of *The Damnation of Faust* by Berlioz, Mendelssohn's *Elijah*, Spohr's *Last Judgment* and Rossini's *Stabat Mater* by a festival chorus composed largely of Choral Society singers. A group of eminent soloists was engaged and the conductor was Charles Hallé who came from Manchester with his band for the occasion. The final concert, consisting of a miscellany of items, was conducted by Joshua Marshall who was, incidentally, also the first conductor of the new Glee and Madrigal Society, members of which would have been in the festival chorus and also belonged to the Choral Society. Hallé and his band had gone by this time and musical accompaniment was supplied by J E Ibeson on the piano and by Henry Parratt on the Father Willis organ, newly installed in the hall, by James Conacher and Sons of Huddersfield, from its first location in Newport, Monmouthshire. Ibeson followed Parratt as Society organist in 1885 when the latter retired owing to failing eyesight. The Town Hall has been the 'concert home' of the Society ever since that opening festival before which it had been obliged to use various unsatisfactory locations after its eviction from the old Philosophical Hall in Ramsden Street when it became the Theatre Royal. It had used this hall since its opening on the 24th May 1837, the 18th birthday of the then Princess Victoria. The Society's first-ever concert was held in Spring Street Infants' School, a building still identifiable and which now bears a plaque

Handel's *Samson* in 1864, recorded that on this occasion a member of the band had used insulting language to both the conductor, Burton and the leader, Mr Thomas. This was Liversidge himself who, in a letter from the Society's President, was threatened with dismissal unless he apologised to both gentlemen. There is no mention anywhere of how the matter was resolved but Luke's name appears on later lists of Society committee members, leaving one wondering where majority sympathies lay. Burton's successor as conductor was Joshua Marshall, a local musician, who, unlike Burton, asked for no fee for his services.

One of the most significant developments in

Plaque over the doorway of the Spring Street Infants School and BELOW *the Infants School, Spring Street today. Photos* SELWYN GREEN

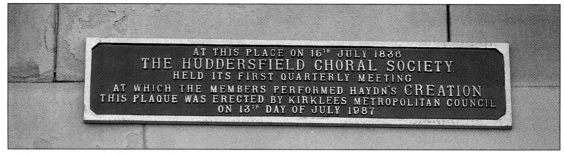

recording the fact, placed there when the Society celebrated its 150th anniversary in 1986.

Joshua Marshall established a new harmonious relationship both between the Society and its public as well as among its members, the number of which increased as did the number of eminent soloists engaged for concerts. There were administrative and financial problems, however, and subscription concerts were reduced in number from four to three per season. When Marshall became ill during the eighties there were pressures to replace him and when his affliction forced him to withdraw in 1885 he was replaced by John North who, like him, took no fee. Both Marshall and North held the post of choirmaster at the Parish Church in succession and just as there were strong links between that church and the Choral Society during the 19th century, so do these two men exemplify the strong links that existed between Wood's music business, which still thrives in Huddersfield and Bradford, and the Society at that time. Joseph Wood, who started the business back in 1850 had received lessons on the organ from Henry Horn, the Society's first conductor, and followed Walter Parratt as organist of St Paul's, where Horn had once played. Wood and his father were both closely associated with the Society, the son serving for a time on its Musical Committee. Shortly after starting his business he went into partnership with

Joshua Marshall who was his pupil. John North, who started working for Wood and Marshall's as a very young errand boy, was helping to run the business when Joe Wood died in 1884. J E Ibeson too studied under Marshall, had been apprenticed to Messrs Wood and Marshall, and received help and encouragement from Joe Wood himself. Wood's were responsible for the publishing of much locally-composed music including that of Battye, Marshall and North. Marshall, who was invited by Ben Stocks to be the first conductor of the Glee and Madrigal Society in 1875, was succeeded in that post also by North. In 1887 North took two choirs to London for the Welsh National Eisteddfod at the Royal Albert Hall. Both choirs, one male voice and the other mixed, which included singers from both the Choral and Glee and Madrigal Societies, won gold medals. John Bowling carried the choir through the nineties until he was replaced by Dr Henry Coward in 1901, disaffection having set in following deterioration in choir discipline and declining concert audiences.

Henry Coward's arrival was without a doubt another significant event in the Society's history. He not only broadened the choir's musical horizons but developed it into a formidable musical ensemble. He instilled a discipline in its ranks to match his own self-discipline which was evidently considerable, as becomes clear from reading his autobiographical *Reminiscences*. Performances by the choir of works by composers such as Bach, Brahms, Beethoven, Verdi, Elgar, Wagner, Parry, Holst &c. were heard either for the first time, or else to an increasing degree. According to Coward's own report, the principal bassoon of the London Symphony Orchestra, which had accompanied the choir's 1907 performance of Elgar's *The Dream of Gerontius*, was so impressed by the choir that he recom-mended that it should be invited to sing Bach's *B Minor Mass* with that orchestra at the Queen's Hall, London later that year under Hans Richter. The choir's first performance of this work had been at home in the previous year. For the London engagement a special train leaving at 9 00 am took them to King's Cross, returning at midnight. They were provided with a hot meal, paid for by John Watkinson, the Society's President at the time, on both outward and return journeys on board the train. With the exception of *The Times*' review, press reports of the concert were all favourable.

The choir sang Bach again in London in 1911 when it performed his *Singet dem Herren* in the Queen's Hall at an International Musical Festival. Because Coward was off on his extraordinary world concert tour at the time the concert was conducted by W G McNaught. This world tour of Coward's, in which some forty Huddersfield Choral Society members joined Coward's Sheffield Musical Union, lasted six to seven months. Coward gives a full account of this trip in his *Round the World on Wings of Song* and the Society possesses the transcript of letters home by a Mrs Beal, one of its members who went on the trip, provided by her grandson, now living in the

Sir Henry Coward LEFT conducts the Hallé Orchestra at the Society's centenary celebration concert in October, 1936 BELOW

The choir en route to Holland, 1928

United States, which is full of fascinating news and gossip but makes slight mention of music!

It was Coward who took the Society on its first foreign trip in 1928 to Holland where it performed Elgar's *The Dream of Gerontius* at the Amsterdam Concertgebouw with Coward conducting the Residentie Orchestra, which had never before played Elgar's music. In The Hague it gave a selection of items including Holst's *Hymn of Jesus*, a work also new to the Dutch. It all went off very well, a report in the Dutch press commenting on 'unrivalled quality and supple pianissimos'. These latter had been nurtured by Coward, who had required the ticking of the clock in the rehearsal room to be heard above the singing when necessary. The choir had had something of a reputation as 'the loudest in the land' and was accused in one London report of 'sledgehammer singing'. Coward changed all that.

The Choir did not travel abroad again until after the second world war when, assisted by grants from the Arts Council, it was able to give concerts in Austria, Germany, Portugal and the USA. during the '50s and '60s. Of these, perhaps the first – to Austria in 1958 – was in many ways the most remarkable. 150 members of the choir travelled to Vienna to take part in the centenary celebrations of the Vienna Music Society. They were away for a week. A performance of *Messiah* was given on Sunday June 1st in the famous Golden Hall of the Vienna Musikverein – made familiar now to such a wide audience through the New Year's Day popular Strauss concert – with Sargent conducting the Vienna Symphony Orchestra. On the following Tuesday in the same hall they sang Walton's *Belshazzar's Feast* together with the Fauré *Requiem*. The soloists for *Messiah* were soprano, Norma Procter, mezzo-soprano,

Elsie Morison, tenor, William McAlpine and bass, James Milligan, the second and last of these also singing the solo parts at the Tuesday concert. Despite the heat, which was considerable, the *Messiah* performance was a triumph. It was reported that the applause lasted just short of a quarter of an hour (Sargent was unrivalled in his ability to keep applause going!). When the orchestra filtered away, the choir alone remaining, the applause and cheering went on. At the end of the Tuesday concert, which was not quite so enthusiastically received, the applause nevertheless lasted for ten minutes. The *Austria News* quoting from the *Messiah* text, reported that the choir was worthy to receive 'power and riches and wisdom and strength and honour and glory and blessing'. Sargent 'almost cheered himself', he said. The Society was awarded the Franz Schmidt Silver Medal of the Gesellschaft der Musikverein of Vienna, a distinction they share with the Vienna Philharmonic Orchestra and the Vienna Boys' Choir. The President of Austria expressed his sense of joy and privilege at having been present to witness the tremendous reception received by the choir.

Begun in Coward's time and continued to a highly successful degree in Sargent's, was the exploitation by the Society of the new technologies of recording and broadcasting. More recent Choral Society recordings on CD of *Messiah*, with Mackerras conducting the Royal Philharmonic Orchestra, or with Harry Christophers conducting the BBC Philharmonic Orchestra, and of *The Dream of Gerontius* with Vernon Handley conducting the Royal Liverpool Philharmonic Orchestra (and its chorus) have none of them eclipsed the brilliant success of the 78 rpm recordings of *Messiah* and *The Dream of Gerontius* with Sargent conducting the Liverpool orchestra, made in the '40s, either commercially, as with *Messiah* in particular, or artistically, as with *Gerontius*. Through the radio broadcasts and the recordings made during and following the second world war the choir's name became known to millions, many of these having but scant acquaintance with the world of oratorio or 'serious' choral music. When the Society celebrated its 125th anniversary in 1961 Sargent received the Freedom of the Borough of Huddersfield and the Society received a testimonial of appreciation of its 'glorious musical achievements' and its 'illustrious contribution to the art of music-making'

Sir Malcolm Sargent is made a Freeman of the borough of Huddersfield, March 1961: ABOVE with the Mayor of Huddersfield and the Choral Society's President G D Haywood. LEFT receiving applause after the concert with the BBC Northern Orchestra where he was granted the Freedom.
Photos THE HUDDERSFIELD DAILY EXAMINER

RIGHT Jane Glover (2nd left) at her final concert, Elijah, as the Society's Principal Conductor, March 1996; with Chorus Master Paul Leddington Wright (centre) and soloists Stephen Roberts (left), Martyn Hill (right) and Inger Dam-Jensen (extreme right). Photo SELWYN GREEN

BELOW a recent performance with Martyn Brabbins

and 'the fame which [it had] thereby brought to the Borough of Huddersfield'.

It was not until the Society approached its 150th anniversary in 1986 that it fully recovered the sense of loss it had experienced following the end of the Sargent era. For more than half a century it had enjoyed continuous excellent direction and good fortune which was not easily sustained after 1967. However, the popular and ebullient Owain Arwel Hughes had infused the choir with a new sense of direction and purpose after his appointment in 1980 and the equally popular chorusmaster Brian Kay turned rehearsals into occasions of a rare combination of hard work and delightful entertainment. Anniversary celebrations began in the autumn of 1985. The season was a star-studded year which included a Messiah performance in the Royal Festival Hall in the presence of the Prince and Princess of Wales; Paul Patterson's specially commissioned *Stabat Mater*; two performances, one in Huddersfield and the other at St David's Hall in Cardiff; of *The Dream of Gerontius*; two performances of Verdi's *Requiem*, one in Cardiff and the other a televised broadcast from Huddersfield Town Hall with a quartet of internationally famous soloists; a civic reception held in Huddersfield; and many other memorable occasions. It ended, however, with something of a bombshell when Hughes, who had so triumphantly conducted the choir throughout this glorious celebration season, announced his decision to resign. In addition to other successes he had crowned the season by producing two best-selling recordings of the

choir, one of hymns and the other of carols. Indeed it was at the final carols recording session that he announced his decision to the members of the choir. Irreconcilable differences, he claimed, between himself and the choir management made his departure inevitable: his request to replace the chorusmaster had been turned down. Despite pleas from all quarters he was adamant, so that once more the Society was faced with the task of re-establishing a secure musical future. At the beginning of the very first concert of the 150th season Hughes himself had said to a capacity and hushed house that 'it is our responsibility to see that there is still a choir here to celebrate 200 years' and that he hoped the Society would have 'the blessing, the honour and the glory for ever

ABOVE each member of the choirs participating in the 1887 Eisteddfod received a certificate like this. The bottom portrait is of conductor John North.

LEFT the Prince and Princess of Wales cut the cake – made to celebrate the Society's 150th anniversary – at the Royal Festival Hall in 1986

ABOVE LEFT *Owain Arwel Hughes.* Photo SELWYN GREEN.

ABOVE RIGHT *Brian Kay*

BELOW *Martyn Brabbins*

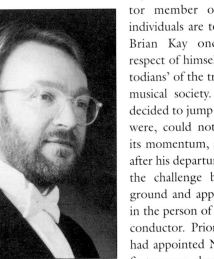

and ever, Amen.' Perhaps he thought that by going he would best ensure its survival.

The Huddersfield Choral Society has, it would seem, after such a long and proud history, a life and being of its own and is in a sense larger than any individuals, whether conductor member or official. Such individuals are to be regarded, as Brian Kay once remarked in respect of himself, merely as 'custodians' of the tradition of a great musical society. Hughes, having decided to jump off the train, as it were, could not thereby destroy its momentum, and not too long after his departure it responded to the challenge by breaking new ground and appointing a woman in the person of Jane Glover as its conductor. Prior to Brian Kay it had appointed Nina Walker as its first woman chorusmaster (chorus person?) and in the last decade of the 20th century it has had two women presidents. As a result of a somewhat bizarre process which left the Society without a principal conductor again for a while, Jane Glover was transmuted, after a period of eight years, from principal conductor to principal guest conductor, which remains her present position. She brought with her, from her background with the London Mozart Players, some exhilarating performances of *Messiah* and, of course, some wel-

come Mozart. She conducted the first-ever performance by the Society of Bach's *St Matthew Passion* and a memorable performance of Britten's *War Requiem*, the latter occurring on the very day, by a poignant coincidence, that the Berlin Wall began to be pulled down. These last two performances were given with the London Mozart Players participating.

Some out-of-the-ordinary engagements in recent years have included a trip to Czechoslovakia (as it still then was) in 1991, to perform Dvorak's *The Spectre's Bride* (in Czech) both in Bratislava and Brno, a work which the Society had only once before performed, in 1895. Another was the UK premiere of Alfred Schnittke's *Faust Cantata* as part of the Huddersfield Contemporary Music Festival in 1990 with the English Northern Philharmonia conducted by Gennadi Rozhdestvensky.

In 1994 at a Royal Albert Hall Promenade Concert came the performance of Ethyl Smyth's *The Wreckers* with the BBC Philharmonic Orchestra conducted by Odaline de la Martinez. A live commercial recording was made of this concert.

Recent collaboration with the BBC PO has resulted in several broadcast concerts by the Society of performances of French music by Berlioz, Fauré and Poulenc with Yan Pascal Tortelier conducting, and Russian music by Rachmaninov and Shostakovich with Vassily Sinaisky conducting.

Currently the Society is in a robust and healthy state under Martyn Brabbins, one of the country's leading conductors, who has come to the Society with what one senses as a genuine commitment to its service and the intention to ensure that it, in turn, serves its public with excellent music-making. The future with him promises well with the prospect of exciting new works, both ancient and modern, for the choir to undertake. With its newly-appointed chorusmaster, Joseph Cullen, who comes with a wealth of appropriate experience, a profound musical instinct and a disarming Scottish charm and intelligence, the choir may hope for a settled rehearsal schedule which will endure for a good while (recent years having seen some strange comings and goings in the appointment of chorusmasters).

Although ultimately the choir's very existence depends on a well-maintained membership level which, as we have already noted, requires continual recruitment effort these days, the Society is fortunate in having taken the wise steps to inaugurate and support two junior choirs, the Huddersfield Choral Society Youth Choir, and its Children's Choir, both of which flourish exceedingly and are an outstanding credit to their founders, managers and musical directors. In such seed-beds lies the future of the performance and the creation of choral music.

In his greetings to the choir on the occasion of its 150th anniversary celebrations, Sir John Pritchard, its principal conductor from 1973 until 1980, said, 'My memories of music-making we have undertaken together and the perennial response of your members to the most demanding vocal difficulties, encourage me to believe that indeed the Huddersfield Choral Society will always be at the spear-head of choral groups everywhere. Congratulations – and go to it!'

As it has done for something approaching one and three-quarter centuries now, who can doubt that Huddersfield Choral Society intends to do anything other than to 'go to it'?

ROBERT A EDWARDS

• *The Huddersfield Choral Society acknowledges with gratitude the support of J Donald Haywood, a Life Member and past President of the Society.*

Huddersfield Methodist Choir

Huddersfield Methodist Choir came into being in 1946 when the BBC invited the local Methodist church choirs to combine for a broadcast of 'Sunday Half-Hour' on the Forces Programme; a further broadcast followed on the Home Service. So successful was this new venture that it was decided to make permanent what had been intended as no more than an 'ad hoc' choir. In December, therefore, 400 voices assembled in the Town Hall to perform Handel's *Messiah* – the first annual performance in what has proved to be an unbroken sequence to this day. Alfred S Frost, organist and choirmaster of the Queen Street Mission, was the conductor (a position he retained for 30 years) and Ernest Cooper, organist at Lindley Zion Methodist Church (and Huddersfield Choral Society's long-serving accompanist) was the organist. The proceeds from the performance were devoted to the Methodist appeal for churches damaged during the Second World War. (Ticket prices then, and for some years after, ranged from 1/- [5p] to all of 3/- [15p]!).

In March, 1952, the choir sang Mendelssohn's *Elijah*, in what was the first of an occasional series of Spring Concerts. In 1975, the Spring Concert became an annual event, featuring a wide range of music, secular as well as sacred and guest soloists, choirs and orchestras – and on one occasion, the Band of the Welsh Guards. In December, 1964, the first annual Sunday Carol Service was held in the Town Hall; in 1969 (and to this day) it was replaced by a Saturday evening Carol Concert

Alfred S Frost, first Conductor of Huddersfield Methodist Choir

The Huddersfield Methodist Choir with INSET *conductor Alan Brierley*

with Lindley Band (who played in every one until 1995; since then, other bands have been engaged).

Since the pattern of three annual concerts in the Town Hall was established in 1975, the choir has further diversified its activities. One of its more unusual engagements was to sing on a train for *Wesley Trail*, a BBC documentary in 1988 commemorating the life of John Wesley. Visits have been exchanged with choirs in the USA, and it has played host to choirs from the USA, the Netherlands and Canada. The Golden Jubilee Year of 1996 was celebrated with special events culminating in a Songs of Praise in the Town Hall, at which the guest speaker was Canon Roger Royle, the well-known presenter of religious broadcasts.

Until 1970 the choir rehearsed at the Queen Street Mission. In that year thia huge chapel (built in 1819 to accommodate 1,800 worshippers) was closed (after endless debate, it was to re-emerge in 1995 as the Lawrence Batley Theatre), and choir and congregation moved to a new, smaller building in King Street. Here the choir remained until 1999, when the King Street Mission was demolished to make way for the Kingsgate Shopping Centre; the choir moved to the new Methodist Mission in Lord Street.

On Alfred S Frost's retirement in 1976 he was succeeded as conductor by Ralph Garside, a former Frost pupil who had been the choir's accompanist for many years. In 1984 Mr Garside was succeeded by his former pupil Alan Brierley, who had been his successor as accompanist: he remains the choir's conductor to this day, assisted by his deputy, Angela Griffith. Since then, Lucius Pearson, Ian Greenhalgh and now Malcolm Hinchliffe, another former Garside pupil, have been the choir's accompanists.

For some years now, although the choir retains its Methodist title, it has been open to anyone who simply enjoys singing and is prepared to undergo a short audition.

Sheffield Philharmonic Chorus

Like all the great towns and cities of Yorkshire Sheffield has a long and distinguished history of choral music-making. It was Sir Henry Coward (1849-1944) who brought the city to the forefront in this field. In 1876 this remarkable man (largely self-taught as a musician) founded the Sheffield Musical Union, and proceeded to raise the standard of choral singing to hitherto unprecedented heights. Coward was to remain its conductor for the amazing period of 57 years, retiring only in 1933. The six-month world tour of 1911 (in which members of the Sheffield Union were joined by singers from other choirs conducted by Coward – notably the Huddersfield Choral Society) is still remembered as one of the most singular events in British musical history.

Slightly older than the Musical Union was the Sheffield Amateur Musical Society (founded in 1864). When in 1935 the Sheffield Philharmonic Society was created to present an annual season of concerts in the new City Hall, the Amateur Musical Society became the resident choir, renaming itself the Sheffield Philharmonic Chorus. In 1937, the new chorus and the Musical Union were amalgamated to form a choir of almost 400 members.

In 1943, the chorus began one of the most fruitful periods in its history. John Barbirolli had returned from the USA to revive the ailing Hallé Orchestra, and the Chorus was to become closely associated with this orchestra and conductor. Apart from its Sheffield appearances the Chorus travelled to many other cities, to widespread national acclaim: '...the Sheffield choir have every quality – power, richness, delicacy. Every section was first-rate.' (*The Daily Telegraph*); '...the Sheffield Philharmonic Choir sang beautifully, almost past belief.' (*Birmingham Post*).

Especially notable were an Edinburgh Festival performance of Verdi's *Requiem* and one in London of Elgar's *The Dream of Gerontius* (a recording of this work, in which the chorus was joined by the Hallé choir and the Ambrosian Singers, is still in the catalogue and still a recommended version). But the chorus sang under many other leading conductors of the day in major choral works such as Walton's *Belshazzar's Feast*; Berlioz's *Grande Messe des Morts* (this in York Minster alongside Huddersfield Choral Society) and *Te Deum* (in the Royal Albert Hall under Sir Thomas Beecham); *Messiah* with Sir Malcolm Sargent; Vaughan Williams' *A Sea Symphony* (conducted by the composer); and Tippett's *A Child of our Time*. For many years the choir's chorusmaster was Herbert Bardgett, the most distinguished choral trainer in the north.

More recent years have seen equally memorable highlights in which the choir has appeared with all the leading orchestras in the north under many distinguished conductors, including the late Arvid Jansons, Tadaaki Otaka, Owain Arwel Hughes and Richard Hickox. On two occasions (1989 and 1992), the men of the choir performed Schönberg's *Gurrelieder* under Sir Charles Groves. In 1994 the chorus commissioned Geoffrey Poole's *Blackbird*: the first performance was later broadcast on BBC Radio 3. In 1996, with the Hallé under Kent Nagano, came Mahler's Eighth Symphony, performed in Sheffield and in Manchester's newly-opened Bridgewater Hall. Members of the chorus were among those who took part in a massive performance of Orff's *Carmina Burana* during the 1998 season of BBC Proms. In the following year the chorus was at York Minster for the opening concert of the Ryedale Festival, singing Berlioz' *Grande Messe des Morts*. More recently, it joined the Leeds Philharmonic Chorus and the BBC Philharmonic Orchestra in Leeds Town Hall for a performance of Verdi's *Requiem* later relayed on BBC Radio 3. During these years chorusmasters included Eric Chadwick, Stephen Westrop and Graham Barber. Its current Musical Director is Darius Battiwalla.

In the 1990s the Chorus embarked on a series of short foreign tours – to Germany, Spain, Donetsk (Sheffield's twin city in the Ukraine), France and the Czech Republic (where it gave a joint concert with the Brno Philharmonic Choir). Since 1992 it has appeared regularly in 'Classical Spectaculars' in the Sheffield Arena, singing to upwards of 10,000 people. In 1995 it sang to an audience of 14,000 at a similar concert in Castle Howard.

The chorus in Sheffield City Hall, 1954, shortly before its trip to the Edinburgh Festival

CHOIRS

RIGHT an 'away day for the choir'.
INSET David Bryan

Aire Valley Singers

In 1970 David Bryan, Head of Music at the Salt Grammar School in Shipley was Chorusmaster of the Bradford Festival Choral Society. Some members of a new semichorus of about 30 voices formed in that year wished to continue as a small group of singers outside the large chorus. In October 1970 this small group together with friends of the conductor started meeting in members' homes. To begin with there were about 16 voices, and the first concert was given at Tetley Street Baptist Church in the spring of 1971; this was followed by a concert at Gomersal and then a programme of sacred music at St Paul's Church in Shipley, which has since become their spiritual home. In the meantime the choir's numbers doubled from the original 16.

Concerts were given at various venues and in 1974 Salt's welcomed an orchestra from the Gymnasium Hammonense in Hamm, Germany; their conductor, Ludwig Ricken, stayed with the Bryans and a friendship was formed resulting in an invitation to visit Hamm in October of that year. Since then David Bryan has led many visits to Hamm with his school choir and the Aire Valley Singers; he was on the original *twinning* committee that arranged the twinning of Shipley with Hamm.

Through various contacts, the Singers have visited in addition, Belgium, Holland, Norway, France, Spain, the USA and Wales, the conductor's native land. They have sung in churches, village halls, cathedrals and even in the British Embassy in Oslo (not forgetting the Norwegian Parliament). In return they have welcomed choirs from Germany, Norway and Spain.

Honours they have received include a first prize at the Rencontre International de Chant Chorale at Tours in the Loire Valley, and an award for Best Chamber Choir at the Royal Albert Hall; they have twice been runners-up in the BBC's 'Let the Peoples Sing' competition. In the course of time they have established a reputation for fine choral singing – amateurs singing to a professional stan-

dard in a largely a cappella repertoire, which ranges from Palestrina, through music of the Tudor period, Bach and Handel, the Classical and Romantic composers, to the twentieth century and arrangements in close harmony of the `standards'. Over the years they have raised thousands of pounds for charities, have appeared on radio and television at home and abroad and have produced three recordings. They will shortly release two CDs, commemorating 30 years of song as Bradford's and more especially Shipley's 'ambassadors of song'.

The Amici Singers

The Amici Singers came into being as a natural progression from a Choral Class which Brenda Hawer was asked to begin some ten years ago at the Horsforth Music Centre in Leeds. Open to all, with or without choral experience or even the ability to read music, class members made progress over the years and took part in a number of concerts. Eventually it was felt that the time had come to expend, open the group up to the community in general and start afresh as an independent mixed voice choir in the Adel/Horsforth/Cookridge area of Leeds.

The group reformed as a choir in 1997, since when its numbers have more than doubled until it now has around 60 members. The name 'Amici Singers' was chosen in order to reflect the essentially friendly nature of the group, whose members consider the social aspect of choir life to be only secondary to their musical endeavours. Anyone

who would like to share the experience of 'singing for pleasure' is welcomed and encouraged – auditions are unheard of! – as this is an essential feature of the choir's policy. While some members have previous choral experience, others have been introduced to singing for the first time, many taking up this new interest in retirement. Although the Singers do not follow the larger choral society tradition of presenting major works such as oratorios, their repertoire is widely varied, encompassing Masses, motets, anthems, cantatas, spirituals, folk songs and songs in lighter vein: something, we hope, for everyone.

Since the early days, when the Singers combined with the Music Centre Band, they have appreciated the value of choir trips, not only as a means of bringing focus to the work done week by week in rehearsals but also from the benefits that ensue from enjoying time in each other's company, sharing musical experiences, getting to know family members and travelling together. The choir's growing membership has enabled it to plan its own independent trips. In its first year it visited Bruges; last year it went to Dublin and Galway; and this year it undertook what is probably its most successful tour to date, when a party of 47 visited the Glasgow area, giving four concerts and raising over £1,600 for charities.

In addition to its holiday trips, the Singers give a number of concerts each year, generally in aid of charity or church fundraising and in residential homes and hospitals. Occasionally they have entered a competitive festival, and they consider themselves to be expert party-givers.

The Holme Valley Singers

Initially named the Holme Valley Choir, the Holme Valley Singers was formed in 1975 by Alan Simmons, then Head of Music at Holmfirth High School, for staff and former pupils. It started with about 15 members and has now grown to its present membership of about 35, seven of whom are founder members.

In 1981, after the choir had sung at the Sainsbury's Choir of the Year Competition in the Royal Albert Hall, Alan relinquished the conductorship owing to his commitments as Kirklees Music Adviser. In his place we were fortunate to have James Morgan, who also replaced Alan as Head of Music at Holmfirth.

James was born in Willenhall, near Walsall, and obtained a first class honours degree from Huddersfield Polytechnic (now University). He undertook further studies in the USA, obtaining qualifications in composition and conducting at Indiana State University. He began his teaching career as a percussion teacher for Kirklees, whilst also playing percussion with the Black Dyke Mills Band. Among his current activities, he is percussionist for Alan Simmons' 'The Mastersingers'; he conducts a local orchestra; and in his 'free time' helps out in a ceilidh band.

The choir is also very fortunate in having the services of Jane Robertson and Kim Kaye, both of whom have been with it for some years now but they continue to amaze us by their versatility and talent. Jane is the regular accompanist, while Kim is both her and Jim's deputy. The choir only hopes that neither Jim nor Jane is unavailable at the same time (so does Kim!).

The group is held in high esteem in local musical circles, and is a respected participant in competitions. It has to its credit successes in the Sainsbury's Festival of Choirs, and the Blackpool, Freckleton and Morecambe festivals. It also appears regularly in Huddersfield's prestigious Mrs Sunderland Competition: among its successes there have been 12 first places in the Mixed Voice Class, and three occasions on which it has won the Choir Challenge Trophy.

It has undertaken exchange visits with Die Boose (not a drinking club, but a group of Belgian folk dancers, flag wavers and singers). On one visit the choir sang in Bruges Cathedral. It plans to visit its twin town of Imphy in Burgundy within the next 18 months.

Amongst many special occasions and funny moments, one embarrassing incident stands out, when in 1999 the choir competed in the Morecambe Festival for the first time. We were to be the first to appear in our class, so we set off in what we thought was plenty of time. Unfort-unately, the coach broke down and we had to wait for a replacement. Thanks to modern technology (a mobile phone) our secretary was able to contact the organisers, and they agreed to delay the start of the class. We climbed aboard our replacement coach and made as much haste as speed limits and traffic would allow. To save time on arrival, we decided to change while still on the coach. Unfortunately we failed to take into account the likely route to Morecambe, and many drivers were astonished to see 30 people doing the 'full monty' as the coach proceeded through Lancaster!

In August 1999 the choir decided to change its name to the Holme Valley Singers, feeling that it better reflected the group's distinctive nature – and in the hope that will stop people from referring to us as the Holme Valley Male Voice Choir!

The Glen Singers

Great choirs don't just happen. They have usually started as small choirs which are the inspiration of one person followed by a committee of hardwork-ing and dedicated members. So it was with the Glen Singers of Shipley.

Maureen Handby, a music teacher and member of a local choir, decided she would like a choir of her own. She placed an advertisement in the *Bradford Telegraph & Argus* asking anyone inter-ested in 'singing for pleasure' to meet at Shipley Community Centre on Thursday 1 March 1984. Not knowing what to expect, Maureen arrived at the Centre, opened the piano and set out her music and half-a-dozen chairs. She then sat with her fin-gers crossed, waiting to see if anyone was interested in 'singing for pleasure'. I suppose that in the dim and distant past the Archangel Gabriel sat 'up

The Glen Singers
July 2000
Photo STEVE MYERS, Shipley

there' waiting for the first members of his Heavenly Choir to arrive; and, of course, they did. Maureen felt very much the same till the door opened and a hesitant figure popped its head round the door asking, 'Is this where the choir is?' Sure enough, one after another they arrived and more chairs had to be set out, until finally 24 people had arrived. Over the years the interest has gathered pace, and Maureen now has a choir of over 80 mixed voices. The choir was christened 'The Glen Singers' and has gained quite a reputation and a great following, having presented many concerts over a wide area. Its success is mainly due to the broad range of music performed at its concerts – from religious to

Maureen Handby, MD the Glen Singers, (right) presenting cheque to Muriel Bendig Chairman, Bradford Branch, Yorkshire Cancer Research campaign.

light popular music, from *Zadok the Priest* to songs from the shows. Its interpretations of the songs from *Les Misérables* and *Phantom of the Opera* are superb.

Over the years the Glen Singers have established themselves as a great Yorkshire choir, having shown the flag throughout the whole of the north of England. They have presented concerts as far afield as St Annes, Darlington, Nuneaton, Wolvey (Leicestershire), Pickering and Fountains Abbey. Many local churches have benefited from their concerts, and thousands of pounds have been raised for a variety of charities.

Our peak moment came in 1995 when the choir presented a highly successful concert in York Minster for Yorkshire Cancer Research. It was a daunting and ambitious experience. Several problems had to be overcome such as the initial cost of £800 for hiring the Minster. The Dean and Chapter laid down strict rules as to the type of music the choir could perform – it all had to be of a religious and serious nature, which didn't fit in with our usual programme content. Another big production problem was the organ's time-lag:

Maureen had to conduct the choir with one ear open waiting for the sound from the organ to circulate the nave and catch up with the choir's singing. Fortunately our organist and accompanist, Ian R Baxter, and Maureen are so professional that the problem was happily resolved. A well-organised transport system enabled hundreds of supporters to be bussed in from all over Yorkshire. The nave of the Minster was full with over 800 people attending, and over £3,500 was raised for Yorkshire Cancer Research. The concert featured very talented guest artists – Mike Leeson, a freelance trumpeter who works with major orchestras and bands, and David Bainbridge, a local baritone from Shipley, who has appeared in concerts and recitals all over the north of England. The compère was Margaret Schofield, known locally to Gilbert and Sullivan enthusiasts for her leading soprano rôles.

In 1988 the choir embarked on its first singing tour of Germany to the Rhine Valley. Kamp Bornhofen was the destination and the base for a number of pre-planned concerts. Unfortunately, the tour company had arranged these at venues over 100 miles away from base; even more unfortunately, all the publicity supplied for the concerts was in English – with one disastrous result. After a journey of several hours, the Singers arrived at their venue, a large hotel on the banks of the Rhine at Königswinter, and found that they were to give the concert in a most beautiful room, all red plush, gold and white – very luxurious. They changed into concert dress – the ladies in their long green dresses and pearls, the men in dinner jackets with bow ties, green cummerbunds and green pocket handkerchieves: a smartly turned-out choir. Maureen spent some time arranging the choir into balanced sections so that the performance would have its usual professional character. As the starting time approached there appeared to be a severe lack of public interest. The tension in the room slowly mounted, the conductor's face more and more flushed by the minute. After waiting half an hour, she finally announced that the concert would go ahead, and so it did – a full concert presented to an audience of…four! They gave us a great ovation at the end, and everyone saw the funny side of the occasion – it has been a standing joke ever since.

There was compensation, however, for the next day, after another 100-mile journey, we had a marvellous reception at an old people's home in Idar-Oberstein. The hall was full, and they applauded every item, especially *The Happy Wanderer*, which we sang in German. We had to encore it several times, as they all joined in and sang with great gusto. Everyone had tears in their eyes after that concert. Our final concert was at Bad Bertrich – which seemed 1000 miles away! Situated south-west of Cochem in the Moselle Valley, it was a beautiful place, but we were too tired to enjoy it.

The choir has made four singing tours of Germany. On one occasions Maureen was presented with the Europa Union Medal by the President of that organisation in Aachen, given in recognition the contribution the choir had made to fostering good relations between the two countries. It was a particularly emotional moment for Maureen: 25 years earlier, her father, Arnold Edwards, had been presented with a similar medal for his work with exchange visits involving the youth and community of Halifax after the war.

During our stay in Camp Bornhofen we had been invited to sing at a special service in the large village church on the Feast of Corpus Christi. The church had a huge organ loft in the roof of the church and there we were perched. When we started singing the congregation thought that the Heavenly Choir had arrived – they had no idea where we were, and couldn't tell from where the sound was coming. They were absolutely enthralled; for the choir this was another memorable and moving experience. The night before the service one of the ladies had suggested, very seriously, that since it was a special service, the choir should sing 'Penis Angelicus!' The choir erupted and everyone burst out laughing; this, too, has been a standing joke ever since.

The choir maintains a strength of over 80 voices and is well balanced in all sections. A very busy programme has been arranged for this Millennium Year, with a highly prestigious concert to start the season. This took place in Manchester's Royal Northern College of Music, where the choir had been invited to perform with the Manchester Recorder Orchestra. This is one of only five recorder orchestras in the country and comprises over 60 members playing instruments which range from the twelve-inch Sopranini to the six-foot Double Bass Recorder.. For its monthly rehearsals in Manchester it draws players from all over the country. This was a marvellous occasion: the choir voices blended magnificently with the orchestra. Its musical director was so impressed that he suggested we present another joint concert, this time in Yorkshire. The concert is being planned for June

2001 in the Great Hall of Bradford University, with proceeds to go to Yorkshire Cancer Research.

Under the inspiration and guidance of Maureen Handby and with the backing of a very enthusiastic committee, the Glen Singers continue to move ahead (we have just set up our own website on the Internet). Maureen has been ably assisted by her husband Ernest, who is the choir's Social Secretary and Transport Manager. Between them, they have created a choir which is rather different – it is a family of singers rather than just another choir. It is significant that ten of the 24 founder-members are still with us, and 68 have received their ten-year service award. From the start, Geoffrey Ellison has been the choir's dedicated chairman, and he has always set a very high standard for us to maintain.

In 1984, Maureen Handby wanted her own choir; now in the year 2000 she has not only a choir but a great Yorkshire choir of 80 mixed voices, the Glen Singers who, under her guidance, are still 'singing for pleasure'.

The Huddersfield Singers

Though acquiring its present title only in 1988 this choral group has in fact been in existence since 1875. In that year Benjamin Stocks (a prominent member of the Choral Society – see elsewhere) entered an as-yet unformed mixed choir for a musical competition in Manchester. Having duly gained the £70.00 first prize the group's 25 members decided to continue singing together under the name of the Huddersfield Glee and Madrigal Society. Its first conductor was Joshua Marshall, the then conductor of the Choral Society.

Initially it was a competition choir with a repertoire of short pieces; it became so successful on the competition circuit that it was able to devote its prize money to commissions of original pieces. Ten years on, its membership was approaching the 100 mark, and it extended its repertoire to standard oratorios such as *Messiah* and *Elijah*; by the turn of the century its performances were being accorded the same lengthy and respectful reviews in the local press as those of the Choral Society. It was increasingly heard far beyond the confines of Huddersfield. In 1916 and 1917, for example, under its then conductor C H Moody (organist of Ripon Cathedral) it performed in Westminster Abbey.

In the 1920s its conductor, the hyperactive local musician Dr T E Pearson, introduced

The Huddersfield Singers with Philip Honor

modern British works into the repertoire, beginning the choir's long and continuing association with living composers including Holst, Vaughan Williams, E J Moeran and Britten and, more recently, John Gardner, John Joubert and Arthur Butterworth.

Dr Pearson's successors have included many musical household names: Roy Henderson (a leading baritone of his day, who died in 1999 at the age of 100); Leslie Woodgate (for many years BBC chorusmaster) and Donald Hunt (subsequently organist at Worcester Cathedral): under the latter's direction the society performed Bach's *St Matthew Passion*. Richard Steinitz (founder and director of the Huddersfield Contemporary Music Festival) was in charge for most of the period 1970-85, and he extended the repertoire still further, bringing Monteverdi's *Vespers* to Huddersfield for the first time.

In the late 1980s the society faced some stark choices brought about by changing circumstances. Membership had steadily declined from its 1950s peak: as a result, the choir was no longer large enough to tackle the really big choral works; and the Town Hall, where it had always given its concerts, was no longer a suitable venue. At the same time 'glees and madrigals', though not entirely neglected, had long since ceased to be a staple part of the repertoire.

In 1988, therefore, the society, now a chamber choir of about 35 members, renamed itself The Huddersfield Singers and moved to the more intimate surroundings of St Paul's Hall in the University. Here, following the appointment in 1990 of its present conductor, Philip Honnor, it rapidly established an enviable reputation for excellence and versatility. In the words of the *Huddersfield Examiner* Mr Honnor 'has proved to be a sympathetic interpreter of music of all styles and periods'; as that newspaper has also frequently pointed out, in the intricate art of programme-planning he has shown unrivalled skill and insight, born of a deep knowledge of every genre of choral music – from early music to demanding contemporary scores (often for unaccompanied voices).

Of their concert in December 1999, entitled *A Baroque Christmas*, for instance, the *Examiner* had this to say: 'Notable ingredients in this imaginatively conceived programme were contrasted settings of *In Dulci Jubilo* (by Buxtehude and Scheidt) and of the *Magnificat* (by Pachelbel and Pergolesi); some of J S Bach's many explorations of the *Nun Komm, Der Heiden Heiland* melody; and instrumental works by, among others, Corelli and Frescobaldi.'

By virtue of their distinctive programmes and high performance standards the Huddersfield Singers have carved out for themselves a unique position in what is Huddersfield's unusually crowded musical market-place.

Colne Valley Male Voice Choir

The Colne Valley Male Voice Choir was officially formed at a meeting at Slaithwaite Liberal Club on May 8th 1922.

A year earlier, Mr Hervey Haigh, secretary of the Colne Valley Mixed Vocal Union, had met together with friends from the valley to make up a male voice group meeting on Friday evenings. The choir which sprang from this background in 1922 elected to rehearse on Monday evenings, and that has been the practice ever since. Another resolution at the first meeting was that the choir should compete in an open-air music festival at Gomersal on July 15th 1922. Conducted by Hervey Haigh, the choir was placed fourth.

The choir was soon giving concerts at local places of worship, in the Liberal Hall, and in Marsden Park. At the annual meeting on January 1st 1923, with a declining membership, the choir came close to disbandment, but a decision was held over until three outstanding engagements had been fulfilled. The delay brought a change of heart and three weeks later it was decided to carry on, with Mr Clarence Roberts as president. On

July 7th that year the choir took second prize at Thornhill (Dewsbury) and the following week won first prize (the princely sum of £7.00) and the conductor's baton at Batley. A year later, under deputy conductor George E Stead, the choir was awarded first prize and the challenge cup at West Ardsley. The partnership between conductor and choir was cemented on September 1st 1924, and by the time of his death 44 years later, George had conducted the choir in scores of concerts and contests, winning over 50 firsts. In the 1930s he led the choir to an unmatched string of successes at the Blackpool Festival, then the top competitive musical festival in Britain.

Despite war-time restrictions and the absence of some members in the Services, Colne Valley Male Voice Choir took part in many charity concerts and musical services, both locally and as distant as Leeds and Ilkley, raising upwards of £3,000 for various funds.

The biggest setback the choir sustained during this period was the call-up of George Stead early in 1944, and it was not until August 1946, on his return, that the choir was able to get back to normal.

RIGHT the choir in its early days

FAR RIGHT Thom Meredith, Conductor

On Mr Stead's return, and with the resumption of competitive musical festivals, the choir entered and were successful once again in being awarded the first prize at Blackpool in November 1946, thus continuing where they had left off in 1939, making it effectively five wins in succession.

The March 1947 Town Hall concert was celebrated as the choir's Silver Jubilee concert. Appearing with the choir were Kathleen Ferrier (contralto) and Cyril Smith (piano). It was an outstanding success, the Town Hall being filled to capacity with an enthusiastic audience. Included in the choir's programme was Wagner's *The Holy Supper of the Apostles* and Brahms' Alto Rhapsody with Kathleen Ferrier as soloist. The concert was also noteworthy for the first public performance of a composition by Mr Stead – *A Song of Thanksgiving* – a setting of Psalm 46, dedicated to the members of Colne Valley Choir 'with grateful thanks for the safe return of our men from HM Forces'. This setting subsequently turned out to be the first of other works by Mr Stead for the choir, mostly based on psalms, which were destined to be published and widely acknowledged as masterpieces of male voice choral writing.

Many other competition victories followed in the 1950s, but it was in the 1960s that the choir gained international acclaim. In that decade it sang nine times at the Llangollen Inernational Eisteddfod and won four first prizes (with a hat-trick of wins in 1961-1963), four seconds and one third, with time also to take first prize at the inaugural Teesside International Industrial Eisteddfod in 1966.

George Stead was in his vigorous prime, conducting other choirs such as the Huddersfield Vocal Union, and chorus master of the Bradford Festival Chorus (where he would always take his place among the basses for the actual performance). He had recently returned to the Blackpool Festival where he won the bass solo competition and had been awarded the MBE for his services to music – when he suddenly died in his chair at home at the early age of 68 to the shock and dismay of the choir.

George Stead came at the end of the amateur tradition – the end of the time when opportunities for even a really talented musician to make a career in music were very limited indeed, and for a chorusmaster virtually non-existent.

His successor John Gulley, appointed in 1969, was in a more modern mould. A man of the West Country, John had originally studied law but switched to french horn and conducting, and was at the time of his appointment a senior lecturer in music at what was then the Huddersfield School of Music (now University).

An able all-round musician equally at home with bands and orchestras, John held the choir together very well. Under him it reached its greatest size with 92 singing members, and competition successes continued, notably one outstanding first prize at the Cardigan Eisteddfod in 1971 and another at the Pontrhydfendigaid Eisteddfod in 1977, plus two entries at Llangollen which yielded second and third prizes. Commercial recordings (some with excellent brass accompaniments arranged by John) continued to be made. Repeated visits to and from Solingen in Germany and to the (non-competitive) music festival in Besançon in France in 1975 were made, and still a very high level of achievement was maintained, even if the sheer supremacy of the Sixties had faded somewhat.

But after ten years John Gulley decided that he had done all he could and tendered his resignation, which was accepted with regret.

In 1988 Colne Valley chose as its conductor a ginger-haired 23-year-old Oxford University graduate, Thom Meredith. From the outset his musicianship and affable personality established a popularity which has gained him high respect both within the choir and in ever-widening musical circles. At the time he was a member of staff at Colne Valley High School; now he is assistant head of Kirklees Music School: in both positions, Thom has made a great contribution to younger people's enjoyment of music.

People change, but the continuing tradition of Colne Valley Male Voice Choir cannot be better expressed than in the words of the author of the 1972 Golden Jubilee souvenir publication. The late Brian Donaldson wrote:

> 'For them, music is a natural form of expression; it is a quest for sweetness and light, an engagement of the human spirit. They are true amateurs – and we must remember that that word really means lovers. They sing because they are lovers of song and it is such a love that is – must be – the foundation of a healthy musical life'.

Gledholt Male Voice Choir

In 1948 a group of men who attended Gledholt Methodist Church in Huddersfield formed a double male quartet under the leadership of a Mr Joe Ripley. They were formed to sing at local churches, old people's homes and hospitals &c. Gradually the original double quartet expanded to become firstly the Gledholt Glee Singers, then the Ripley Singers and finally the Gledholt Male Voice Choir.

From an early enthusiastic beginning with a choir that gave annual concerts in Huddersfield Town Hall, the membership began to decline and in 1977 it had only 28 singing members and appeared close to collapse. Joe Ripley retired and a committee was formed to find a replacement conductor. It chose Malcolm Fairless, who was already singing with the choir as first tenor, and appointed him musical director in October 1977. He has remained the choir's conductor ever since.

Malcolm's effort and drive had an immediate impact on the choir and the number of singing members increased so that by the late 1980s the numbers had increased to nearly 70 singers.

Early in the 1980s the annual concerts which had previously been held in Huddersfield Town Hall were moved to the Great Hall at the Polytechnic, and then to St Paul's Concert Hall

Gledholt Male Voice Choir

ABOVE *Malcolm Fairless, (Conductor).* RIGHT *Monty Segal (President)*

and part of Huddersfield University. In 1989 these concerts were moved to December and featured carols and other seasonal items within the programme. Then in the 1990s there was a move to stage the annual concert again at the Huddersfield Town Hall while still retaining the Christmas concert each year in St Paul's Hall.

The new series of annual Gala concerts began in 1996 and featured many guest artists, amongst them Brass Bands, visiting Male Voice Choirs and organ solos. Amongst the choir's visitors was a male voice choir called *Les Chenestrels* from Besançon in Eastern France, Huddersfield's twinned town, with whom the choir has formed a long-standing friendly relationship as an exchange. The first attendance of *Les Chenestrels* was in May 1996 at the Gala Concert at the Town Hall, with a return match arranged for the Gledholt Male Voice Choir for the spring bank holiday the following year. The choir publishes its own magazine *The Temeraire* , now in its 18th year.

Most important of all, the choir hosts the Northern Male Voice Choir Championships. This was begun in 1985 and has become a highlight for all Male Voice Choirs. The choirs compete by invitation in Huddersfield Town Hall and sing the same two test-pieces. There were 13 competing choirs at the first championship in 1985 with four prizes of £1,000, £650, £400 and £300. The celebrity concert in the evening becomes the highlight of the day and the prize-winning choir along with Gledholt Male Voice Choir sing selected items to a select audience, introduced by Geoffrey Wheeler. In the ten years that these championships have been held, new test-pieces have been commissioned and some of them used regularly by choirs at other major festivals since.

Gledholt Male Voice Choir has been long-standing supporters of charities, raising money for churches and particularly Yorkshire Cancer Research Fund.

The choir celebrated its golden jubilee in 1998 with a series of concerts throughout the year.

Honley Male Voice Choir

While maintaining strong links with the its past, Honley Male Voice Choir prides itself on its forward-looking thinking, combining tradition with innovation. Since its birth in October, 1936 the choir has ended each of its rehearsals with the singing of *Deep Harmony*, ('Sweet is the Work...'), the favourite hymn of the choir's founder Ben Kinder, and the title of the first of five recordings made by Honley between 1977 and 1999.

And in recent years, while retaining a strong traditional male voice choir repertoire, the choir, under its present Musical Director Alan Jenkins, has branched out into musical theatre – performing, as well as singing, excerpts from well-known shows. The choir regularly sings to packed houses in Huddersfield Town Hall with the country's leading brass bands but it also shares the concert stage from time to time with swing, jazz and steel bands. The choir is always willing to try something new in its quest to provide entertainment for its audiences.

While the choir has had its fair share of first prizes in competitions over the years, providing entertainment has always been more important than winning trophies, and the choir believes its greatest success is the rapport it continues to achieve with its concert audiences.

Since Ben, a local music lover, founded the choir in October, 1936 and became its first secretary, it has built part of its reputation on raising funds for good causes in the local community and at the same time achieved national fame with appearances at international Rugby Union and Rugby League events at Wembley Stadium, Twickenham, Old Trafford and Huddersfield's Alfred McAlpine Stadium, towards the end of the last Millennium.

Over the years the choir has enjoyed exchange visits to other choirs in Bath, Cornwall and Wales and has been on concert tours to Florida, Holland and Germany and competed at music festivals in Malta and Southern Ireland.

The choir receives a great deal of support from its thriving Ladies Circle, formed in 1970, and which choir members' wives or partners can join, and has more than 600 subscribers.

Ernest Armitage, who like Ben had sung with the now defunct Holme Valley Male Voice Choir, become the first Musical Director of the new choir. The first practice was held in the Southgate

Honley Male Voice Choir.
Photo TREVOR BRAY, Huddersfield.

Methodist School (now the Honley Theatre) attended by 18 men, most of them drawn from local churches. It was decided that members should pay a subscription of 3d a week – the annual subscription is now £30 – and gradually more members were attracted.

When the Second World War broke out in September, 1939, the choir had about 45 members. Twelve joined the Armed Forces and many others were working overtime on war work and in September, 1941, the choir's activities were suspended. However, rehearsals began again the following year and in December, 1942, the choir made its first broadcast with 38 members travelling to Leeds BBC studio to record six songs which were broadcast in the USA in a 'Britain Sings' programme.

Following the death of Ben Kinder in September, 1952, Ernest Armitage resigned a month later and was replaced by Ronald Daniel, a former tenor soloist with the Holme Valley Male Voice Choir. He took over the choir as it was entering into a period of doldrums when attendances at rehearsals were averaging only 16 or 17.

But gradually attendances improved and in 1964 the choir won a first prize at the Blackpool Musical Festival. In 1968 the choir appeared on Yorkshire Television's *Choirs on Sunday* programme and in the following year, John Oldfield was appointed piano accompanist (he was also made deputy conductor in 1970) following the death of his uncle Clifford, who had accompanied the choir since 1938.

Roy Firth, deputy conductor of the Colne

Ben Kinder

51

Valley Male Voice Choir, succeeded Ronald Daniel in 1974 as Musical Director of Honley and in the same year George Marsden was appointed deputy accompanist and organist. Roy gave the choir fresh impetus, taking it from Section B to Section A status and charmed audiences with his wit and extrovert personality. It was during his time in charge that the choir made its first visit to the Ulfts Mannenkoor choir in Holland – the two choirs have retained their close links to this day – made three recordings, took part with Richard Stilgoe in BBC TV's *Nationwide*, recorded a 45-minute programme about life in the choir for BBC Radio Leeds and as part of its golden jubilee celebrations presented a trophy to the Mrs Sunderland Musical Festival.

Ill-health forced Roy Firth to resign in 1988 and he was succeeded by Alan Jenkins who led the choir to success in the first National Male Voice Choir Championship in 1990, and in the Champion of Champions Contest at Widnes in 1991. Alan Jenkins left in September, 1997 and was replaced by Sean De Burca who arranged the music for the choir's last recording in 1999, *The Pride and Passion*, which was produced by a London record company in time for the Rugby Union World Cup. Following Sean's departure towards the end of 1999, John Oldfield took over the duties of Musical Director until May, 2000,

ABOVE Alan Jenkins TOP RIGHT the choir at the Rugby Union World Cup Final at Wembley and BELOW with Richard Stilgoe on BBC's Nationwide.

when Alan Jenkins returned for a second spell.

The choir now numbers around 70 – about ten fewer than when it celebrated its golden jubilee. It rehearses twice a week on Tuesdays and Fridays at the Honley Nursery and Infants school and believes it has successfully achieved the twin aims set out by Ben Kinder in 1936 – 'excellence in male voice singing and good fellowship'.

Skelmanthorpe Male Voice Choir

First referred to in the Domesday Book, the village of Skelmanthorpe lies near the eastern edge of the Pennines, eight miles east of Huddersfield, in an area long renowned for its choirs and brass bands.

'The name of this choir shall be Skelmanthorpe Male Voice Choir': so runs Resolution 6, the final resolution of the inaugural meeting held in Skelmanthorpe Working Men's Club (now the Parish Council Offices) on Monday, October 29th 1934. At this meeting attended by some '30 odd people', it was decided that a male voice choir should be organised in Skelmanthorpe Whether the 'odd' refers to an inaccurate count, or to the idiosyncrasies of the people present is not stated, but one thing is certain: the choir continues today with 50 individuals committed to providing the best in Male Voice singing.

It is interesting to note that Resolution 1, under the heading 'Subscriptions' stated that each member should pay an entrance fee of 1/-, and then 1d per week. At the end of the first year of activity, only a handful of members lived outside the village, whereas at the present time the reverse is the case

with by far the greater part of the members coming from the surrounding areas. Two founder members of the choir still live in Skelmanthorpe.

In the early years the choir concentrated on a repertoire of traditional male voice music, and corn petitions, with many successes, being a large feature of the choir's life. This continued after the war and from 1962 to 1976 no fewer than 29 first places were recorded, under the musical direction of Jack Haigh.

In 1976, Alan Simmons was appointed Conductor and this saw a change in the choir's approach to repertoire. New music or arrangements of more popular songs were virtually non-existent, and Alan brought about a change by composing and arranging many pieces which are now standard repertoire for Male Voice Choirs all over the world, but which were pioneered by Skelmanthorpe Male Voice Choir.

The choirs first recording in 1979 entitled *Movin' On* gave an indication of the wish to broaden the repertoire. *Portrait*, which followed, continued the theme.

1990 saw a change of Conductor with Stephen Williams taking over the role of Musical Director. The introduction of new music was again the priority. Two further recordings were made and the choir again excelled in the competition field, the highlight being first place in the National Male Voice Championships in 1991.

December 1995 saw the departure of Stephen Williams, but, after much negotiation, in June 1996 came the appointment of our present Musical Director, Steven Roberts. His interest in musical theatre has enabled the choir to introduce a further dimension to the concert programme, and, whilst not abandoning 'the tradition', the broader spectrum has brought pleasure to choir and audience alike. The most recent recording, *This is the Moment*, is further evidence that the choir is still *Movin' On*.

Although originally a local choir, Skelmanthorpe now has a much wider audience, not only in the UK but also in Europe and North America, with specific contacts in Germany, Sweden, Russia, Toronto, Ottawa and Montreal, having either visited and/or hosted choirs from these places.

No history of Skelmanthorpe MVC would be complete without reference to the 32 years of friendship which have existed between the choir and MGV Nordbogge in Germany. Since 1968, when the first visit to Germany took place, there have been 13 exchanges between the two choirs, the latest being in July 2000 to celebrate our continuing friendship into the new century.

These notes are but a brief insight into the musical progress of the choir since its inception. Many other factors have contributed to its life; lack of space, alas, precludes their inclusion.

Steeton Male Voice Choir

For 93 years the village of Steeton has nurtured its male voice choir, originally an 'ad hoc' group of a dozen local men, but now with a membership which tends to hover around the 80 mark and is drawn from a catchment area well beyond the village. Its reputation has grown along with its size and it has won many plaudits, particularly for the richness of its sound and the clarity of its words. As one member famously put it when complimented by a reporter in another part of the country, 'Oh aye, we've allus been renowned for us diction'.

The choir has been singularly fortunate in having had only four conductors in its entire history. Hulme Wrathall founded the choir in 1903 and led it until his death in 1952. This was a remarkable contribution which gave the choir a firm foundation. Arthur Wilson, who had originally joined the baritone section in 1922 before pursuing a solo career, came back as conductor in 1952, and led it successfully for 25 years. John B Smith then took over, and the choir grew, improved and broadened its outlook throughout his 18-year tenure. In the five years in which Alan Clark, the current conductor, has been in charge, he has shown the same commitment, and in such a relatively short time has made a significant contribution to the choir's further development.

All choir members and supporters were delighted at the announcement in this year's Queen's Birthday Honours of the award of the MBE to Arthur Wilson, the choir's President and,

*LEFT
Skelmanthorpe
Male Voice Choir
in rehearsal*

at 96, still singing in the baritone section.

Steeton MVC performs about 30 times a year in venues of all kinds – from large concert halls and cathedrals to small chapels and nursing homes. It has appeared with virtually every top brass band in the country including World and European champions.

In recent years it has been the guest choir in a series of military band concerts in St George's Hall, Bradford, and Leeds Town Hall, with the bands of Her Majesty's Royal Marines (three times), the Swedish Navy, the Hungarian National Guard and the Russian Army (three times). Steeton MVC has also been pleased to support the Yorkshire Campaign for Cancer Research by sending large contingents to each of the four massed choir events given for that cause in the Royal Albert Hall (it will be no less strongly represented at the 2000 Sheffield Arena concert).

In Britain, the choir has sung in places as far apart as Berwick-upon-Tweed and Swansea, its three visits to South Wales being particularly successful. Five continental tours have taken members to the cathedrals of Ypres and Cologne, as well as to other excellent venues in Germany, Belgium and the Netherlands. Very few choirs have been privileged to sing in the famous 'Last Post Ceremony' at the Menin Gate in Ypres, but Steeton has done so twice – in 1991 and 1999.

The choir currently holds three trophies from Blackpool Festival, though it competes less frequently nowadays, mainly because of the heavy demand it receives to give concerts, almost all of them in support of some charity or other. Nonetheless, Steeton has a good competition record and has taken on choirs from all over the world at Llangollen International Eisteddfod, where an adjudicator described it as a 'fine, fine choir'. But even competition victories have their downside. On one occasion in the 1950s, the choir won its class at a festival in Rhyl and celebrated by gathering on the promenade for an impromptu performance of *Ilkla Moor baht 'at*. Meanwhile thieves were ransacking the coach – and the choir returned to Steeton baht 'ats, baht coats...baht everything!

Worrall Male Voice Choir

The Worrall Male Voice Choir cele- brated its 30th anniversary in grand style by making its first foreign con- cert tour in May, 2000. Such an enterprise would have been far from the minds of the 13 men who gath- ered in Worrall Independent Chapel, on 7th September 1970, to form another male voice choir. They were more concerned with local opposi- tion in an area where almost every valley fielded a brass band, competing for audiences with the choirs which formed in the hill-top villages around Sheffield.

Bill Thompson led the choir in its early months but he was soon succeeded by Doug Crossland who was to remain until 1995, when until ill health forced his retirement. By the mid 1980s, when the well structured choir became a registered charity, it had sixty members. Under Doug Crossland's inspired direction the young choir gained a sound reputation at concerts and by coming first in numerous competitions. The Worrall Choir broke new ground by becoming the first English choir to win the Cornish Open Choral Championship for Male Voices in 1987, previously the exclusive preserve of Cornishmen.

Closer to home, in 1988 the choir became involved in the fundraising concerts organised by the Lyceum Theatre Trust to restore the fine old theatre in Tudor Square, Sheffield. The choir proudly recalls being accompanied by the bands of the Coldstream Guards and the Duke of Wellington's Regiment on these prestigious occa- sions. These events led to invitations for the choir to participate in ITV's 'Telethon '90' and BBC Radio Sheffield's concerts and Christmas celebra- tions.

Once the restoration was completed the Worrall Choir participated in the first choral per- formance held in the re-opened Lyceum, a grand charity concert on 8th March 1992. It was accom- panied by the James Shepherd Versatile Brass and Mary-Louise Aitken, a promising young soprano from nearby Stocksbridge. The full house of nearly 1,000 at the concert raised £3,000 for the local Weston Park Hospital Cancer Fund. Both per- formers and audience particularly appreciated the theatre's fine acoustics, which are rated second to none in the country.

The Choir celebrated its Silver Anniversary on 5th February 1995 with a repeat per- formance of this Lyceum con- cert. Miss Aitken, by then in her final year at the Royal Northern College of Music and a member of the Glyndebourne chorus, was again the soloist.

Since then the Worrall Choir has fulfilled some 35 engage- ments a year including weddings, after-dinner shows, concerts – and to keep its members on their toes – competitions. Such a com- mitment would not be possible without the loyal support of the non-singing Friends of the Choir and members' wives. The Ladies Support Group helps by organ- ising fundraising and social events and providing Yorkshire teas for these, and for the annual Cricket Match against the Grenoside Male Voice Choir from across the Don Valley.

LEFT Coat of Arms embroidered by Ada Nears of Worrall WI

BELOW Cornish Open certificate 1987

Keen to foster amateur music-making in other fields, the Choir has developed links with Bradfield Comprehensive School. These enable this rural school's choristers and instrumentalists to join the Worrall's public performances at Firth Hall and elsewhere under the 'Developing Musical Life' initiative. Local enterprises of this nature are sponsored by the National Federation of Musical Societies, in association with British Telecom and the Arts Council of England, as part of 'The Music Experience', a three-year community project involving youngsters. For its part in this scheme, the choir gained one of 22 regional awards made in 1999.

The Millennium was celebrated by the Worrall's first overseas tour to Catalonia, where venues included Barcelona Cathedral and the monastery of Montserrat. By way of contrast the Choir participates regularly in the important carol singing season which ranges from Carol Concerts to the more homely 'Sings' in local pubs. These have their own tradition of local Christmas Carols rarely heard in churches. Some of these were incorporated in the Choir's 'Blue Book' entitled *The Joy of Christmas* which, since Christmas 1982,

has sold in its thousands both at home and to Yorkshiremen settled in Australia and the USA.

Worrall MVC supports the David Clover Competition, the Sheffield Spring Music Festival, practically, financially and by providing the Doug Crossland Memorial Shield for the most promising female entry. This thoroughly versatile choir performs not only the traditional works associated with the male voice but a wide range of popular songs and arrangements. The appealing South African song *Homeless*, normally a solo piece, is one of the favourites at Worrall concerts, where the Worrall family crest of a golden lion rampant to denote excellence, is always displayed.

A choir's sustained excellence depends not only on the vocal qualities of the members but upon the skill and devotion of its leadership. Today the choir is very fortunate in having Elizabeth Hampshire as its musical director and Michael Peaker as its accompanist. In meeting the challenges of high standards and demanding judges the Worrall Male Voice Choir has earned a firm place in the musical history of the former West Riding of Yorkshire.

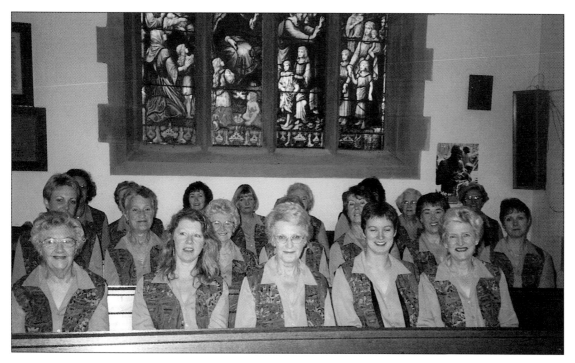

Almondbury Ladies Choir

The choir's history goes back to 1964 when a splinter group of about twelve members broke away for a Townswomen's Guild Choir because they felt restricted by the narrow range of repertoire and venues for concerts. The new group decided to call themselves 'Aymbry Ladies Choir', after the old spelling of Almondbury. However newspapers always 'corrected' this spelling so it soon became, and has remained, Almondbury Ladies Choir.

When the new group began it had no music or piano so it was decided each member would pay 6d a week towards music. Some members lent £5.00, and each time that amount was raised in sixpences the £5.00 loan would be returned. When Milton Church in Huddersfield closed down, the choir acquired all its music and a piano.

Rehearsals were originally held in the Parish Room but later moved to the schoolroom of Almondbury Methodist Church where they remain to this day. The choir has always had strong links with the church and the community. Several concerts have been held in the church, with a Christmas one planned for December 2000; and the choir has often had a fund-raising stall at the Annual Almondbury Gala. We even have in our repertoire the *Almondbury Carnival Song* with its cheery chorus:

TOP Sept 2000 at a wedding.

BELOW three founder members cut the 25th anniversary cake

LEFT carol singing in Sainsburys

There's no reason why as through life we go
We should lose the happy knack of giving a
smile.
As sure as we're alive it's on sunshine that we
thrive,
A singing heart will shorten many a mile.

In its thirty-six years the choir has had only three conductors. Enid Nicholls conducted the original breakaway group. She was followed by Isobel Rossell. A highlight of her time as conductor was an invitation to perform at the Bishop's Palace at Bishop Auckland. The third and current conductor Angela Griffith joined the choir in 1985 and is still going strong.

The choir has a long history of competing in local festivals – at, for example, Harrogate, the Mrs Sunderland in Huddersfield and Penistone. In 1998 we had a memorable win at Penistone when the audience was electrified by the performance of a new work, a slave freedom song called *Yonder Come Day*.

Performances at weddings and residential homes as well as fund-raising for charities also feature on the list of choir activities. We are usually to be found in the weeks before Christmas giving our all to *White Christmas* or *Rudolph the Red-nosed Reindeer* outside Asda or Tesco.

It is often said that the choir's repertoire ranges from Bach to Bacarach, and we do take our music-making seriously as Angela Griffith leads us through our paces with singing and sight-reading exercises and attention to tone and technical detail. We also frequently expand our repertoire having just premiered an arrangement by Alan Simmons of songs from *Oliver*. A concert programme from 1978 'Brass and Voices' at Huddersfield Town Hall shows our choir with three other ladies' choirs presenting *Rock a My Soul*, *Panis Angelicus*, *The Snow* and *Scarlet Ribbons*, all of which we still perform. At the 1999 Penistone Festival we were congratulated by the adjudicator for our adventurous and challenging choice of an Estonian *Milking Song*!

Now 40-strong, the choir always welcomes new members, but we are also proud to have long serving members like Mrs Kath Bray who is the only surviving founder member; Gwen Taylor who joined in 1970 as a middle soprano and is now a stalwart in the altos; and Mary Holt, who joined in May 1977: a year later she became secretary and is still giving sterling service in 2000.

The Lawnswood Singers

Perhaps we should lay one ghost at the outset – no, the Lawnswood Singers do not have a connection with the Lawnswood Crematorium, at least not yet, although we have sung at services there. But we do have a connection with Lawnswood School in Leeds or, as it was in our day, the Lawnswood High School for Girls.

A chance remark at a school reunion dinner in Silver Jubilee Year (1977), and a 'testing of the waters' with a paragraph in the Yorkshire Evening Post led to a group of around 40 ex-pupils, all past members of the school's prestigious choir, meeting some 20-plus years on in the home of their former music teacher, Mrs Agnes Grisdale. She it was who had first inspired in her young pupils an enthusiasm for music and a love of choral music in particular.

Memories of works sung in the school choir many years previously came flooding back afresh, and when the reminiscing and news exchanges were done, it was decided to sing together just once more under Mrs Grisdale's (neé Clayton) direction. As a result, a 'Silver Jubilee Concert' was given in Headingley Methodist Church, a venue of many previous school concerts.

Singing together again was an experience too good to give up, and so the group, many now wives and mothers and following a diversity of careers in teaching (several now music teachers themselves), floristry, the law, pharmacy, commerce, journalism and the civil service, began rehearsing on a regular basis. It has since given concerts throughout the West Riding, raising many thousands for charities and other worthwhile causes.

Alongside hundreds of recitals in churches and chapels, highlights have included radio broadcasts, performances in Leeds Town Hall, Civic Hall, Civic Theatre and Temple Newsam House, and successful competitive festival appearances. An ITV Sunday morning broadcast service remains engraved particularly on the memories of certain choir members who returned from August holidays for the recording, only to find that a technicians' strike had caused the session to be cancelled, and the date rearranged.

After some years, Mrs Grisdale's health deteriorated and she eventually retired to live in Windermere. There she continued to share a home with her close friend of many years and a former president of the Lawnswood Singers, Mrs Elizabeth ('Daisy') Bardgett, widow of the late renowned chorusmaster Herbert Bardgett. At this time (1984), Brenda Hawer, a founder-member of the school choir and now also following a career in music education, took over from Mrs Grisdale with her blessing and continues to conduct the choir today.

The loss of members over the years inevitably threatened the choir's future and so it was decided some time ago to 'open up' the membership to non-Lawnswood former pupils, since when the choir has been delighted to welcome new sopranos and altos. This has ensured the continuation of a group which not only unites musically but in which its members support each other both socially and personally. So, 23 years on, the Lawnswood Singers continue to enjoy fun and fellowship of making music together and to be able to assist in so many worthwhile causes.

Mingled with the wealth of happy memories are inevitably the sad ones. In 1999 the Singers paid their last loving respects to the lady to whom they owed so much, when they sang at the funeral of Mrs Grisdale (aged 83) in Windermere. In that same year they lost another dear friend of the choir, Miss E Kelsey, a former teacher of Modern Languages at the school to whom many of the choir, as pupils, were indebted. She had always retained a great interest in the activities of the Singers, and had given them unfailing support from the choir's inception up to the time of her death.

As with all choirs, the anecdotes abound and certain events are engraved deeply on the memory. Many are the times we have trailed in our long skirts out of vestry doors at Christmas time, to plough through churchyards deep in slush and snow in order to enter at the west door and proceed in a dignified (?) manner up the aisle, with hair and carol books dripping – an experience from which many a copy of *Carols for Choirs* has never recovered.

There was the unforgettable Christmas when the choir took part in a Christingle-type service, each member having been asked to bring an orange by way of a candle-holder. The symbolism of this 'Light of the World' suffered somewhat when an enterprising member, having forgotten to purchase her orange, showed true 'Lawns-wood' determination and arrived at the church with the only available substitute: a Terry's chocolate orange.

On another occasion we shared a concert with Leeds Police Band. Rehearsal time was short, so there were few qualms about taking a joint performance of Elgar's *Land of Hope and Glory* 'on trust'. The folly of this became clear in performance when it was found that the band's chosen

key left sopranos and altos imitating basses as they growled their way to the end with increasing apprehension and difficulty. We have experienced stilettos stuck in gratings; we have had members slip through staging tiers; we have coped with pianos of every type imaginable, even being greeted with the words, 'You're not going to play THAT piano, are you?'; like all choirs, we have had interminable discussions on uniforms. We have agreed to turn up for an engagement in our cream blouses only to find that one member had forgotten and tuned up in our alternative red (we got out of that one by telling our audience that she was our mascot!).

We have provided 'the entertainment' after dinner and been thanked by a chairperson, who had clearly spent a very 'celebratory' evening, with the words, 'I want to thank you all very much – well, I've enjoyed it anyway.' We've sung unabashed with music folders clutched to bosoms as bent-double teamakers crept kitchenwards between choir and conductor to answer the call of a whistling boiler

Yet through it all, we have kept on singing and enjoying our music. It is all part of the camaraderie of being a member of the Lawnswood Singers. Long may it continue!

Church Music & the Sings

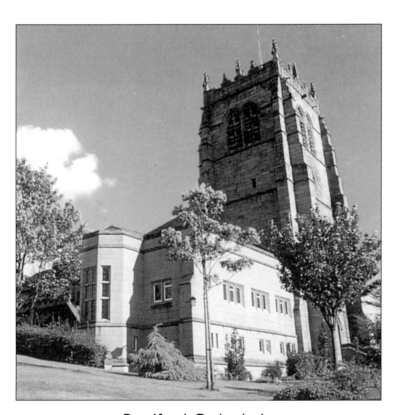

Bradford Cathedral

St Peter's Cathedral at Bradford, West Yorkshire is the second smallest of England's parish church cathedrals. Elevated to Cathedral status when the Diocese of Bradford was formed in 1919 it occupies the oldest site of Christian worship in the city. Parts of the building date from the early 14th century and many alterations and additions have been made during the intervening years particularly in

the late 1950s and early 1960s, when the East End was rebuilt and enlarged to designs by Sir Edward Maufe. In addition to its rôle as the Mother Church of the Diocese, the Cathedral has a large regular congregation and a lively ministry as the parish church of the city centre. The Cathedral services recognise this dual rôle, some being fully choral and using traditional forms of worship with others reflecting recent liturgical trends.

The Cathedral Choir is entirely voluntary, as there is no Choir School attached to the Cathedral. The boys and girls attend over twenty different schools in Bradford and the surrounding areas, and their work necessarily takes place outside school hours. The students and adults of the Choir are drawn from a wide area around the city; strong links are maintained with the universities of Bradford and of Huddersfield. The Full Choir numbers around seventy-five singers who operate a flexible rota system to share the considerable workload whilst ensuring that an optimum number is present for each service.

In addition to their work of singing at the Sunday and mid-week services in the Cathedral the Choir regularly appears in concerts, often in support of local charities. The Choir also tours both in England and on the continent, and broadcasts on the radio and on television, most notably the 1977 Service for the Royal Maundy which was held in the Cathedral as part of the visit to Bradford of Her Majesty the Queen.

It is known that in 1850 St Peter's Parish Church, Bradford had a Choir of mixed voices, adult men and women, who occupied the two pews in front of the organ in the West Gallery. The first organ in the Parish Church was installed in this gallery in 1786 having been built by Donaldson of Newcastle and shipped to Bradford by sea to Hull, and from Hull to Bradford by river and canal. It had three manuals extending down to G, with the Swell extending to fiddle G, and no pedals.

The first organist was William Speight, of whom nothing but his name is known save that he held office for thirty years. He was followed in 1819 by John Simpson. He is described as 'a most amiable and courteous gentleman'. He was a leading figure in the musical life of the town and was much in demand as a recitalist in the town of Bradford and the surrounding area. A stained glass window (the first of its kind in the Parish Church) records the date of his death as 18th November 1860, and that he had been organist for over 40 years.

The first mention that we have of the establishment of a robed choir at St Peter's Parish Church, Bradford is in 1853, when on the first Sunday of the New Year, 2nd January, 'twelve surpliced boys, reverently filed out of the present clergy vestry, separated at the chancel steps into two streams, Decani and Cantoris, as in the Cathedral Churches, walked along the north and south aisles, mounted the gallery steps to the two pews assigned to them, in front of the men, who were not yet surpliced; an incongruity amended on the Easter Day following, when the full choir men and boys walked in proper order...'

Simpson was followed by Mr Absalom Rawnsley Swaine, a school-master by profession whose disciplinary methods (sic) with the chorister boys were described as 'highly successful'. On his appointment the salary of the organist was raised to £52 p a, augmented later to £60 and finally to £75. He is attributed with having said, '...You cannot expect to get an S S Wesley for £21 a year...' which was the sum paid to his predecessor. Swaine resigned his appointment in 1893, having served for 33 years. He died at Trowbridge, Wiltshire, where he had retired with his wife whose family were from that town.

Dr Henry Coates (1858-1938) succeeded Absalom Rawnsley Swaine in 1893, retiring in 1938, just a few months before he died. The Song Room added at the West End of the Cathedral in 1954 is dedicated to his memory.

Dr Charles Hooper (1896-1963) succeeded Coates in 1939. Born in Plymouth, he was educated at Manchester and Leeds Universities, and was Music Adviser and Inspector of Schools, Leeds. He composed many anthems, and his educational publications (*Teaching Music to Classes and School Music Readers*) were highly rated. He resigned in 1963. A stained glass memorial in the Oriel window of the Song Room is dedicated to him

He was succeeded by Bradford-born Keith Vernon Rhodes (1930-1992). He was educated at Leeds University, was a lecturer at the Royal Northern College of Music and served as Organist of the Cathedral until 1981. On leaving the Cathedral he founded the Bradford Choristers and was Director of Music at Ashville College, Harrogate. For 21 years he was also Deputy Chorus-Master, Organist and Accompanist to the Huddersfield Choral Society. He contributed widely to the musical press and his acclaimed manual *The Musical Training of Choristers, RSCM* was published in 1974 and 1987. He died following a short illness in 1992 and a memorial glass in the Oriel window of the Song Room bears his name. An outstanding choir-trainer, under his leadership the Choir flourished and established an enviable reputation, at one time numbering over 100 singers, boys and men, in two fully balanced four part choirs. They recorded and broadcast regularly and toured at home and abroad, most notably to Jamaica in 1974.

Rhodes was followed by Geoffrey Weaver (b 1943), educated at Gonville and Caius College, Cambridge. He taught at Maidstone Grammar School (1966-69), Bristol Grammar School (1969-74), and at St Catherine's School, Hong Kong (1975-81) on behalf of the Church Missionary Society. During these years he was Conductor/Director of many amateur and professional choral groups, in addition to which he was a noted orchestral conductor. He was Organist of Bradford Cathedral from 1982-1986 and a lecturer at Leeds University. During his time at Bradford he rebuilt the choir, which had suffered a period of immense difficulty after Keith Rhodes' departure, inspiring loyalty and a renewed sense of purpose where for a while there had been despondency and insecurity. He took it on tour to France and twice to Germany establishing its musical viability once more. In 1986 he moved to

Birmingham to join the staff of Crowther Hall, a CMS Training College. In 1996 he became Warden and Director of Education for the Royal School of Church Music in which role he has travelled widely; he has published two collections of Christian songs from churches across the world, in particular from the developing countries.

Alan Horsey (b 1955) succeed Geoff Weaver in 1986 as Organist and Master of the Choristers and lecturer at Leeds University. He had studied at the Royal College of Music, then taught at Leeds Polytechnic while assisting with the music at Leeds Parish Church. In 1979, he had returned to London as Director of Music at St James's Church, Muswell Hill. Together with Martin D Baker, the Assistant Organist (appointed at 22 having been Organ Scholar at Huddersfield University for three years, and now Deputy Headmaster at Penistone Grammar School) he has continued the rebuilding work that Weaver had begun, expanded the network of local schools from which choristers were drawn, and in 1992 founded the Cathedral Girls' Choir. Under his direction the Choir has appeared on television and radio, has recorded commercially and toured in Denmark, Belgium, and Germany In 1996 he became Conductor of the Ilkley and Otley Choral Societies on the sad death of their much-loved conductor, John Coates.

His is, at the time of writing, still in office at Bradford Cathedral.

The Organ

The organ was built in 1904 by William Hill and Son of London. A fine example of that notable firm's work, it had 40 speaking stops, three manuals and pedals and was tightly packed into what is now the North Ambulatory.

In the 1958s and early 60s when the East End of the Cathedral was developed, the organ was rebuilt and enlarged (with the addition of a fourth manual and a solo trumpet) by William Hill & Son, Norman and Beard. At this time it was installed in a new organ chamber twenty feet above the Ambulatory where it speaks directly into the resonant Chancel. Further work was carried out on the organ by the firm of J W Walker and Son in 1977, and J Clough and Sons in 1993. There are now 58 speaking stops spread over four manuals and pedals. As part of the redesigning of the organ in 1962 an Antiphonal Section, the

Nave Organ, was installed at the West End of the Cathedral. It had 13 stops and was played from the main organ console in the Chancel. It proved very effective in leading the singing of large congregations and for enriching the sound and flexibility of the organ in concerts and recitals. In 1987 it was removed when the Cathedral underwent a major re-ordering, and in 1992 a Bradford Computer Organ (electronic) again playable from the chancel console, was installed to take its place.

ALAN HORSEY

Halifax Parish Church

Music-making in Halifax Parish Church goes back to 1766 when the organ was built by John Snetzler, the Austrian organ builder. (There was known to have been an organ prior to this, in 1502, but this was destroyed in 1650 under a Parliamentary order by Cromwell.) The first organist of the church was William Herschel, the astronomer, who was to discover the planet Uranus. Shortly after his appointment in November 1766, a performance of Handel's *Messiah* took place in the Parish Church, presumably by local choral societies. The earliest record of a choir at Halifax Parish Church is in the period from 1868 to 1882 when Dr John Varley-Roberts became organist. Dr Roberts was to compile his own hymn book for Halifax Parish Church, many copies of which still exist. In October 1879 services were held to celebrate the restoration of the church, when there were reputed to be 70 choristers in the choir. The choir was generally considered to be of a high standard. This was stated recently by a Mrs P Martin of Devizes, Wiltshire, whose father, Charles Mumford, was Head Chorister in the late 1880s.

Since then, very few records of the choir are available other than some weekly music lists of 1907-08 which show regular performances of many anthems and service settings. An outing to Blackpool for 28 choirboys in 1936 was recorded in the parish magazine. No records of choristers were kept prior to 1971 when the present organist, Philip C Tordoff, was appointed. Since then the choir has maintained its tradition of choral music with boy trebles (currently 17 in number) and men, with some lady altos.

Three years ago the girls' choir was formed and they rehearse and perform separately with their own repertoire, joining with the boys on a few occasions.

The organ as it stands today is a four-manual Harrison & Harrison of Durham, incorporating a number of stops from the original Snetzler instrument of 1766. The last major rebuild took place in 1928 but there was also a thorough renovation in 1976. Since 1965 the organ has been in the care of Mr John Clough, of Bradford, who is not only an independent builder of repute, but also one of England's leading euphonium virtuosi. The organ is dignified and beautifully balanced with a great range of tone from the lovely soft swell strings and quiet flute stops to the powerful Solo Tuba and heavy pedal reeds. It is used almost every day of the week, whether for service accompaniment, recital work, private tuition or organ practice.

esting old town. Composite recitals (not necessarily all for organ) are held periodically, giving amateurs the chance to play alongside the professionals. The organ has become widely known as one of the finest Parish Church instruments in the country and it has been highly praised by such distinguished musicians as Carlo Curley, Jennifer Bate, Gillian Weir, Francis Jackson, Simon Lindley and many others. An updated history and specification of the organ is currently being produced.

PHILIP TORDOFF & MARGARET WHITELEY

Leeds Parish Church

The history of music at one of England's most famous Parish Churches can with certainty be traced back to the plans laid in 1713 for the first organ in the church of Saint-Peter-at-Leeds. A Place of worship has stood on the banks of the River Aire for over a thousand years. On arrival as Vicar of Leeds in 1837, Dr Walter Hook set about making improvements to 't'owld Church'. This was done for two reasons – the building was very

Guided tours of the interior are available by arrangement and most of the 3,000 pipes may be viewed. The 32-foot pedal open wood lies horizontally along the back of the organ, there being insufficient height for it to be placed vertically.

For the last quarter of a century a regular pattern of weekly organ recitals from April to October has become firmly established. Such recitals are held in the evening on the first and third Saturdays in the month and at 12 00 noon on the second, fourth and fifth. They are supported not so much by the church's own congregation but mainly by the 'Friends of the Music' (founded in 1976) and by the increasing number of visitors to this inter-

LEFT Leeds Parish Church.

FAR LEFT Halifax Parish Church

dilapidated and required urgent repair, and, secondly, on account of its inherent unsuitability for forms of worship placing equal emphasis on sacrament as well as word. Holy Communion in the old Church involved administration of the sacrament in the Chancel, in effect a separate building, and then only once every three months. Hook required a facility by which Altar and Pulpit, on equal terms, were to be visible all over the building. He re-formed the Choir of Boys and Men founded in 1815, and arranged for the singing of Choral Services on weekdays as well as Sundays and Holy Days. This is a tradition continued today, and one sustained without the advantage of a resident Choir School or large-scale endowments.

Its continuance is sustained by parishioners, well-wishers and others who subscribe specifically for the purpose to the Friends of the Music of Leeds Parish Church (a Registered Charity) and through the generosity of a number of national trusts and charitable bodies, principally The Friends of Cathedral Music, The Ouseley Trust and – particularly – the Billing Trust.

The Boys attend schools all over the Leeds area, and many of the Lay Clerks and Choral Scholars are students in full-time education. To this nucleus are added supernumerary gentlemen for Sundays and special services, recitals and concerts.

Simon Lindley

A separate Girls' Choir was established in 1997 to sing regularly at services as an independent unit, and with the Gentlemen. All singers combine each term for divine worship, and girls and boys (separately and together) participate in concerts requiring a group of upper voices; they are to be heard to good effect on the Chandos recording of Mussorgsky's *Boris Godonov* from Opera North, conducted by Paul Daniel. Other commitments have included Orff's *Carmina Burana* for a Radio 3 broadcast, Andrew Carter's *Benedicite* at the Leeds Summer Heritage Festival and the world premiere of Philip Moore's *From Earth to Heaven*.

The Boy Choristers attend each day after school on Mondays, Tuesdays and Wednesdays with other services on Friday evening and on Sundays. Visiting tutors in piano, theory, voice and violin provide individual tuition for boys in conjunction with normal choir attendance, while others study at lessons taken in school or the home environment. The boys are busy folk and pursue a wide range of interests outside choir including sports of all kinds, recreations and computing.

Organists since 1841 are headed by Samuel Sebastian Wesley (1842-49), Dr (later Sir) Edward Bairstow (from 1906 to 1913) and in more recent times Dr Melville Cook and Dr Donald Hunt – both Conductors of the Three Choirs' Festivals (respectively at Hereford Cathedral from 1956 to 1966 and Worcester Cathedral from 1975 to 1996). The present Organist and Master of the Music, Mr Simon Lindley, was appointed in 1975.

Two other ensembles enjoy a close relationship with Leeds Parish Church – St Peter's Singers and St Peter's Chamber Orchestra. The Singers (a mixed choir of some 36 members founded in 1977) have developed a wide-ranging repertoire – from the baroque to the contemporary – and play a prominent role in the Leeds Concert Season. For large-scale works they are augmented by the Leeds Parish Church Festival Choir.

The Orchestra regularly accompanies the Singers, but it also appears in its own right either with other choirs or for orchestral concerts.

SIMON LINDLEY

St Anne's Cathedral, Leeds

Situated at the heart of Leeds, the Cathedral has been for many years a pioneer of music-making in the city. In 1995, it was the first Catholic cathedral in the country to establish a girls' choir, and it lays claim to an unusual world record – that of having had the youngest ever Cathedral Organist, Henry Chambers, who at the time of his appointment in 1913 was aged eleven.

The Cathedral, built in 1904, is widely hailed as the country's finest Catholic Cathedral after Westminster and has one of the greatest acoustics in the city.

Music is currently produced by three choirs containing boys, girls and adults respectively, who provide music for two sung Masses (Sunday 9 30 & 11 30) and two sung offices (Thursday 5 30 & Sunday 4 30) each week, using repertoire of all periods and styles.

The choir has toured widely to Ireland, France and most recently to Spain, where it was invited to deputise for the choirs at Montserrat and Barcelona's own Cathedral.

In July 2000, it was proud to host the first Catholic Three Choirs' Festival in conjunction with the cathedral choirs of Liverpool and Birmingham.

The cathedral itself is about to undergo substantial restoration and rebuilding, a major part of which will be the installation of a new mechanical action organ and new facilities for its choirs, the latest testament to the ever-increasing profile of music in the Cathedral and City of Leeds.

The cathedral is staffed by a full-time Director of Music, Stuart Thompson, who is responsible for music in the Cathedral and the Diocese of Leeds (his immediate predecessor was Joseph Cullen, now, amongst other things, chorusmaster of Huddersfield Choral Society). He is assisted by a part-time organist, an organ scholar, a vocal trainer and eight choral scholars.

Ripon Cathedral

It is likely that there was a choir when a cathedral was first built on the site by St Wilfrid (678 AD), although no surviving records mention the choir until the time of Archbishop Romanus (1286-1296) at which time the existing building was built. Chapter minutes first mention an organist as one Thomas Litster (1447). At the time of the Reformation the choir comprised six songmen and six singing boys but after the Chantries Act (1547), Ripon Minster – then a collegiate church – disbanded its choir for a time. It was refounded during the reign of James 1 (1603-1625) and from then until the 1940s daily sung Mattins & Evensong was offered. The Minster regained its own see in 1836, becoming a cathedral once again. Daily sung Evensong has survived as the choir's most significant musical offering.

The magnificent four-manual, 65-rank Harrison & Harrison organ on the central screen dates from 1878 when T C Lewis built a three-manual 49-rank instrument there. In the 1920s Harrisons enlarged and rebuilt it, revoicing it to sound characteristically bold and noble.

In 1960 the Dean and Chapter sold, amongst other valuable books, two 'Caxton' bibles to buy the site of the choir school, situated in the southern part of the city, now the only boarding choir school in Yorkshire. Ripon remains one of the smallest cathedral cities in Europe with a population of only 15,000, but its cathedral choir has become widely broadcast and recorded. Recent concert tours have taken them to Holland, Germany, the Czech Republic, Slovakia and Luxembourg.

In 1996 a separate choir, the Cathedral Girls'

Ripon Cathedral Choir

Choir (girls aged 8-15, non-boarding) was founded under the direction of the Organist & Master of the Choristers, Kerry Beaumont, to complement the existing choir. The girl choristers sing one or two services each weekend with or without the lay clerks.

Aside from singing 8-9 cathedral services each week, the cathedral choir performs in three annual festivals: the Northern Cathedral Festival (Ripon. Durham, York – early summer), the Yorkshire Three Choirs Festival (Wakefield, Leeds – early October) and the Yorkshire Cathedrals' Girl Choirs Festival (York, Sheffield, Wakefield, Leeds – early spring).

KERRY BEAUMONT

Sheffield Cathedral (Anglican)

The present church of SS Peter and Paul in Sheffield dates back to the early l5th century, indeed the chancel of the building is the only entire piece of medieval architecture left in the city centre.

The first reference to music in the building is in 1528 when John Wickersley gave the means to build a new organ. A choir is mentioned in 1770 when the singers and instrumentalists occupied a gallery over the west window. Sheffield Parish Church became the cathedral for the Diocese of Sheffield in 1914, to recognise Sheffield as an important city needing such a spiritual focal point. By 1920, the choir contained 24 boys and 12 pro-bationers as well as 18 men. The boys (as they are now) were drawn from various local schools, including Firth Park, High Storrs and Abbeydale. The workload was however more like that of a parish church, with one weekday evensong and two Sunday services.

At the time of World War II, the choir numbered 20 men and 20 boys. However, under Tustin Baker, it was involved with more city events, a notable example being the boys' partici-pation in the premiere of Honegger's *Christmas Cantata* under the baton of Sir John Barbirolli. The choir continued to sing for the civic events, chiefly The Judges' and Master Cutler services. In 1947 it made a recording of Mendelssohn's *Hear my Prayer.* The famous solo was sung by Neil Wilkinson.

1966 was a very busy year for the city, both The Queen Mother and Princess Margaret attending on state occasions. It was also the year that the Mander Organ was inaugurated by Dr Francis Jackson, Graham Matthews being the Director of Music. In the 1970s, the choir enjoyed its participation in the much-missed West Riding Cathedrals' Festival, alongside the choirs of Bradford and Wakefield Cathedrals.

In more recent times, the Cathedral choirs have become far more active, singing four weekday evensongs and two Sunday services. In 1995 Simon Lole launched a Girls' Choir, one of the first cathedrals to do so. The choir toured South Africa in 1995 and subsequent visits have been made to Germany and Holland as well as taking up residence in other British Cathedrals, most recently Portsmouth and Exeter. Next year the choir plans to tour the USA.

In addition to touring, the choirs have made a number of recordings, namely *Nunc Dimittis* in 1997, and with Neil Taylor as Director of Music, *Excelsis* in 1998 and *A Ceremony of Carols* in 1999, which includes a first-rate performance by the girls

of Britten's *Ceremony of Carols*. This year the choir has made *Et in Terra Pax*, a CD of contemporary English Mass settings, with music by George Malcolm, Lennox Berkeley, Grayston Ives and Mark Blatchly. The cathedral choir has featured on the BBC World Service, Songs of Praise and Radio 3 Choral Evensong.

Sheffield Cathedral is now in the middle of a development campaign, and hopes to raise £6.5 million to enhance and improve the building and musical life. As well as essential maintenance work, a new cathedral centre is proposed which will continue to serve the disadvantaged. Musically, a new organ will be built and an endowment find created to facilitate the growth and future development of music in the cathedral.

JOHN SWINDELLS
(organ scholar 1998-2000)
with the memories of
MELVYN STAFFORD (OC Sheffield)

Sheffield Cathedral (Catholic)

The Diocese of Hallam was founded in 1980 and chose as its Cathedral Church the Church of St Marie in the heart of the city of Sheffield. Built in 1850 by M E Hadfield, St Marie's is a masterpiece among his works. The design was based on a study of fourteenth-century churches in Yorkshire and Lincolnshire, especially St Andrew's, Heckington.

The organ built in 1875 by T C Lewis was donated by the Duke of Norfolk and is housed in a carved ease of Austrian Oak designed by John Bentley. Its 24 stops are distributed thus: Great 9, Choir 6, Swell 7, Pedal 2. The organ received some attention in rebuilds of 1975 and 1986. Unfortunately this work did not improve the playability of the instrument though happily the pipework. which remains the instrument's most remarkable aspect, was left untouched. There are plans to do a major rebuild which will retain the pipework and mechanical action but substantially reduce the weight of the action.

Apart from the Master of Music and Cathedral Organist all the musicians serve on a voluntary basis. Membership of the musical groups is open to all who are willing to offer their skills regardless of age, gender, ethnic origin or Christian denomination. Term-time membership for students is welcomed.

LEFT the Anglican Cathedral church of SS Peter and Paul

The Cathedral Choir rehearses on Thursday evening and sings at Sunday Morning Prayer and at the 10 30 am Mass as well as at the major celebrations of the liturgical year. It is a mixed choir and membership is open to anyone who enjoys singing. A regular commitment to attendance is expected. The wide-ranging repertoire includes music from the Renaissance to more contemporary liturgical composers from Britain (notably from the St Thomas More Group and Iona Community) and America.

The Cathedral Music Group rehearses on Sundays at 5 pm and sings at the 6 30 pm Mass. Instrumentalists and singers are welcome to join at any point in the year. Regular attendance is invited but a commitment to attend whenever responsibilities allow is expected. The repertoire includes music from the St Thomas More Group of composers and their American counterparts, and from the Iona Community. Among the many additional opportunities there is a regular monthly Taizé Prayer Service at which ecumenical involvement is particularly welcome.

Philip Jakob, who has been Master of Music since 1994, is committed to supporting the liturgy with music which reflects the vision of the Second Vatican Council. He is also Music Adviser for the Diocese, which work involves him with churches and schools of the Diocese of Hallam. He is an organist and frequent speaker at liturgical conferences. The Cathedral Organist is Hugh Finnigan who has served the community at St Marie's for over 25 years.

PHILIP JAKOB

Wakefield Cathedral

Wakefield Diocese, formed in 1888, was originally part of the diocese of Ripon and before that of York. The Cathedral (formerly the Parish Church) dates back to Saxon times and has the highest spire in Yorkshire. The five-manual organ can be heard in the free summer recital series on Saturday mornings. The Cathedral Choir consists of twenty boys and fourteen layclerks. Most of the boys are educated at Queen Elizabeth Grammar School and receive valuable choral scholarships. We also welcome boys who may attend other schools. The layclerks in some cases travel vast distances in their devotion to the musical worship of the Cathedral. The regular choral services are the Solemn Eucharist and Evensong on Sundays and Evensong on Thursdays; in addition the boys attend for practice on Tuesdays, Wednesdays and Fridays.

The Cathedral Girls' Choir was formed in 1992, shortly after the foundation of Salisbury Cathedral Girls' Choir. The twenty girls, aged from 8 to 18, are recruited from various schools. They sing at the Sunday Parish Eucharist and Wednesday Choral Evensong and practise on Fridays. Sir John Tavener's *Ikon to Saint Hilda* was specially written for them. Both choirs undertake a full programme of services, concerts, recordings and TV appearances.

The Cathedral has had only four Organists: Joseph Naylor (1888-1930), Newell Wallbank (1930-1946), Percy Saunders (1946-1970) and Jonathan Bielby (1970-present). The formidable list of past Assistant Organists includes John Scott (organist of St Paul's Cathedral), Peter Gould (organist of Derby Cathedral), the Revd Gareth Green (one of the music directors for the BBC Daily Service), Keith Wright (assistant organist of Durham Cathedral), and Sean Farrell (assistant organist of Rochester Cathedral). The Archbishop of York and the Bishop of Lincoln are former Wakefield choristers.

The music department seeks to uphold and renew the liturgical traditions for which Wakefield Cathedral is famous. It follows an innovative programme of commissioning new music. The following have written works for the Cathedral Choir: Kenneth Leighton (himself a Wakefield old chorister), Paul Drayton, Philip Moore, Andrew Carter, Richard Shephard and Philip Wilby. Over the years Jonathan Bielby himself has written many pieces to commemorate special events at the cathedral, ranging from Bishops' enthronements to layclerks' wedding anniversaries! To mark his Silver Jubilee as Organist these were published as a three volume subscription edition entitled *25 Years at Wakefield*.

In the 1970s the Cathedral Choir took an active part in the West Riding Cathedrals Festival (together with the choirs of Bradford and Sheffield Cathedrals). Since 1981 it has teamed up with the choirs of Ripon Cathedral and Leeds Parish Church in the Yorkshire Three Choirs Festival. There is an annual carol concert in Huddersfield Town Hall. The first Yorkshire Girls' Choirs Festival took place at Wakefield in 1998 (girls from York Minster, Ripon, Sheffield and Wakefield Cathedrals, and Leeds Parish Church).

National tours started in 1975 with a visit to

Wells Cathedral (also in 1976); Winchester, Salisbury, Chichester, Portsmouth and Arundel followed in 1977, and St Paul's Cathedral in 1980. Overseas tours started with two visits to Germany: Unna in 1979, and Braunschweig in 1981. The 1983 tour was to Le Puy in France, and three years later the choir made a return visit to Unna. The two American tours in 1991 and 1995 were to the eastern seaboard of the United States, from Boston through New York and Baltimore to Washington. A tour of Scotland in 1993 featured the music of Leighton. At Easter 1999 the Choir visited Salzburg and southern Germany. The Girls' Choir has gone on tour to Ely and London. Their first overseas tour will be to Sweden in 2001.

Despite these various extra activities, which enable the Cathedral's ministry and worship to be spread more widely, the choirs' primary work remains, and will always remain, the offering of the highest standards of music in the regular services of the Cathedral.

JONATHAN BIELBY (Organist & Master of the Music)
LOUISE MARSH (Assistant Organist & Director of the Girls' Choir)
ALWYN CLEGG (Deputy Assistant Organist)
KEITH BROWN (Organ Scholar)

The Royal School of Church Music in West Yorkshire

From the mid-nineteenth century, it became fashionable for Anglican churches to have robed choirs and organ accompaniment, this taking the place of groups of instrumentalists and unrobed singers ('west gallery minstrels'). Nonconformist churches also supported choirs (the preface to the 1933 edition of the *Methodist Hymn Book* begins with the statement 'Methodism was born in song'). By the inter-war years, most churches could boast an enthusiastic choir. Some were of a very high musical standard (that of Holy Trinity church, Huddersfield won prizes in church choir competitions, and was declared the best choir in the country). Most sang, in addition to hymns and in Anglican churches, psalms, mainly Victorian anthems, typified by the work of Goss, Barnby, Maunder, Stainer, Elvey, Macfarren &c – mostly easy pieces churned out in their hundreds to satisfy the needs of enthusiastic choralists. Most Anglican choirs were of boys and men; mixed choirs became more common from the 1950s onwards.

Sir Sydney Nicholson founded the Royal School of Church Music in 1927 to help all engaged in church music to appreciate the spiritual basis of music in worship, achieve higher standards, and discover the glories of church music (Victorian anthems are often associated more with Gilbert & Sullivan-like ditties than spiritual music, and the best of them constitute only a very small part of that heritage of English church music which in 1927 was unknown to most parish choirs). Based eventually near London, the RSCM set up area committees to coordinate local events for choirs. West Yorkshire is currently covered by the Bradford, the Leeds & Ripon, and the Wakefield Area Committees. The Wakefield Area was a merger of the former Halifax Area (formed in 1968), and the Pontefract Area (formed in 1971).

The RSCM has since its inception organised choirs festivals (the writer recalls a packed nave in Wakefield Cathedral around 1960 for which three conductors were needed – Dr Percy Saunders was the main conductor on a central rostrum, with relayers of the beat covering the side aisles. Mr A Hanley Lawrence of Huddersfield Parish Church was the organist.) It has also run training courses at various levels for choristers, both junior and adult. These have ranged from single sessions at local churches, through three-day courses at regional centres, to one-week residential courses with services sung in a cathedral (again the writer recalls singing the glorious music of Howells in York Minster).

During more recent years, depletion of church choirs has gone hand-in-hand with depletion of church congregations. Many churches which formerly had large choirs now rely on single vocalists, or a very small choir. In some churches, 'music groups' (guitar, drums, synthesiser, microphone-bound vocalist) have supplanted traditional choirs. However where viable choirs have survived, musical standards have often risen. In the Anglican church, the RSCM may have contributed significantly to this, but it is also true that performing groups of any type have to compete with the professional standards broadcast on radio and TV, and this has also helped to encourage an improvement in standards.

GEOFFREY LOCKWOOD

The Sings

There is one musical tradition which, more than any other, is very much unique to the old West Riding and which illustrates very succinctly the endemic need for the population in the area to 'make music'.

This music and social phenomenon, which has simply become known as 'the Sings', seems to have been originated in Longwood, when Jabez Iredale, secretary of the then Longwood Working Men's Club, met with a group of friends to sing outside the Thornhill Reading Rooms (now a hairdresser's shop) one day in 1873! This would not have been considered unusual – 'Everyone loved to sing, they were people of the hills, a love of singing was innate' (Esme Shackleton). Besides being members of the Longwood Choral and Philharmonic Societies, people used to meet to sing and play in each other's houses and gardens. Other kinds of meetings would often finish with a sing-song. The following year, the men decided to hold their Sing at the foot of Nab End Tower at 7.00 am on a Sunday morning as no one would be at work or church. It was not unheard of to sing hymns outside – Salendine Nook Baptist Church held an outdoor service once a month – but the Sings at Longwood had no particular religious affiliation. From Jabez Iredale's first germ of an idea, all other Sings emanated. A collection was taken and distributed to the local sick and needy. Later, with police permission, there was sometimes a house-to-house collection, and occasionally tins were placed in local hostelries. Many people remember large sheets held between four poles at the entrance to the Sings, with money being thrown into the middle. Sing Sunday was usually, though not always, held at the same time as the village feast. It was a time of great rejoicing, an open-house, and a meeting with friends and relations not seen since the previous Sing.

So, what exactly is a Sing? A Sing consists of a choir drawn mainly from local churches and chapels, which performs a few well-known choruses (*Hallelujah*, inevitably, but the Gloria from Mozart's Twelfth Mass is a particular favourite) and is joined by all other participants for the singing of the hymns which are printed in a programme. A hymn 'in memoriam' is sung, should anyone have died during the year, one of the most popular being *Deep Harmony*. Sometimes there is an address, sometimes prayers, and often the

National Anthem. The Sing takes place either early on Sunday morning (for example, Mollicar Woods near Castle Hill at 7 30 am, or Honley at 7 00 am), or more commonly during Sunday afternoon, in order that church services may still be attended. The only exception appears to be Hepworth who still hold their Sing on Feast Monday, necessitating time off work or school for participants. The conductor is usually a local musician; the Skelmanthorpe balance sheet of 1924 unusually shows him being paid 12/- for his services. The accompaniment was originally provided by a harmonium, band, orchestra or string group, with the exception of Mollicar Woods which has always been unaccompanied.

Unlike the Whitsuntide Walks, when everyone sings hymns in their church or chapel groups, the Sings are characterised by a lack of banners denoting a particular church or chapel. Instead, all denominations walk, stand and sing mingled: an observer would be unable to distinguish their individual religious affiliations. Although predominantly middle-class and chapel, the Sings were

(and in some cases still are) an important factor both in bringing together people of every class and every religion, and in raising funds for local charities. Although not originally formed with a view to fund-raising, this soon became one of the main functions, most of the money raised prior to the introduction of the National Health Service being donated to the local hospitals and Nursing Associations. Because of this, many became known as 'Hospital Sings' or 'Hospital Sunday Festivals'. Other charities which benefited included the Huddersfield Deaf and Dumb Institute, the Bradford Eye and Ear Hospital and Manchester Eye Hospital.

The relationship between the Sings and the Health Service

In order to attend a hospital as an in- or out-patient, it was necessary to be recommended by two 'upstanding' members of the community. Such was their position that the members of the Sing committees could be called upon to perform this very necessary function and indicated this on their

programmes. By 1935 this was no longer required, a doctor's letter being all that was necessary. Sing committees were also allowed to have representatives on the hospital Boards of Governors, Jabez Iredale of Longwood fulfilling this position from 1895.

The Sings continued throughout both world wars but, as with so many similar institutions, have reduced in numbers for a variety of reasons over the years. Many chapel choirs, the former nucleus of the Sings for instance, no longer exist. In their heyday, vast numbers of people attended the Sings. In 1929 a Sing made headlines with the damage that 7,000 people caused to walls and crops, and in 1930 it was decided to hold the Sing only in the first stopping point.

Angela Griffith's excellent work on the Yorkshire Sings (the basis of an MA thesis) lists no fewer than 53 villages in the Huddersfield area which at one time previously held Sings, and a further 30 in the Barnsley area. Of the Huddersfield Sings, only a handful now survive.

Opera & Operatic Societies

Huddersfield Amateur Operatic Society

The oldest amateur society of its kind in the district and one of the oldest in the country, Huddersfield Amateur Operatic Society may justly be called the parent society of the Town's amateur musical theatre. Founded in 1896, the Society is understood to have been one of those represented at the meeting in Manchester that led to the founding of the National Operatic and Dramatic Association (NODA) in 1899.

The Society began by establishing a tradition of fine performances, and it was taken for granted in those days that an amateur operatic show 'would be efficient in production and thoroughly musicianly in performance'. That tradition has been well maintained ever since. Since those days also, the Society has been a training ground for artists who helped to found other societies and so make amateur productions such a feature of the life of the town.

Sadly the Society's early records cannot be traced but newspaper cuttings from around its founding suggest that making a start was not at all easy. The 'prime mover' seems to have been a Mr Harold Wheawill. In November 1895 he sent out a circular announcing the proposal to form the Huddersfield Amateur Operatic Society but received so little encouragement (only two ladies attended the first meeting) that the project was dropped until the following Spring. A general meeting was held on 14 May 1896. Fourteen enthusiasts turned up and, though so small an attendance could hardly have been encouraging, it was decided to go ahead.

Thereafter all went well, though a proposal that principals should be selected by people outside the Society suggests that there were some teething troubles! Membership grew rapidly and in September rehearsals were started on *Iolanthe* which from the start had been the only show suggested. The then Mayor, Alderman John Lee Walker, was the President, and the Presidents of the Huddersfield Choral Society and the Huddersfield Philharmonic were Vice-Presidents. A Conductor was appointed and the Society also allowed itself the luxury of a Chorus-Master. A coach (or director as he would now be known) was also appointed, but before he arrived the ubiquitous Mr Wheawill conducted rehearsals as well as playing a part and acting as Secretary.

The first performance of *Iolanthe* was staged at the Theatre Royal on 16 February 1897. It excited great enthusiasm and was so well patronised that a hundred guineas was distributed to charity. Not all productions were at the Theatre Royal. The Society for some years went to the Hippodrome, later to become the Tudor Cinema, and also to the Palace Theatre, but for many years the 'Royal' was felt to be its proper home. Following its closure and subsequent demolition, the Society then moved to the ABC Cinema until its modernisation led to a further move. There followed a succession of venues including, among others, the Venn Street Arts Centre and the Town Hall, until the opening of the Lawrence Batley Theatre in 1994, which is now home to the Society's productions.

OPPOSITE
Huddersfield AOS's
1906 production of
Utopia Limited

From the outset the Society has always been fortunate in having loyal and long serving members in all spheres; musicians, performers and those attending to the business and technical side of its affairs. Over the years the Society has been host to many well-known local performers and also some who have gone on to further fame – Thelma Barlow of *Coronation Street* played with the Society as did David Bintley (as a boy), now internationally renowned for his work in the world of ballet.

The Society has always maintained touch with the musical life of the town. In 1954 it made a presentation of a silver rose bowl to the 'Mrs Sunderland' Musical Competition to be offered for the annual competition in the men's operatic solo class. It continues to enjoy close and valuable links with other societies and individuals in the

THE HIPPODROME, RAMSDEN STREET, HUDDERSFIELD,

20th, 21st, 22nd, 23rd and 24th FEBRUARY, 1906.

"Utopia Limited,"

OR, "THE FLOWERS OF PROGRESS,"

BEING

THE TENTH ANNUAL PERFORMANCE,

It is earnestly hoped that the kind patronage of the public will be increasingly extended, so that the total amount distributed amongst

LOCAL CHARITIES
will be at least **£1000.**

The Opera will be Produced under the Stage Direction of **Mr. H. LINDSAY HARMAN** (late of D'Oyly Carte's Opera Companies).

Magnificent Costumes, Wigs, &c., by B. J. SIMMONS & CO., Covent Garden, London.

Augmented Orchestra. Powerful Cast and Chorus. Special Scenery.

SUBSCRIBERS' TICKETS Half-a-guinea each, entitling each Subscriber to attend Four Rehearsals and the Dress Rehearsal, and to Two Reserved Seats.

BOXES (two), One Guinea each, entitling holder to same privileges as Subscriber's Ticket.

STALLS' TICKETS (Reserved), Two Shillings and Sixpence each.

Tickets and copies of this Souvenir may be obtained of Members of the Society and at the Music Shops.

Miss SPENCE has kindly undertaken the arrangements for sale of

TEA, COFFEE AND BISCUITS DURING THE INTERVAL,

Assisted by the following ladies:—Mesdames DEAN and LITTLEWOOD; Misses ARMITAGE, BROADBENT, HOLROYD, LEAROYD, LITTLEWOOD, LOCKWOOD, RILEY, IDA RILEY, SENIOR, SHAW, WADE, WHITTELL, WOOD; and Masters BERNARD CROWTHER RONALD CROWTHER, LESLIE CROWTHER, FRANK SYKES and BERTIE FAULDER.

Follies Girls from Huddersfield AOS's production of Crazy for You

town who are closely involved with singing, drama and instrumental music.

Since the first hundred guineas given to charity the Society has made many further large donations (though sadly not in recent years owing to the high costs of mounting productions). A look at past accounts and a comparison with those for more recent years highlights the increasing costs of presenting shows. In 1955 a production of *King's Rhapsody* cost in the region of £1,800 to stage; in 1999 the production of *Crazy for You* cost some £27,000!

Over the years the Society has never been afraid to rise to new challenges (none more so than *Show Boat* and *42nd Street*). It has presented a range of shows from Gilbert & Sullivan (very popular in early years but not performed now as there is a G & S Society in the town) through the Romberg shows, Rodgers & Hammerstein, Lerner & Loewe and Bernstein. Wherever possible shows newly released for amateurs have been presented (*Mack & Mabel* back in 1984, *Anything Goes*, *42nd Street*, and in the Centenary year, *Follies*, followed by *Me and My Girl* in 1997 and Gershwin's *Crazy for You* in 1999).

While with their first production the Society stood alone, their example has been such that the district now flourishes with amateur operatic societies greater in number than ever before.

Having completed its first 100 years, the Society looks forward to its next centenary!

Haworth West Lane Baptist Amateur Operatic Society

The strength and versatility of church choirs following the last war meant that in addition to performing old favourites such as Handel's *Messiah*, Stainer's *Crucifixion* and Maunder's *Olivet to Calvary*, many also gave pleasure by presenting popular works such as *Merrie England* and *The Rebel Maid* in concert form.

Such was the position at Haworth in 1948 when the choir of the West Lane Baptist Chapel broke with tradition and staged *The Pirates of Penzance*: conducted by Joseph Snowden and produced by Arthur Hird – a show totally cast from choir members. During the next decade (and before the spread of TV) there was much musical interest in the Worth Valley, with five societies within a radius of four miles performing Gilbert and Sullivan operettas each year. The Haworth choir performed many G & S works, but in 1958 *Rose Marie* was chosen, at which point the first chapter of the story comes to an end.

The second chapter opened in 1964 when choir members, with support from other churches, formed the Haworth West Lane Baptist Chapel Amateur Operatic Society. The first production to be chosen was *The Mikado*, conducted by our present Joint Musical Director, Terence Lofthouse, and produced by Frederick Pye. Shows at this time and for many years thereafter will be remembered for stunning stage designs by Stanbury artist Ken Jackson, who has also produced shows and frequently joined the ranks of the amateur musicians who have served the society so well over the years.

In 1985, after 22 years as Musical Director and Chairman, Terry Lofthouse decided to take a well-earned rest. Pamela Dimbleby took over the baton; later Terry Lofthouse returned to share conducting duties with her. Producers who have made their mark over the years are Derrick Fuller, Jean Holdsworth, Walter Anderton, Mollie Thornton and, from 1992 to the present day, Michael Lofthouse.

In recent times the Society has performed shows and concerts at a variety of venues. In 1998, for example, when the Chapel was not available because of redevelopment work, the choir presented *Trial by Jury* and 'Songs from the Shows' at Skipton Auction Market. A number of members also battled through snow and ice in a borrowed Landrover to Halifax in 1979 when they joined with other societies and the BBC Concert Orchestra for a live G & S broadcast on Radio 2. The Society returned to a much changed Baptist Chapel in 1999 with no proscenium arch,

a flat playing area, an orchestra divided on two sides and an audience very close to the action. Initial concerns about the new environment changed to delight when the production of *Iolanthe* was voted a success.

Principals, chorus members, accompanists, helpers and supporters too numerous to name have given sterling service over the years and the Society looks to the future with confidence in providing many more performances in Haworth of the imperishable Gilbert and Sullivan operettas

LEFT Haworth West Lane Baptist Society AOS perform Iolanthe *and ABOVE* Patience *in 1969*

Great Horton AOS production of Anything Goes *set on board a ship*

Great Horton Amateur Operatic Society, Bradford

Formed in 1904 as a Glee Union, the society is the oldest of its kind in the city. In 1905 the society's first production was *Sherwoods' Queen*. Gilbert and Sullivan operas were performed annually in local halls until 1939, by which time the society's size and repertoire had expanded: *Rose Marie* was the first show to be performed by the society in the city's professional theatre, the Alhambra.

Reformed in 1950 after the war, the society used four different venues for its shows, all of which closed after we used them. Was it something we said? Or did? In 1961 we returned to the Alhambra which has been our home ever since.

Show week is always February. Our 1954 production of *Land Of Smiles* was set in China. In oriental costume the cast had to cross the stage outside, re-entering covered in snow! A dress rehearsal of the 1996 *The Pirates Of Penzance* was also hit by snow. Everyone walked (complete with costumes) from all over the city at 6 00 pm. Seven members made it – by 10 00 pm the last cast member arrived. The city was gridlocked. The theatre was opened by the police as a refuge for stranded commuters and the tea team moved front of house to serve hot drinks to very cold motorists.

Back stage at the theatre can be dangerous, so new members are always shown round. One member was shown the trapdoor (used for the Genie in a pantomime). She spent the whole week's production avoiding it (not realising it was locked) in case she disappeared down the hole! Many quick changes take place at the side of the stage by torchlight. One member dashed off stage, by which time the scenery had changed and his costume was up in the roof.

In the 1990 production of *Oliver* boys and girls (playing the role of orphan children) were used for the first time. The 1992 production of *Anything Goes* was set on a ship. The orchestra was on the bridge with the MD having his back to the audience. The orchestra saw the theatre emptying! When told, he replied, 'Keep playing, keep playing.' Eventually the safety curtain dropped: there was a bomb scare. He said he felt as if he was on the *Titanic*. The cast ended up practising their tap dancing skills in Morley Street to keep warm until they could re-enter the theatre and carry on with the performance.

Our 1994 production – *Barnum* – was the most taxing of all. The members learned balloon sculpture, juggling, unicycling, stilt-walking, and trapeze, and Barnum walked the tightrope every night. Hours of rehearsal paid off: it was a raging success and we all had a ball.

1997 brought *Singing In The Rain*. 'Would we have rain?' everyone asked. 'Of course', was the reply. There was just one snag: the leading man had to mime the song – otherwise he would have been electrocuted by the rain on his mike. Recently we have performed new shows, but our millennium production, *Me & My Girl*, was a 'golden oldie' enjoyed by all. Our next show in February 2001 at the Alhambra is *The Sound Of Music*.

Many professional actors have learnt their craft in the society.

Opera North

The first major excitement at Opera North was at a choral rehearsal David Lloyd-Jones took in a relatively small hall. Here was the choral sound the Company longed for from a northern chorus, here was the attention to detail (including the French for *Samson et Dalila*) expected from its Music Director. What a start! And it was followed by an early hearing of the orchestra, which was everything hoped for from a group of young professionals; generous of sound, technically adept, involved. Everyone since – supporters, public and critics – have noticed the huge contribution made by both arms alike.

Hits in early seasons included *A Village Romeo and Juliet* and *Rigoletto*, the former being the only truly 'northern' opera the Company has scheduled, whilst the latter was mounted in a temporary structure, part tent, part aircraft hangar in Sheffield. Both of them were serious successes and popular with a growing, subscription-based public. Wagner, not easy for an opera company with a relatively small orchestra, has rather surprisingly featured in six of the Company's twenty one years, but extra costs rather than artistic doubts have

Opera North's Wozzeck *by Alban Berg with Wozzeck played by Andrew Shore, Marie: Josephine Barstow. Photo* DONALD COOPER

inhibited a revival of *Die Meistersingers*, reasonable in orchestral demands but hard on extra-chorus numbers and overtime alike. Nonetheless it was a milestone.

Wagner postulates mountain-climbing, part of the responsibility of every opera company, and has not been shirked at any stage of its development by Opera North. *Prince Igor*, a work on the biggest scale came after only four seasons, the first time since the war that the opera with all its awkward ramifications had been tackled by any British company. It was staged as a direct result of the Music Director – David Lloyd Jones's – Russian expertise. To this day, his edition of *Boris Godunov* is the one used at the Bolshoi Theatre in Moscow. Prokofiev's *The Love for Three Oranges* was the next addition to the Russian repertory, dazzlingly

Benjamin Britten's A Midsummer Night's Dream, *Winter 2000. Titania: Claron McFadden, Bottom: Jonathan Best.* Photo STEPHEN VAUGHAN

directed by Richard Jones, televised by the BBC, and starting to occupy a secure place in audience affections. The jewel in Opera North's Russian crown has nevertheless been *Boris Godunov*, dominated by a towering performance by John Tomlinson. How many people ever expected to experience Musorgsky's original seven-scene version in the theatre, let alone in a production which put forward such punch and conviction?

Verdi has naturally figured with some prominence in Opera North's lists – achieving nearly one out of every seven performances, the identical proportion accorded to Mozart. It is typical of the Company that *Nabucco* arrived almost coincidentally with *Rigoletto*, and has moreover aggregated thirty performances in three seasons. If the seldom performed *Jerusalem* clocked up only nine in its single season it was a courageous choice, billed at the time as the only one of Verdi's operas not previously produced in the UK. If the production baffled some – de-construction on a major scale – the score delighted many and it was not surprising to find *Attila* and *Don Carlos* following in the next seasons and providing Verdian triumphs both for John Tomlinson and Paul Daniel, the new Music Director. The Company has particularly happy memories of a streamlined *Aida*, marvellously set by Philip Prowse, very well sung, and for once recognising that only two scenes of this basically intimate piece can properly accommodate spectacle.

Twentieth-century work features prominently in these first twenty one seasons, accumulating 617 performances from a total of 2,378, the 617 swelled by over 150 Puccini performances (of *Tosca, Butterfly, Fanciulla, La Bohème, La Rondine* and *Gianni Schicchi*), but with due respect paid to Walton, Tippett and Britten. Wilfred Josephs' *Rebecca*, Robert Saxton's *Caritas*, Michael Berkeley's *Baa-Baa Black Sheep*, Benedict Mason's *Playing Away* and Simon Holt's *The Nightingale's to Blame* are the only world premieres so far, but each can be seen as a shrewd addition to the Company's list. Roberto Gerhard's *The Duenna* almost comes into the category as a world deuxième, a work of considerable stature and a belated reparation to the composer for years of neglect in his adopted country.

This is an article about landmarks, not personalities, and should include a glance at enterprising choices in the repertory, works which years of operatic globe-trotting might not bring you.

Chabrier's witty *L'Etoile* certainly counts as a rarity and it is good that it was followed by the composer's other and more substantial comedy *Le Roi malgré lui*. If that was mild trail-blazing, the inclusion in successive seasons of Dukas's *Ariane et Barbe bleu* and Schreker's *Der ferne Klang* – masterpieces of *art nouveau* – qualify without a shadow of a doubt. You could have had long odds against seeing either of them in the North when the Company started in 1978! Long odds too against Krenek's *Johnny spielt auf*, even Strauss's *Daphne*, and maybe against that Tchaikovsky double bill, *Yolande* and the *Nutcracker*, which climaxed the Russian master's stage career. To commemorate Tchaikovsky's death, other companies dutifully trotted out *Onegin* and *Queen of Spades*, but it is likely that nobody else would have contemplated the affectionate 'cod' of *Nutcracker* unveiled at the Edinburgh Festival, to the total stupefaction of critics who didn't know whether the joke was on them, Tchaikovsky, or merely on years of prettification of a masterpiece which copes with anything dished out to it and still delights its audience. Neither Mozart's *Il re pastore* nor Ponchielli's *La Gioconda* occurs very frequently nowadays in British operatic lists, and Opera North's revivals of these brought nearly as much credit as did that of Britten's *Gloriana*, a major salutation to a surprisingly neglected masterpiece.

British opera companies have not foraged much in the field of the Musical, but Opera North blazed a trail in the much-praised *Show Boat*, and has followed up with Gershwin's *Of Thee I Sing* and the outstandingly successful *Sweeney Todd*. Opera North's most determined, most typical gesture in its fifteenth season was the wonderfully successful assault on *Wozzeck*, that Eiger climb which stands between any opera company and maturity. Master-minded as it was by Paul Daniel, that was as heart-warming a portent for the future as you could wish for.

The regime of Paul Daniel and Nicholas Payne was notable for Daniel's graduation from the most promising conductor in the UK to acknow-ledgement as one of the very best. Opera North played its part in that step, just as Daniel played his in Opera North's advance. It was rounded off by a bold and illuminating new staging of *Pelléas et Mélisande*, as much an eye-opener as *The Trojans*, *The Love for Three Oranges*, *Boris Godunov* and *Yolande/Nutcracker* had been before.

Paul Harrhy as Truffaldino in Opera North's 1988 production of Prokofiev's The Love for Three Oranges

During the Company's 21st season in 1999-2000, the 'three-in-one' autumn season (*La Traviata, Katya Kabanova, Don Giovanni*) suggested that new productions staged with super-economy did not preclude prime imagination, and on top of it all a new Music Director, Steven Sloane, arrived to put a firm personal imprint on musical matters. Britten's *A Midsummer Night's Dream* in a new production, to which neither conductor, Steven Sloane, nor production team, Patrice Caurier and Moshe Leiser, brought the accumulated Shakespearean baggage inevitable to any British-reared group, formed the centre-piece of the winter season. That was salutary – and fresh – which is what is hoped and believed that Opera North's productions tended to be in the past and will continue to be in the future.

The 2000/2001 season bears out these intentions by beginning with a new production of Schuman's only opera, *Genoveva* directed by David Pountney before joining revivals of *The Marriage of Figaro* and *La Rondine* for the Autumn tour. Winter 2000 brings a new production of Donizetti's *Elixir of Love* directed by the winning combination of director Daniel Slater and designer Robert Innes Hopkins, who created a striking *Bartered Bride* two years earlier; and Richard Jones' gripping production of *Pelléas and Mélisande* coupled with a specially devised dramatised concert version of *Tristan und Isolde* in the newly refurbished Leeds Town Hall. The Company continues to further its commitment to the Musical with a new production of Shostakovich's operetta *Moscva Cheryomushki*, retitled *Paradise, Moscow* directed by David Pountney and conducted by Steven Sloane in Spring 2001, leading the Company confidently into the future.

Orchestral Music

INTRODUCTION

The principal beneficiaries of the explosion in musical activity which took place in the second half of the nineteenth century, discussed elsewhere in this book, were choral societies and brass bands. Orchestras, too, advanced, but for various reasons their development was by no means as assured (even London had to wait until 1904 for the establishment of the London Symphony Orchestra, the capital's first professional orchestra to achieve permanence). There was no shortage of instrumentalists or of teachers, but in the English concert hall the orchestra was generally regarded as no more than a necessary adjunct to a choral society.

At the great triennial music festivals (at Leeds, Norwich and Birmingham, for instance) orchestral music was a poor relation to the great oratorios of Handel and Mendelssohn (and the not-so-great works of Spohr, Costa, Sullivan and a host of now-forgotten English composers). Few impresarios were prepared to face the financial risks of putting on orchestral concerts, and it was only in 1895,

Halifax Square Chapel Orchestra

when Robert Newman launched the Henry Wood Promenade Concerts, that a concert series of enduring success was born.

The main source of employment for professional players was the theatre (and later, in the days of silent films, the cinema). The summer season, when no self-respecting holiday resort was without its resident orchestra, offered further employment (Bournemouth was one of a handful of such places to mount orchestral concerts in the winter: the Bournemouth Municipal Orchestra, founded by Sir Dan Godfrey in 1893, is the only one to survive today: its present title – the Bournemouth Symphony Orchestra – dates from 1954). The superior sort of café or hotel also boasted a 'Palm Court' Orchestra.

For many years, therefore, the Hallé Orchestra (founded by Sir Charles Hallé in 1858 and the country's oldest professional orchestra with a continuing history) was unique, though it was only after the Second World War that it gave concerts all the year round and its members received annual salaries (as opposed to concert-by-concert payment).

From early in its history the Hallé established strong links first with Bradford and subsequently with Sheffield (with occasional visits to other Yorkshire towns). Otherwise, professional concerts were provided by 'ad hoc' orchestras (often quaintly named 'Permanent Orchestras'): their members would be drawn from local players in theatres and so forth and they would assemble for a 'same-day' rehearsal (usually on a Saturday).

The best example of this practice comes from Leeds. The Leeds Permanent Orchestra was founded in 1903: it was subsequently renamed the Leeds Symphony Orchestra and, in 1935, the Northern Philharmonic Orchestra (it appears to have been wound up in 1950, three years after the appearance of the Yorkshire Symphony Orchestra). It presented an annual season of six or seven subscription concerts in Leeds Town Hall, engaging top conductors and soloists. Its financial state seems to have been always parlous (see illustration), particularly in the notably difficult interwar years, when the advent of 'the wireless', the ever-widening dissemination of increasingly sophisticated gramophone records and the lure of 'the talkies' (to mention merely the most immediate rivalling demands on people's leisure-time) resulted in falling audiences for its concerts.

Other towns with 'permanent' (in the event,

FACTS ABOUT YOUR CONCERTS

Estimated Average Losses:

		£10
1st CONCERT		£10
2nd CONCERT		£22
3rd CONCERT		£56
4th CONCERT	(StringConcert)	Slight Profit
5th CONCERT		£24

6th CONCERT Taken at doors and programmes £62 nett. Subscribers £82. Broadcast Fee apportioned from String Concert and other economies effected. **Estimated loss £13**

7th CONCERT ??

You are reminded that the figures which have been given on this page are **ESTIMATES**. They have been given so that the audience may appreciate the financial difficulties which the Management have to face and to show what a very narrow margin there is between the yield of **AN ABSOLUTELY FULL HOUSE** and the average cost of a Concert.

(Average cost £182. Full House £200 nett).

The Management hope that many casual attenders will become subscribers next year, and that all old subscribers who dropped out this year will return next season.

THE SUBSCRIBERS ARE
THE BACKBONE OF THESE CONCERTS.

---

short-lived) orchestras included Bradford, Huddersfield and Wakefield.

There was to be no full-time professional orchestra in Yorkshire until the establishment of the Yorkshire Symphony Orchestra in 1947. Many who read this will have fond memories of this ambitious but ill-fated enterprise. Launched on the wave of enthusiasm generated by the wartime boom in classical music, it was subsidised by a Leeds-dominated consortium of local authorities. It was undermined from the start by the fact that neither Bradford nor Sheffield (with their long-standing association with the Hallé) supported the project. Maurice Miles was a respected conductor

In the early 1930s the Leeds Symphony Orchestra's programmes regularly carried announcements similar to the above (March, 1932). In 1933, however, it was able to state that at the first concert of the new season 'door receipts were a record...and a margin of profit was attained', with 1,890 out of 2,058 seats filled.

but lacked the charisma which might have given a provincial band the national status enjoyed by the Hallé Orchestra. Though the YSO was disbanded in 1955, it did bequeath a substantial legacy. It had brought regular concert seasons to many towns for the first time, and such seasons have been maintained, in one form or another, to this day.

Only in 1978, with the establishment of the English Northern Philharmonia, the orchestra of Opera North, did the county at last have its own orchestra – from the start, committed to giving orchestral concerts as well as playing in the theatre-pit. It has greatly enriched the country's, as well as the county's, musical scene.

The fitful progress of professional orchestras – regionally and nationally – has been mirrored in the amateur sector. Throughout the nineteenth century (and even earlier) amateur orchestras came and went, but in the 1880s and 1890s, several societies were established which, having endured serious vicissitudes (not always merely financial), are today thriving as never before. Among them must be listed the Huddersfield Philharmonic (1862), Hull Philharmonic (1881), Halifax Orchestral Society (1882), Leeds Orchestral Symphony Society (1890), Slaithwaite Philharmonic (1891) and York Symphony (1897). (Curiously, Bradford – in so many respects an eminently musical city – seems never to have generated an amateur orchestral society of any note, and does not possess one today. Sheffield possesses several, but none with a continuous history going back to the nineteenth century)

Amateur orchestras are decidedly unpredictable beasts: their success depends on so many variables – membership, rehearsal attendance, conductor, repertoire, but above all, on their philosophy. Do they open their doors to all-comers, or are they selective? Do they pursue an 'adventurous' repertoire, or, in order to attract a large audience, are their programmes 'populist'? And, given that though their members are not paid, even amateur orchestras' concerts are expensive to mount, can they balance their books? All the orchestras mentioned above – and others – have found differing formulae for meeting these sometimes conflicting considerations.

For the present writer, if the orchestra possesses adequate resources, repertoire presents the most fascinating challenge. Over the years, the programmes of amateur orchestras have tended to follow the pattern established by the professionals.

Thus, amateur programmes from the 1890s are no different from that of the first Henry Wood Prom in 1895, with its multiplicity of soloists and mainly short items (some decidedly ephemeral in nature). Such programmes were still common up to and even after the Second World War, by which time the professionals had abandoned them, concentrating on the mainstream symphonic repertoire. In due course (in the 1950s and 1960s) amateur orchestras had caught up with this trend; by that time, however, the professionals had become more adventurous (Bruckner and Mahler symphonies, once rarities, were now commonplace, and the *avant-garde* was beginning to make its noisy presence felt). Here, the amateurs were quick to catch up (except that they did not embrace the *avant-garde* – your average string-player wants to produce beautiful sounds from his instrument, not demented shrieks…): look, for instance, at the programmes of the Huddersfield Philharmonic in Arthur Butterworth's time.

There is no doubt that the standard of amateur orchestral playing improved immeasurably from about 1960 onwards – not surprisingly, given the heavy post-war investment in 'youth' orchestras and the stream of talent which emerged from them. And all this has taken place when, for decades, the survival of some of our longstanding professional orchestras has been under constant threat; and also, when local authority support has notably dwindled (in Yorkshire, Leeds is an honourable exception).

Now, in the year 2000, we have reached a most interesting position. Outside London (a law unto itself), the provincial orchestras appear to concentrate their resources on their 'flagship' concerts in their home towns: the CBSO at Symphony Hall, the Hallé at the Bridgewater Hall. 'Out-of-town' concerts have become predictably 'safe'; and it seems increasingly to be the role of the well-founded amateur orchestra to bring to the public large-scale masterworks which though by no means 'obscure' are unlikely to be programmed by a visiting professional orchestra. In the current Huddersfield season, for instance, Suk's *Asrael* Symphony, Prokoviev's Fifth, Bruckner's Ninth and Mahler's Third figure: all presented by the town's two amateur orchestras.

The future of the amateur orchestra seems brighter than ever before.

ADRIAN SMITH

Halifax Symphony Orchestra leaves for Germany

Halifax Symphony Orchestra

The Halifax Orchestral Society (at first named the Northgate-End Orchestral Society) was founded in 1882, but for many years before that there had been a succession of short-lived orchestras in the town. A 'Harmonic Society', for instance, had flourished in the 1790s, performing works by Bach, Handel and Haydn. Like many other old societies, it laid down rules which strike us today as comical:

> '...That every member coming intoxicated, or making himself so during the concert [sic], shall forfeit two shillings and sixpence'.

From 1866 to 1880 a Philharmonic Society enjoyed considerable success. Concert programmes in the early 1870s carried the following announcement:

> 'For many years past, Halifax has been the only town in the West Riding possessing a complete resident Orchestra, and the musical public of the town and district are appealed for support, that the local reputation be maintained.'

However, falling membership and increasing reliance on imported professionals led to the society's disbandment in 1880.

The new orchestra was formed largely on the initiative of the Rev F E Millson, the minister at Northgate-End Unitarian Chapel (interestingly enough, the Huddersfield Philharmonic was similarly indebted to a Unitarian minister for its foundation). The members were to bring their own instruments, except for double basses, side drums and 'clarionettes', which were provided by the Society. There was a weekly subscription of 3d. At its opening concert, 31 players presented a programme of a light nature. In the 1890s more solid orchestral fare was being tackled. The prestige of the orchestra was such that its concerts were reviewed not only in the two local papers (the *Guardian* and the *Courier*) but also the *Bradford Observer*, *The Yorkshire Post* and the *Leeds Mercury*. In an orchestra of 65 players, a quarter were professionals.

In 1909, the association with the Unitarian Chapel ended, and the orchestra was renamed the Halifax Orchestral Society. Like many similar organisations, the Society was badly affected by

Halifax Symphony Orchestra at rehearsal

the First World War, and struggled to keep going. There was a steady recovery in the 1920s (though it was not until 1925 that a full public concert was given – the first in 11 years).

In 1927, James Bates, who had been a member of the society for over 30 years, became conductor and the orchestra began to regain its pre-war reputation, though its rigid adherence to the all-amateur composition of the orchestra posed problems of balance, and restricted the choice of repertoire.

After the disruption caused by the Second World War, the society resumed full activity. Important decisions were made: the 'all-amateur' policy was abandoned, and a career conductor was to be appointed. In fact, there was to be a rapid turnover of conductors, as successive 'apprentice conductors' of the newly-established Yorkshire Symphony Orchestra were engaged. It was in this period that the orchestra paid two visits to Lüdenschied in West Germany.

Subsequent conductors included David Jordan, Arthur Butterworth (under whom there were many exciting 'firsts' for the orchestra) and Frank Cliff (who also pursued an adventurous repertoire). In 1976, Anthony Ridley, a former violinist with the Royal Liverpool Philharmonic with considerable conducting experience, was appointed conductor – a post he holds to this day (the present leader, John Marshall, has been in post almost as long).

In 1982, the Society celebrated its Centenary in style, with a commissioned Overture *The Brontes* by Wilfred Josephs, Moura Lympany in Rachmaninov's Second Piano Concerto and the *Symphonie Fantastique* of Berlioz.

Since the Centenary, the orchestra has continued to give three concerts each season in the Victoria Theatre and remains central to the musical life of Halifax. Inevitably, as with most amateur orchestras, the going has not always been smooth. Today, nevertheless, the Halifax Symphony Orchestra, already well into its second century, faces the future with confidence.

Huddersfield Philharmonic Orchestra

1862 is an important date in the musical history of Huddersfield. Though there is clear if sketchy evidence to show that 'ad hoc' orchestral ensembles came and went in the town before that year, it was then that the first (and indeed only) orchestra to achieve lasting permanence was established – 'Mr Thomas's Band'. Later this became the Fitzwilliam Street Philharmonic Society and ultimately the Huddersfield Philharmonic Orchestra, which can therefore claim to have had an unbroken existence over a period of 138 years.

It is now possible to establish beyond doubt a matter previously disputed – exactly when the orchestra became the 'Huddersfield Phil'. S H Crowther, in *An Orchestral Centenary*, his regrettably brief sketch of the orchestra's history, claimed 1871 as the date, and the orchestra duly celebrated its centenary in 1971. However R A Edwards later pointed out in *And the Glory* (his history of Huddersfield Choral Society) that this claim was simply inaccurate (Crowther had got a vital date wrong); and Ruth Holmes, the society's present archivist, now confirms that it was shortly after Thomas's death that the orchestra renamed itself the Huddersfield Philharmonic, giving its first concert under that name on 7 February, 1885.

Be that as it may, it is clear that like those of many other now distinguished organisations, the orchestra's beginnings were humble enough. The Rev J H Thomas was a Cambridge graduate, expert linguist and accomplished musician, who was initially ordained into the Church of England but who later abandoned Anglicanism in favour of Unitarianism. In 1862 he came to Huddersfield as Unitarian minister in Fitzwilliam Street, where he remained until his death in 1884. According to the *Huddersfield Examiner* obituary notice,

'...he got a number of lads and young men around him... For five or six years he gave lessons gratuitously...and bought many instruments for the band out of his small means... For the first few years the music of the band was exceedingly crude and often painfully out of tune; but the band was always an improving one...'

Among the Rev Thomas's successors as conductors were several who were intimately con-

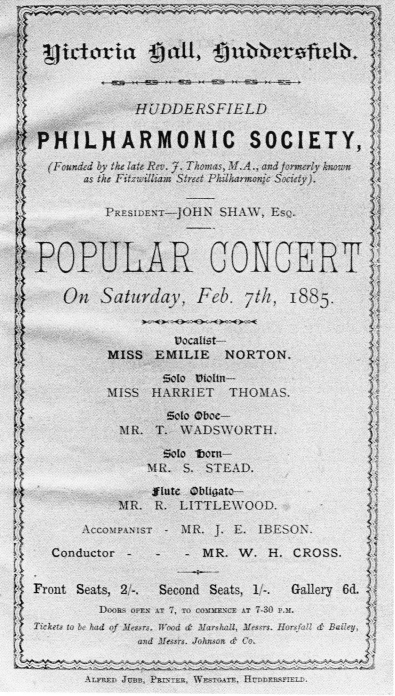

The programme for the 'Phil's' first concert, 1885

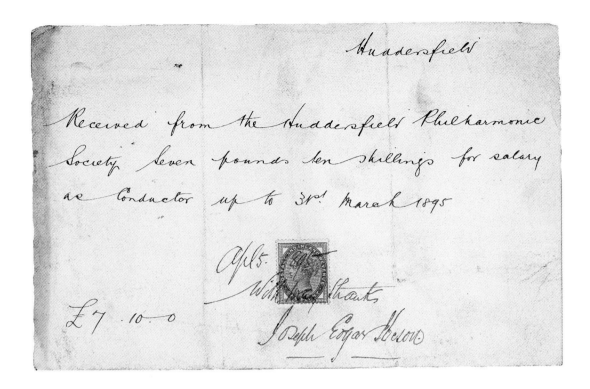

An 1895 receipt
from J E Ibeson

nected with the town's other leading musical organisations. One of the most remarkable of these was John North (conductor also of the Choral and Glee & Madrigal Societies). He began his working life as a butcher's errand boy at the age of nine. A vacancy soon arose for an errand boy at Joe Wood's music shop (founded in 1850, and today still in the hands of his descendants) and Johnny North was taken on. This was to transform his life completely. He at once revealed great musical gifts, and encouraged by Joe Wood, he became an adept pianist and reliable tuner; he also took up the cornet and developed into a fine violinist.

Following the death of Joe Wood, North joined Wood's sons as a partner in the business, where he proved to be no less adept as a businessman than he had already shown himself to be as a musician. In his short and crowded life (he died at the age of 39) he held various posts as organist; in addition to the Huddersfield Choral, he conducted the Holmfirth and Keighley Societies, and also further afield.

The programmes given by the orchestra in John North's day were typical of the period with a multiplicity of items: the orchestra played nothing more substantial than an overture, and vocal and instrumental solos predominated. The October 1888 concert, for instance, featured two

vocalists, two pianists and a violinist: the purely orchestral works ranged from Rossini's *Semiramide* overture and a gavotte (*True Love*) to a selection from Cellier's *Dorothy* and a Waldteufel waltz. Three years later a similar programme was given, though this did contain a full concerto – Mendelssohn's First Piano Concerto played on the 'grand pianoforte' by Master G G Stocks.

The orchestra's archives covering the years up to 1935 are decidedly thin: only a painstaking trawl through microfilms of past editions of the *Huddersfield Daily Examiner* and other local newspapers (more than one in those days) can establish a firmer picture. For many years before and during World War I the orchestra was conducted by another prominent local musician, J E Ibeson. At some time he was succeeded by Frederick Dawson, a leading concert pianist and former pupil of Grieg. He in turn was succeeded by J Fletcher Sykes in 1920; some time in the early 1930s the latter was briefly followed by F W Sykes, about whom nothing is known.

For reasons given elsewhere in this book, the inter-war years were a difficult time for orchestras, professional as well as amateur, and the Huddersfield Phil was no exception. One factor peculiar to Huddersfield exacerbated matters. Arthur Willie Kaye was a local musician of humble origins who by dint of self-sacrifice and sheer hard work had turned himself into one of the country's greatest violin teachers (it is estimated that he launched over 100 violinists on professional careers); and in Huddersfield at any rate, he had become a 'legend in his own lifetime'. He formed his own symphony orchestra with enormous string sections drawn mainly from his own pupils: for concerts, brass and woodwind were imported from the Hallé. Though this orchestra's ascendancy in the 1920s was short-lived, at that time it completely eclipsed the Phil. The Phil also faced competition from another body about which little is known – the Huddersfield 'Permanent' Orchestra. In the '30s, says Crowther (*op cit*), the orchestra's fortunes fell further: '…on one occasion it looked as if there were more players on the platform than there were men and women in the audience'.

But despite the depressing outlook, the members of the Phil persevered and their persistence was to be rewarded. Some signs of better days ahead had already appeared when T H Crowther became the orchestra's conductor in 1935 (a concert in 1936, for instance, included Franck's Symphonic Variations and Tchaikovsky's 'Pathétique' Symphony). During the Second World War, the orchestra continued to rehearse, but gave only one concert (in April, 1943, when the Town Hall was filled to capacity). In the absence of Crowther through illness, this concert was conducted by William Rees.

At the end of the war the Society was determined to raise both its standards and its profile. A major decision was that the Society should engage a professional conductor and in 1946, following the resignation of T H Crowther, William Rees took up the post. A one-time student under Felix

At rehearsal in the 1950s

Weingartner and former violinist with the Hallé, Rees was an experienced musician who quickly became a firm favourite with orchestra and audience alike. His appointment marked a definite turning-point: from then on, the orchestra's rise to its present eminence as one of the country's leading non-professional orchestras was steady and assured. A notable early concert occurred in 1947 when Margaret Binns made her first appearance as Leader, a post she was to hold with great distinction until her retirement in 1982. Also in that year Geoffrey Phillips was appointed Treasurer: he was to remain a member of the committee for over 40 years until his death. The concert of 1 May 1995 was dedicated to a celebration of his life.

In 1952 the orchestra gave the first performance in Huddersfield of Beethoven's 'Choral' Symphony (the choir was the now defunct Huddersfield Vocal Union). In 1954 the Brunswick Symphony Orchestra came to Huddersfield as guests of the Phil, and the Phil visited Brunswick in the following year. The programme, which included Dvorak's Eighth Symphony and soloist Margaret Binns in Mozart's Violin Concerto in A (K219), was very well received.

A characteristic feature of the Rees years was the development of a repertoire which was both solid and enterprising. In 1956, for instance, works ranged from Brahms' Fourth Symphony to Rodrigo's Guitar Concerto (at the time both the work and the soloist – Julian Bream – were relatively unknown). In 1958 a bold programme featured Brahms' *Alto Rhapsody* and Wagner's rarely-heard *Love Feast of the Apostles* (in which the orchestra was joined by the Colne Valley Male

Voice Choir). The orchestra was responsible for the first Huddersfield performance of the Beethoven Triple Concerto (with 'local' soloists Margaret Binns, Pauline Dunn and Keith Swallow). William Rees's retirement in 1964 was a matter of great regret: for almost twenty years he had enjoyed an exceptionally warm rapport with members of the orchestra, but it was understandable that the time had come when he wished to be released from the strain of the road journey from his home in Lytham St Anne's for rehearsals and concerts.

His successor, Arthur Butterworth, had already acted as the orchestra's associate conductor. Originally a trumpeter with the Scottish and Hallé orchestras, he had given up his playing career in order to concentrate on conducting and composing, in which his reputation was steadily growing. (His skill as an orchestrator was recognised by Barbirolli who more than once called upon him, in the Hallé's cash-strapped 1950s, to cue the parts of unaffordable 'extras' into those of standard instruments.) Butterworth was to conduct the Phil for the next 30 years. He inherited a well-established, confident orchestra – already large, it was to grow under him still further (in the 1971-72 Centenary [sic] Season no fewer than 113 players are listed in the programme, including an amazing 81 strings).

As discussed elsewhere in this book, the 1960s saw amateur orchestras beginning to leave the safe havens of the classical core repertoire, and Butterworth relished the opportunity to steer the orchestra's great potential into previously uncharted waters. Not that he had a free hand in the matter: nowadays conductors are usually styled 'artistic directors' and wield the powers implicit in that title, but in 1964, as was then the way with organisations like the Phil (especially in Yorkshire!), 'the committee' reigned supreme – even in the choice of repertoire and soloists. The conductor was consulted on these matters but he had no executive powers. The present writer recalls a conversation he had with Butterworth some years ago. Soon after his appointment to the Phil, he suggested that the orchestra should play Elgar's *Enigma Variations* for the first time. His proposal was accepted, though, as he said, not without some misgivings on the part of the committee that such a 'difficult' work should be tackled. Nowadays, the programming of such a work would be seen merely as routine.

A youthful Arthur Butterworth. Leader Margaret Binns

In the Town Hall with William Rees

In fact Butterworth was able to persuade the committee to expand the repertoire in all directions. Standard classics were not neglected (there were memorable performances of Beethoven's *Eroica* and, in the Centenary [sic] Season, with the Huddersfield Choral Society, that composer's Ninth Symphony), but works as diverse as Hindemith's *Symphonic Metamorphoses*, Berlioz's *Harold in Italy*, Prokoviev's Fifth Symphony, Respighi's *The Pines of Rome*, Janacek's *Sinfonietta*, Holst's *The Planets* and the Mussorgsky/Ravel *Pictures at an Exhibition* figured in Butterworth's early years. His predilection for the music of Sibelius was also gratified: over the years four of the seven symphonies were played. His own music was occasionally performed and he was commissioned to write a work for the Centenary Season. *From the Tower of Winds* was the result (Butterworth later frankly admitted that the work was probably his least effective orchestral score, and it has never been revived).

If memory serves correctly it was in the late 1970s that the orchestra first tackled a Mahler symphony – the First – though under a guest conductor: Butterworth was notoriously allergic to

this composer's music, though this did not prevent him from conducting Mahler's Fifth some years later! At that time *The Daily Telegraph* produced a northern edition: it was edited by the well-known music critic and author, Michael Kennedy. He ran a weekly 'Music in the North' column, and in one such he drew attention to the performance, noting that he would never have anticipated the day when an amateur orchestra could play a Mahler symphony. He was making the general point, of course, that the standard of amateur orchestral playing had risen by leaps and bounds; but in singling out the Phil he was according it a well-deserved accolade.

Later years brought performances of Bartok's *Concerto for Orchestra*, Elgar's *Falstaff*, Debussy's *La Mer* and Britten's *Four Sea Interludes* – pieces which would have been regarded as 'unplayable' in earlier times. In 1989, after 25 years in office, Arthur Butterworth gave hints that he did not plan to go on indefinitely; but it was not until 1993 that he gave his final concert (choosing the same symphony, as it happened, as had Margaret Binns for her farewell concert as Leader in 1982 – Elgar's First). His successor, Rupert D'Cruze, was presented with a splendid inheritance. What would he make of it?

The answer was soon apparent – a great deal. Originally trained as a trombonist (as principal trombone in the European Community Youth

'Are you sure you want it this way?'

Rupert D'Cruze

Orchestra, he played under Abbado and Maazel), D'Cruze soon turned to conducting, and his growing stature as a conductor was quickly signalled by his prize-winning performances at conducting competitions in Hungary and Japan (both in 1992). Since his appointment to the Phil in 1993 he has continued to broaden the range and diversity of his conducting career. He is particularly active in Hungary and has also worked in Slovakia and Germany. He is no less busy as a choral conductor, notably as Director of the Portsmouth Festival Choir, and he has a continuing interest in young musicians (his most recent appointment in this field being that of Director of Reading Youth Orchestra). He has also found time to become a qualified air-pilot (a rare distinction for a conductor which he shares with the late Herbert von Karajan). Given such a heavy demand on his services, might he not have moved on from the Phil (a mere *provincial* orchestra in the eyes of the metropolitan *glitterati*) after seven years?

That he hasn't tells the present writer two

things: D'Cruze holds the Phil in the highest regard, and as its Artistic Director is able to choose a hugely diverse repertoire. True, many of the works he has programmed appeared in the Butterworth years: Holst's *The Planets*, for instance (nearly 30 years ago) or Bartok's Concerto for Orchestra (in the 1980s), but D'Cruze has broken new ground, showing an especial proclivity for the music of Gustav Mahler (Butterworth's *bête noire*). As early as 1995, for instance, David Hammond rhapsodised in the *Huddersfield Daily Examiner* over the Phil's Mahler Sixth ('...conductor Rupert D'Cruze, who is taking this orchestra to new heights...led his serried ranks...in a convincing performance... which kept me, for one, completely absorbed for the full 80 minutes of its duration.') Another aspect of D'Cruze's programming – his affinity with contemporary music – was evidenced by the world premiere given in 1997 of *All The Long Night Through*, a commissioned piece from Bill Connor for piano, percussion and orchestra. Perhaps the most impressive of all the Phil's 'firsts' under D'Cruze was Stravinsky's *The Rite of Spring* (also in 1997) of which Patric Standford had this to say in *The Yorkshire Post*: '...[this work], long feared by the best of performers, was undertaken with immense confidence and vigour. This performance worked because D'Cruze not only knew the score extremely well but succeeded in shaping its disparate sections into a satisfying whole...'

Another tribute to the orchestra's current high standing is the generous sponsorship it has attracted in recent years from Peter Hawke Garages – remarkable in itself, but made even more so by the fact that commercial sponsorship on this scale is nowadays very hard to come by. This sponsorship has enabled the orchestra, amongst other things, to recruit the 'extras' necessary for doing justice to large-scale works such as *The Rite of Spring*.

Let Chris Robins, reviewing the orchestra's April 2000 concert in the *Huddersfield Daily Examiner*, have the last word. On the orchestra as it stands today he wrote: 'what a fine orchestra Huddersfield Philharmonic has become in the seven years since Rupert D'Cruze became artistic director – and with such imaginative programmes!'

Leeds Symphony Orchestra

Founded in 1890, the Leeds Symphony Society, as the orchestra was called until 1970, gave its first concert in November, 1891. The programme was a typical 'miscellaneous' one of its day: 'a very successful debut, skilfully devised to show the varied ability of the 90-odd musicians', reported *The Yorkshire Post*. At first the new society flourished, but in 1896 serious financial difficulties almost brought about its disbandment.

With the appointment of a new conductor – Arthur Grimshaw, the long-serving organist of St Anne's Cathedral – the crisis was overcome, but by 1903 the society was again in financial difficulty, and the committee voted four-two in favour of disbandment (incidentally, oh that committees were as small today!). However, the two dissentients (one of them the conductor) defied this decision, and on their initiative the society was soon back in business. In Grimshaw's fifteen years as conductor, the orchestra enjoyed considerable stability. In some respects the repertoire was quite adventurous (a performance of Bach's Concerto for Three Pianos and Strings was a particular 'novelty' at the time); press reports suggest that playing standards were variable.

On his retirement in 1911, for the third time the orchestra faced the prospect of disbandment. This did not happen, but it was not until 1920 and the appointment of Harold Mason as conductor, that the orchestra again became a major musical force in Leeds. A particular feature of Mason's direction was a determined attempt to attract children to the society's concerts, despite complaints about their behaviour ('the irrepressible chatter of the children left the conductor in some doubt as to how to set about his task').

The orchestra remained active during the Second World War (among soloists to appear was Fanny Waterman). By 1948, though Mason had been conductor for 28 years, members appeared to have lost confidence in him, and he resigned his post. In the ensuing 22 years, under three successive conductors, the repertoire gradually expanded (Shostakovich's Fifth Symphony made its first appearance) with a matching growth in playing standards.

In 1970, Martin Binks, already the conductor of West Riding Opera (with which the orchestra had long been associated) became conductor – a post he retains to this day – and a new era in the orchestra's development unfolded: the orchestra made rapid progress and attained playing standards previously unknown. Such was the growth of the orchestra's reputation under Binks' direction that from 1977 onwards it was frequently invited to play in venues outside Leeds.

Binks has consistently pursued a challenging repertoire; his marked penchant for French music was rewarded in 1993 when the French government appointed him *Chevalier de l'Ordre des Arts et des Lettres*.

Today, the Leeds Symphony Orchestra has a playing strength of 90 members and gives a season of eight concerts. The quality of its performances may be illustrated by a quotation from a recent review in *The Yorkshire Post*:

'…In a programme of spectacular difficulty, the orchestra showed a breadth of style and beauty of expression what was impressive and satisfying… Martin Binks calls upon a large, substantially-assured string body, and secures consistent, deeply-felt responses from his orchestra as a whole.'

Martin Binks

The Paddock Orchestra

The Paddock Orchestra enjoys a distinctive place in the Huddersfield musical landscape. It was formed in 1975 by its first conductor, Eric Cooper, a peripatetic string teacher, as an Adult Education class held at Moor End High School and quickly became known as the 'All Comers' Orchestra' ('Have you an instrument? Well, just come!'). Other orchestras already catered for amateur instrumentalists who wished to explore the 'heavyweight' repertoire and take part in regular concert-giving. The All Comers' Orchestra was rather different: it was in effect a training orchestra and particularly welcomed 'lapsed' and 'second study' players. Public concerts were occasionally given, but essentially the members played its generally 'light' repertoire simply for fun.

The organisation flourished to such an extent that before long a second orchestra was established (for beginners, who were also given individual tuition). Sadly, cuts in public funding led to the demise of the adult education class. However, a number of players were keen to continue the orchestra so they decided to become self-supporting and moved to Paddock Village Hall.

Today the orchestra (whose President, Geoff Wood, was one of its founder members) is thriving as never before. For this happy state of affairs it owes much to its present conductor, Alfi Glendenning, who succeeded to that post in 1991 by chance. She explains:

'I had retired from school teaching through ill-health and started giving private music lessons. Amongst my pupils was the daughter of Humphrey Bolton, and one day he came to me with doleful news. Colin Sutcliffe, the conductor of an orchestra he played in, was retiring, and with no replacement in sight it seemed that the orchestra would have to disband. Having plenty of conducting experience behind me both in school and with adult amateurs I immediately offered my services as a 'stand in' until a permanent conductor could be found. Now nearly ten years later, I am still here – and enjoying every minute of it!'

At that time the orchestra had few members, so it gave informal concerts in small venues such as retirement homes or hospitals. Soon it grew too large for such venues, so we devoted our efforts to giving our concerts in churches, helping them to raise funds. Today, the orchestra, numbering

about 30 players, is reasonably well-balanced, though it still seeks to enrol additional brass, percussion and strings. Some of its members belong to the Slaithwaite Philharmonic, welcoming the opportunity to play a somewhat less strenuous repertoire; other members of that orchestra help out at concerts. The orchestra tackles anything and everything, as the following items from a recent Christmas concert show: Gershwin's *Summer Time*, Coleridge-Taylor's *Petite Suite de Concert*, movements from two of Brahms' symphonies, Fauré's *Pavane* and Holst's *Suite in E flat*.

The special character of the orchestra is best indicated by some members' recollections:

'I joined Paddock Orchestra because I was press-ganged into it by my wife. At this time the 'orchestra' consisted of about ten members on a good night: there were no cellos, so I played the cello part on my bass clarinet... Eventually, as a result of my wife's enthusiasm, numbers grew... [The arrival of three cellists made my bass clarinet redundant so] I bought a good second-hand oboe and taught myself to produce a decent sound... The repertoire was not altogether to my liking, but I have come greatly to enjoy both the playing and the social side.' (**Alan Glendenning**)

Betty Porritt (violin) joined the orchestra in the early days. '...So, for a quarter of a century, apart from summer breaks, I spent every Tuesday happily playing – in various venues, under various conductors. They were always a caring group, but since the advent of our present conductor, apart from improved playing, it has become a much more friendly and social group.'

'I learned to play the clarinet to a rather modest standard as child and played second clarinet in the school orchestra', says **Richard Redman**. 'I was rather overshadowed by the person playing first, [who was none other than] Gervaise de Peyer!' After leaving school he gave up playing, but kept his clarinets. Fifty years later he resumed playing and joined the Paddock Orchestra at the age of 69. 'Now I look forward to, and enjoy, our Tuesday evening rehearsals and occasional concerts.'

The Paddock Orchestra is a splendid example of an unpretentious and friendly organisation that meets a real need.

Alfi Glendenning

Todmorden Orchestra

The Todmorden Orchestra was originally part of the Todmorden Musical Society, but in 1915 the members decided to split the society into two: thus both Todmorden Orchestra and Todmorden Choral Society were born.

For over twenty years the orchestra was conducted by Dr Ben Horsfall, a highly respected musician who played violin in the Hallé and later the BBC Northern Orchestra (of which he became deputy leader); and, while serving in the RAF during the Second World War, viola in the Cairo Symphony Orchestra. Since his death in 1986, the orchestra has been conducted by a series of young musicians – many studying at the Royal Northern College of Music in Manchester, some of whom have gone on to further studies elsewhere in the world.

The orchestra gives three concerts a year, two of which take place in the Town Hall and usually contain symphonies

RIGHT Percy Dobson who retired recently after 70 years with the orchestra.

BELOW 1932 programme

CENTRE VALE PARK.

PROGRAMME OF CONCERTS BY

TODMORDEN ORCHESTRA

(President—Dr. J. de Ville Mather).

AFTERNOON AT 3 O'CLOCK.

1.	March	"London Scottish"	Haines.
2.	Overture	"Hamlet"	Gade.
3.	Selection	"Cavalleria Rusticana" (pt. 1)	Tavan.
4.	Valses	"Amorettentanze"	Gung'l.

INTERVAL.

5.	Tangled Tune (pt. 1)		Ketelby.
6.	Pathetique Symphony (2nd movement)		Tschaikowsky.
7.	Flute & Clarinet Solo "Lo Hear the Gentle Lark"		C. Le Thiere
	MESSRS. P. DOBSON and C. LEE.		
8.	Selection	"Madame Butterfly" (pt. 1)	Tavan.

God Save the King.

EVENING AT 7-45.

1.	March	"Pomp and Circumstane" (No. 1)	Elgar.
2.	Selection	"Cavalleria Rusticana" (pt. 2)	Tavan.
3.	Capriccio Espagnol (first 3 movements)		Rimsky-Korsakow.
4.	Selection	"Geisha"	Jones.

INTERVAL.

5.	Tangled Tunes (pt. 2)		Ketelby.
6.	Homorous Sketch	"Southern Wedding"	Lotter.
7.	Selection	"Madame Butterfly" (pts. 1 & 2)	Tavan.

God Save the King.

Conductor--Mr. F. LEACH, A.R.M.C.M.

W. SUTCLIFFE, Hon. Treas.

W. ASHWORTH AND E. MITTON, Joint Hon. Secs.

Cunliffe Brothers, Printers, etc., Fielden Square, Todmorden.

and concertos. A variety of instrumental soloists perform, but here again young people are encouraged, and use is made of the excellent National Federation of Music Societies scheme to promote promising young talent. The third concert, which takes place in the summer, is of a lighter nature; recently it has been given in St Mary's Church, Todmorden.

The orchestra is fortunate to enjoy the financial support of Calderdale Leisure Services and the National Federation of Music Societies. It also runs a Patrons' Scheme: patrons currently pay £30.00 a year, for which they receive two tickets for each of the three concerts. This brings in an assured income, and helps to build a larger audience.

The orchestra is a friendly society and looks forward to the future with enthusiasm. It would welcome additional players, particularly in the string sections.

Slaithwaite Philharmonic Orchestra

'I do not know where Slaithwaite is, but musically it is bigger than Birmingham', declared Sir Granville Bantcck (Professor of Music at the University of Birmingham) on 18 May 1912. Earlier that day the Slaithwaite Philharmonic had won first prize of £100.00 in the Orchestral Class at the Midland Music Festival. The adjudicator, Dr Herbert Brewer (organist at Gloucester Cathedral), urged Bantock to attend the grand concluding festival concert, for he would hear Wagner's *Die Meistersinger* Overture (the test piece) '...played as Wagner wrote it – free from the idiosyncrasies of modern conductors'.

This victory launched a remarkable run of five successive first prizes at three of the country's leading music festivals. Such achievements could scarcely have been envisaged in the orchestra's early days. It had been founded in November 1891 by a small group of enthusiasts led by a cellist named John Taylor who felt that 'the lack of an orchestra was a reproach to the village'. The first problem was financial: the income derived from the subscriptions of the small number of members sufficed only to pay for the rent of a rehearsal room; and until they had sufficient funds to build up their own music library, they had to make do with whatever pieces the members could lay their hands on. They therefore decided to appeal to the public for support: in April 1892 one hundred leading Slaithwaite residents and tradesmen were 'memorialised' in the following terms (somewhat quaint to modern ears, but touching, too):

'SIR,

Excuse the liberty we take in sending you this circular. [This] Society which has been in existence over six months, and consisting of about 20 members...desires to approach you asking for your assistance. It has been formed to satisfy a long-felt want in the village in the way of rendering such music appreciable in many ways and as a means of practice, thus adding knowledge and refining the taste of persons desiring to excel... Two members will have pleasure in waiting upon you in a few days, when your favour, however small, will be gratefully acknowledged...'

The appeal was successful: it enabled the Society 'to purchase the music which had formerly belonged to individual members of the band, pay off all debts, purchase new music and place the Society on a firm financial basis.'

Rather more serious, however, were two other problems – insufficient members and poor rehearsal attendance. The first concert was given in December 1892 by an ill-balanced ensemble of 30 players in a programme of 16 items, of which only Mendelssohn's *War March of the Priests* might be heard today. The *Huddersfield Examiner* was somewhat dismissive: 'the band requires sev-

Slaithwaite Philharmonic Society.

THE

FIRST CONCERT

Of Season 1892-3, will be given in the

LIBERAL HALL, SLAITHWAITE,

ON

THURSDAY, DEC. 1st, 1892.

ARTISTES:—

Bass: Mr. JOHN BROWNING,
Principal Bass, Leeds Parish Church.

Soprano: Miss THERESA HAYNES,
of the Manchester Concerts.

Violoncello: Mr. NATHAN CROWTHER,
Huddersfield.

Flute: Mr. F. W. BROOK,
Huddersfield.

Mandoline: Miss R. HELLAWELL.

Hull Orchestra of 30 Performers.

Conductor: Mr. J. T. FERRIOR.
Accompanist: Mr. E. P. ROTHERY.

Front Seats, 1s. 6d. ; Second Seats, 1s. ; Gallery, 6d.

Doors open at 7 ; Concert at 7-30.

T. COCKS, PRINTER, SLAITHWAITE.

Programme cover for the very first concert, December 1892 and, INSET, Arthur Armitage

eral instruments to make it complete, and the players already in it require to give attention to refining their tone and style and to improving their intonation…' Throughout the 1890s membership never exceeded 25: by 1899 it had fallen to 18. The constant refrain in the Secretary's annual reports was poor rehearsal attendance: '…it is little short of a disgrace that a society with 24 members can only muster an average attendance of only 13. It is no use appealing to the public for support if we care so little for the Society ourselves as to neglect its rehearsals…'

By 1897, the ship seemed about to sink, but the members somehow succeeded in keeping it afloat. The turning point in the Society's fortunes came in 1899, when Arthur Armitage was appointed Conductor. This remarkable man was not, strictly speaking, a professional musician (he worked in the textile industry), but in an area boasting many fine musicians, he was one of the most talented. He had been one of the orchestra's founding fathers, becoming at the age of 22 its first leader and secretary; but in 1898, he had resigned from the Society. The reason given was 'other engagements', and it is true that at this time he was setting up his own business as 'Messrs A Armitage & Co, flock, worsted and woollen warehousemen'; I suspect, however, that disillusionment with the Society's lack of progress also played its part.

Intimately acquainted though he was with the society's inherent weaknesses, it is probably the case that he relished the challenge as conductor, and had the self-confidence to believe that he could take it forward. There was no instant improvement, but the concert given in 1903 was an encouraging pointer: the first ever to show a profit (all of 1/8d on a turnover of £9/19/6d) and, more importantly, it revealed a major upgrading of repertoire – for the first time, the programme featured a symphony (Schubert's *Unfinished*). This modest success appears to have galvanised the members into determined action and 1904 must be regarded as the year in which the Society 'took off'. Administration and promotion, previously largely hit-and-miss in character, were at last put on a vigorous footing so that the concert given on 1 December 1904 attracted an audience of over 300 and made a handsome profit. From then on, the orchestra's progress rapidly accelerated: membership steadily grew (though serious instrumental gaps persisted); the repertoire became increasingly substantial (in 1909,

Tchaikovsky's 1812 *Overture*, no less, was featured); finances were buoyant (the 1910 concert made a profit of almost 50% – 'the hall was packed, many people being unable to find sitting accommodation'); and newspaper reviews more and more enthusiastic.

In October 1911 the orchestra entered a competitive festival for the first time, gaining second place in its class at the Blackpool Festival. Four days later the Annual Concert in Slaithwaite Liberal (now Civic) Hall drew an audience approaching 500 (for the 1913 concert, 561 tickets were to be sold: the *Colne Valley Guardian* reported that 'the audience crowded every part of the hall and its approach, while many were unable either to see or hear'. It is worth noting that in these health-and-safety-obsessed days, the maximum permitted audience is now 260!). The Blackpool success was but the prelude to the remarkable run of competition victories already alluded to: in 1912, at Birmingham and Blackpool and in 1913, at Morecambe, Birmingham and Blackpool. In 1914, however, victory at Birmingham and Morecambe eluded the orchestra; and the outbreak of World War I led to the cancellation of the Blackpool festival, and indeed all three festivals 'for the duration'.

In September 1916 the Society was stunned by the premature death at the age of 47 of Arthur Armitage, the man who had raised the orchestra from a position of near-extinction to that of being widely regarded as one of the foremost amateur orchestras in the country. As the Secretary put it a few months later:

> '…the death of our beloved, and deeply lamented, conductor came with the suddenness of a thunderbolt, and we stood aghast and unnerved at the awful news…he was at the zenith of his manhood, possessing remarkable powers of the art of imparting the knowledge, of which he was so ripe, to others, and withal a man of great tact, sound judgment and understanding'.

Though more than 70 years were to elapse before the orchestra could claim to have regained the distinguished reputation which Arthur Armitage had given it, its history in those years is full of interest. Unlike many local musical organisations, the orchestra survived the First War intact; but the inter-war years were difficult times for

The orchestra at Birmingham, May 1913

both professional and amateur orchestras. The coming of the wireless, the gramophone and 'talkies' were only some of the forces to bring about a profound change in the general public's attitude to leisure-pursuits in general, and opportunities for listening to music in particular. A professional orchestral musician, for instance, was far more likely to be appreciated for his services at the seaside in the summer season than in the concert hall during the winter. (It was not until 1932 that the BBC Symphony Orchestra became the first orchestra whose members received a full-time salary). If professional orchestras struggled, it was hardly surprising that the amateur orchestra in a small village in the West Riding would have found the going even more difficult.

From 1920 to 1924 the orchestra was conducted by Slaithwaite-born Dr Thomas Edward Pearson, a multi-talented musician who pursued the highest ideals, but whose sensitive nature was easily bruised.. His term began promisingly: the orchestra returned to Blackpool in 1920 and won the orchestral class with its performance of Elgar's *Froissart*. But the costs of 'contesting' proved to be beyond the society's resources and it was not until 1950 that the orchestra again entered com-

petitive festivals (and then only briefly). Dr Pearson also introduced some highly successful children's concerts and pursued an adventurous repertoire. However, he had a finger in so many simultaneous musical pies (*inter alia*, for instance, conductor of the Huddersfield Glee and Madrigal Society and the first conductor the Colne Valley Male Voice Choir) that some were neglected – and the Slaithwaite Phil was one of these. He regularly failed to turn up for rehearsals; and in January 1925, he was summarily dismissed.

His successor was Lewis Eagland, another Slaithwaite-born musician of versatile talent but very different in temperament; he remained conductor until the orchestra was 'temporarily' disbanded in 1941 because of the war. Under him, the orchestra settled into a humdrum existence. Soon, the repertoire became one more accurately described as being in the main 'light' rather than 'symphonic', and increasingly limited and predictable. (It is said that on arriving at rehearsal one member would greet another by asking: 'Well, is it to be the *Unfinished* tonight or *The Water Music*?'). Still, in almost every season, two concerts were given, and the generally preferred vocal soloists engaged constitute a veritable roll-call of

ORCHESTRAL MUSIC

OPPOSITE *Programme cover for the Haydn Wood concert November, 1934*

the finest of the period. One of these, Norman Allin, the well-known bass-baritone, made a particularly lasting impression. Some years later, when lamenting the Society's ever-recurring financial plight, the Secretary claimed that some people come to the concerts but listened to them outside the hall on the grounds that, 'You can hear Norman Allin from Slawit Brig!' (a bridge nearly a quarter-mile away). There was one indisputably golden moment, recalling the pre-war 'glory days', when Slaithwaite's most famous musical son, Haydn Wood, came in November 1934 to conduct the orchestra in some of his own music (including *A Manx Rhapsody* and the inevitable *A Brown Bird Singing*): 'it was a real pleasure', reported the Secretary later, 'to read the advert in the local paper – *All Seats Sold*'.

Of the conductors mentioned so far, only Arthur Armitage seems to have been able to command high rehearsal attendance: otherwise, by today's standards, rehearsal attendance was unacceptably erratic. Nothing better illustrates the difference in temperament between Dr Pearson and Lewis Eagland than their approach to this intractable problem (one which, I believe, results in an amateur orchestra rarely reaching its full potential). Mr Eagland was remarkably relaxed about the matter: at the 1929 AGM he said he enjoyed a rehearsal even if only a quartet was present – but that if a different quartet attended the following week, it took twice as long to get through the work! Dr Pearson, however, had been altogether less tolerant. The following tale dates from 1924. In the orchestra's ranks was one Harry Johnson, a violinist (remembered as being a somewhat 'wild' character). One night, Dr Pearson was making his way to rehearsal; as he passed the swimming baths he met Harry who was about to go in. 'Aren't you coming to the rehearsal?' asked Dr Pearson. 'Bugger the rehearsal!' was Harry's reply. He was forthwith expelled from the Society.

The outbreak of World War II in 1939 brought immediate problems, and after desultory attempts to keep the orchestra going had come to nothing, in 1941, when it should have been celebrating its golden jubilee, the orchestra was disbanded 'for the duration'; and it was not until 1949, after many unexpected difficulties had been surmounted (many members, including the long-serving secretary, Maurice Sykes, were opposed to its revival) that the orchestra finally reassembled.

The new conductor was Wyndham Williams, who had just been appointed by Huddersfield Corporation to develop what soon became known as the 'Huddersfield School of Music'. 'I think we can make a go of this', he was reported as saying, and such proved to be the case. In December 1950 the orchestra was joined by a 100-strong invited choir in a performance of *Messiah* which was a sell-out (to accommodate those unable to obtain tickets, the final rehearsal was opened to the public). But other commitments led to Mr Williams' abrupt resignation in 1951; and the stay of his successor, Raymond Roberts (a lecturer at Bretton Hall College) was equally brief. Enter now the colourful personality of George Cottam, bass trombonist of the BBC Northern Orchestra: his 11-year reign as conductor began promisingly, survived many crises (often arising from the thorny question of rehearsal attendance), but ultimately ended in grief.

Once again, as after World War I, the entertainment climate had changed. On the one hand, following the unprecedented explosion of 'live' music-making generated during the war years, there was an unprecedented availability of 'live' professional orchestral concerts. On the other hand, the advent of television had persuaded many of the population to remain firmly indoors of an evening. In the circumstances, the Slaithwaite Philharmonic found it increasingly difficult to survive as a symphony orchestra. The financial position was fragile (in 1956 the Treasurer reported that the balance of £1/12/3d 'was quite inadequate for the normal working of the Society'). Membership was ageing and dwindling. Erratic rehearsal attendance not only drove Mr Cottam to the verge of apoplexy, but seriously impaired efficiency. To add to this, his BBC commitments meant that he could give the Committee only three weeks' notice of his availability for a concert, which constituted an organisational nightmare. There were a few highs in these years, but rather more lows; eventually, after 11 tempestuous years, Mr Cottam resigned – specifically, it seems, on the question of repertoire. The Secretary (Hilton Hirst) gave a bleak assessment of the situation:

'...[For various reasons] people who love orchestral music can hear symphonies played much better than we can play them; and I am of the opinion that many people are support-

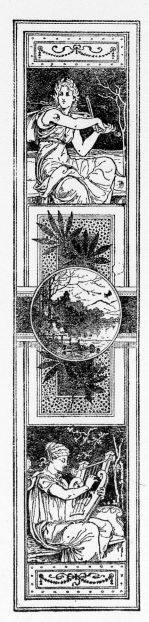

Slaithwaite Philharmonic Society.

President - JOE WILKINSON, Esq.

Vice-Presidents :—
Mrs. M. E. Horsfall, Cr. J. Woodhead, Cr. J. A. Cock, Cr T. W. Varley, Cr. Joe Pogson, J. W. Roberts, Esq., Elon Crowther, Esq., F. Haigh, Esq., D. H. Firth, Esq., J. W. Matthewman, Esq., H. Pearson, Esq.

First Grand Concert

IN THE LIBERAL HALL, SLAITHWAITE,

On WEDNESDAY, NOVEMBER 21st, 1934,

at 7-30 p.m.

Mr. HAYDN WOOD,

The World Famous Composer, Violinist and Conductor.

Mr. FRANK TITTERTON,

The Famous Tenor.

ACCOMPANIST :—

Mr. ERNEST COOPER, F.R.C.O., L.R.A.M.

THE SOCIETY'S FULL ORCHESTRA

Leader - MR. FRANK PIPER.

Conductor, Mr. L. H. EAGLAND, Mus. Bac. (Oxon),
F.R.C.O. L.R.A.M.

Hon Secretary :—MR. MAURICE SYKES, "Holywell," Slaithwaite.

J. W. Roberts & Son, Ltd., Slaithwaite.

Eleanor Moorhouse (left) and her sisters. Photo HUDDERSFIELD DAILY EXAMINER

ing us out of sentiment rather than from the pleasure they get out of listening to us... Should we continue to inflict [*sic*] good classical music on a public that doesn't seem to want it? Should we have better support if we put on music of a lighter character?

John Taylor, grandson of the founder, had been principal clarinet since the mid-20s, and, more recently, deputy conductor as well. To him now fell the task of holding the orchestra together. But after some early signs of new life, the remorseless cycle of decline resumed and by 1968 the orchestra, whose numbers had fallen to 12, seemed doomed – a prospect given added poignancy by the fact that among those gallant few was Eleanor Moorhouse (violin) whose membership of the orchestra stretched back to the 'golden years' of 1911-1914. The main reason why the Society had survived, albeit precariously, against all the odds was almost certainly the existence of its 'light division', which had been active from the beginning. Full-scale concerts were now out of the question, but 'ad hoc' small ensembles could still be fielded

for a variety of social functions – old folks' treats, church bazaars, flower shows and the like; there was also a demand for their services from the numerous amateur light opera societies in the area.

Help was at hand, however – and from a totally unexpected quarter. In that same year (1968) there had been a small but significant influx of new members: Fr Alex Macdonald, a Huddersfield Catholic priest, teacher and keen amateur viola player, had discovered by chance that there was an orchestra in, of all places, Slaithwaite ('village' orchestras being by now a long-forgotten phenomenon), and had persuaded some of his students and friends to join this unlikely ensemble. One of these was a teaching colleague of his, Adrian Smith, who came in on the express condition that he should sit on the back desk of the second violins. He was not a professional musician, but had considerable experience of choral and orchestral conducting.

At a meeting called in November 1969 it was Fr Macdonald who boldly asserted that the orchestra had no future under its present conductor, and nominated the virtually unknown Mr Smith to succeed him. It was a tense, even dramatic moment – John Taylor, a man who had given almost half a century's service to the orchestra and who more than anyone else had fought to keep it going when times were hard, was present at the meeting; after an emotional speech he accepted the proposal. Mr Smith was appointed 'for one or two months'. 31 years later, he's still there.

In effect, the position in 1969 was much as it had been in 1899 – a struggling orchestra, a largely unknown and inexperienced conductor, rudimentary organisation (the annual subscription of 5/-, for instance, had remained more or less unchanged since 1891!), and an indifferent public. As after 1899, so after 1969: the immediate recovery from a parlous state of affairs was slow rather than spectacular, but, despite the occasional setback, an upward curve was firmly established.

The revival of the orchestra's fortunes in the past 30 years falls roughly into three stages. In the 1970s, firm foundations were laid; the 1980s (when the orchestra moved its concerts from Slaithwaite to the newly opened St Paul's Concert Hall in what is now the University of Huddersfield) were a period of consolidation; and the 1990s (when the orchestra finally arrived at Huddersfield Town Hall), where it has sustained an ambitious level of concert-giving inconceivable in 1969.

This progress can be attributed to many factors: the growing size of the orchestra (now complete in virtually all sections); a high degree of commitment from key players; dedicated officials (especially after 1978, when the orchestra was put on a business-like footing); a willingness to take risks and 'think the unthinkable'; a refusal to allow the inevitable financial constraints to be the sole arbiter in deciding what could be done; the development of a distinctive repertoire; and, others might say, the untiring zeal of the conductor.

But other, equally important if less tangible, forces have been at work. It is often forgotten that

Slaithwaite Orchestra, June 1999, with the Parish Church in the background.
Photo GREAVES OF HUDDERSFIELD

an organisation such as an amateur orchestra is as much a social as a musical phenomenon. Excellence matters – but people matter even more. In 1953, when newly-appointed conductor George Cottam's uncompromising ideals were already provoking dissent, an Extraordinary General Meeting was called to discuss a 'six-point plan' he had submitted (his minimum demand was 100% attendance at rehearsals!). David Arthur Garside, principal bassoon for over 50 years, was clearly concerned over this looming rift between conductor and members, and alluded to 'the happy family atmosphere which existed at Slaithwaite and which he considered it the duty of both the players and the conductor to uphold.'

This 'happy family atmosphere' has remained our watchword. We hold no auditions: members are almost invariably admitted simply if there are places available, and they remain in the orchestra as long as they wish to do so. Some members may therefore be less proficient than others – but any consequent diminution in the orchestra's effec-

tiveness is outweighed by the fact that it exists primarily to satisfy their personal musical aspirations rather than become some kind of alternative to a professional orchestra.

A second intangible element was best pinpointed recently by a soloist of international fame on a return visit. 'Why', I asked, 'when you must have more offers of engagements than you can fulfil, do you choose to "go slumming" with an amateur orchestra?' 'In playing with an orchestra like this', was the reply, 'I enjoy being involved in the players' love of music and their clear determination to give of their best – not always my experience with professional orchestras.' This point is reinforced by another fact: 'extras' recruited for concerts invariably return when asked.

There were many milestones in the 1970s and 1980s (these are charted in the present writer's *An Improbable Centenary*, the full-scale history of the orchestra, published in 1990) but I will end this brief survey by confining myself to some of the highlights of the 1990s.

The orchestra performs Mahler's Third Symphony in Huddersfield Town Hall, January 1995. Photo HUDDERSFIELD DAILY EXAMINER

The decade began with the orchestra's final season in St Paul's. Vaughan Williams' *Sixth Symphony*, Prokoviev's *Third Piano Concerto* (soloist, Ian Monro) and an all-French programme which included d'Indy's *Symphony on a French Mountain Song* (soloist, Keith Swallow) are outstanding memories of that season. We were sorry to leave St Paul's – a hall notable for the intimate contact it affords between performers and listeners, but one which had in truth become too small to accommodate our growing audience. In 1991 we moved to the Town Hall to celebrate our Centenary.

At the Centenary Concert itself we were joined by Holmfirth Choral Society in performances of Elgar's *The Music Makers* and Verdi's *Te Deum*. Later concerts included Shostakovich's massive *Leningrad Symphony* and Rachmaninov's *Second Piano Concerto* (in which the soloist was Peter Donohoe) and a Gala Concert hosted by Richard Baker. The season also brought us a Performing Rights Society award for adventurous programming (a second was to follow in 1996). In 1993 we were awarded the NFMS Sir Charles Groves Prize (internal) for outstanding services to music in the community.

The Centenary Season programmes established a pattern for the remainder of the decade. Large-scale works performed – many of them for the first time in Huddersfield – included Mahler's Third and Fifth symphonies, Shostakovich's Eighth and Twelfth, Elgar's Second and Anthony Payne's realisation of his Third, Panufnik's *Sinfonia Sacra*, Arnold's Second, Fourth and Fifth (the two latter in the composer's presence), Rachmaninov's Second and Third, Vaughan Williams' Second and Fourth, and Walton's First. Shorter showpieces have included works by John Adams (*Short Ride in a Fast Machine* and *The Chairmen Dances*), Britten, Ravel and Stravinsky.

Soloists of national repute have been engaged from time to time – Peter Donohoe, Pan Hon Lee (then leader of the Hallé), Dennis Simons (then leader of the BBC Philharmonic), Felix Schmidt (in Shostakovich's First Cello Concerto) and Joanna MacGregor (twice – her brilliant performances of Gershwin and Shostakovich capped by dazzling jazz encores). But local soloists have

not been overlooked, and we have been fortunate to be able to engage a succession of rising stars sponsored by the Countess of Munster Musical Trust, beginning with Philip Duke, now one of the country's leading viola players. The most remarkable soloist of all, however, has been Julian Bliss, who at the age of eight performed as an encore to Arnold's Fifth Symphony the finale from that composer's Second Clarinet Concerto, returning two years later to play the entire concerto.

Infant prodigy: Julian Bliss. Photo ALAN SOUTHGATE

Over the years the orchestra has attracted much favourable press comment. Let this one extract suffice:

> 'Saturday's concert by the SPO generated twice as much enthusiasm and excitement as the one given by a professional orchestra in the same venue nine days ago.' DAVID HAMMOND
> *Huddersfield Daily Examiner*, 12/04/00

The present conductor has indicated that he intends to retire in October, 2001. His successor's inheritance will be undeniably and incalculably richer than that of any of his predecessors.

ADRIAN SMITH

Postscript

No account of the orchestra's recent history would be complete without a special tribute to the part which the writer of the above has played in its current success. His vision, his drive, and his dedication have raised the Slaithwaite Philharmonic Orchestra from the very brink of extinction when he took over as conductor, to a position of high regard among other amateur music-making organisations, the local community at large, and the many soloists and other professionals who have worked with us.

If the first golden age of music-making in the orchestra's history was achieved under the direction of the great Arthur Armitage, then the second has surely been achieved under Adrian Smith. His general philosophy and approach has fostered an *esprit de corps* and a friendliness which we like to think of as a special feature of the SPO. At the same time he has consistently challenged the orchestra's players and audiences alike in the field of orchestral repertoire, by performing works which others have left untouched.

In these days of commercial constraints it is increasingly the role of the adventurous amateur orchestra to perform the large-scale or less popular works. Adrian Smith has long been a pioneer of this approach and has been responsible for the first performance in the Huddersfield area of a number of major works. His guiding hand has undoubtedly led us to our two awards from the Performing Rights Society, and to the National Federation of Music Societies' prestigious Sir Charles Groves award for services to music in the community.

Not only does the orchestra owe a tremendous debt of gratitude for all that he has achieved over the years, but his impact on music-making in the Huddersfield area in general and the Colne Valley in particular has been immense. We can truly say that under the musical direction of Adrian Smith the aims, objectives, and the aspirations of our founding fathers have been fully realised.

IAN N DENTON (Past President)

Adrian Smith – conductor since 1969. Photo GREAVES OF HUDDERSFIELD

Sinfonia of Leeds

The Sinfonia of Leeds was originally formed in 1972 by Graham Bennett, its objectives being to afford high-calibre local musicians the opportunity to meet together to play music and provide quality performances of symphonic music, both classical and modern. In 1991 David Greed joined as Musical Director. David is the leader of the English Northern Philharmonia, the orchestra of Opera North. His appointment has enabled the orchestra to work with international soloists and Opera North members, together with up-and-coming talented local young musicians.

Since its formation, although based in Leeds, the orchestra has performed widely throughout West and North Yorkshire and participated in several music festivals including the Leeds Music Festival, Grassington Festival, Heptonstall Music Festival, the Leeds Summer Heritage Festival and Orchestral Adventures 2000 at Leeds Town Hall.

In 1995 Sir Ernest Hall asked Sinfonia to record all three Bartok Piano Concertos together with the Lutoslawski Concerto. A double CD of these is now on general release.

When Sir Ernest embarked on recording the complete works of Chopin, Sinfonia was, once again, asked to accompany him. Recordings of the two Chopin Piano Concertos took place during November 1999 and a CD will be released during the year 2000.

Having performed a number of Opera Galas in recent years, this next season will bring yet another new departure for Sinfonia, a full concert version of Puccini's opera *Gianni Schicchi*. This performance will be directed by Michael Rolnick of Opera North.

It is now twenty years since the orchestra performed a piano concerto with Michael Roll, the very first winner of the Leeds International Pianoforte Competition. In June 2001 we will be delighted to work with him again and, as on that previous occasion, back in Leeds Town Hall.

The Orchestra of the Square Chapel, Halifax

The Square Chapel in Halifax is a Grade II listed building dating from 1772 which, like the Pease Hall adjacent to it and probably built by the same architect, came perilously close to demolition only a few decades ago. Both have been brought back into use, through the full cycle of neglect and lack of appreciation for what they were to the recognition they now both enjoy as being amongst the key landmarks of Halifax, if not the county.

The Square Chapel was acquired by the then Halifax County Borough in 1969 which at the time, however, was unable to find a use for it despite its status as an important listed building. It remained seriously threatened for several years until 1988, when it was bought by the Square Chapel Trust who saw the potential of the building and who commenced immediately to make plans to save the Chapel. The structure had sunk into a precarious condition with the giant roof trusses warped and threatening to dislodge the pediment.

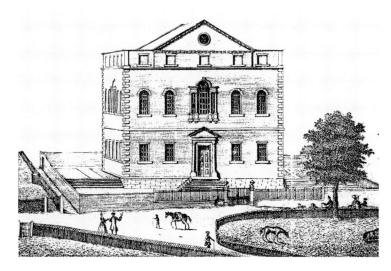

Despite the ruinous state of the Chapel it was clear to the Square Chapel Trust that the building showed exceptional promise as a space highly suitable for the performing Arts. It was at this time that the idea of an annual Chamber Music Festival was conceived. The Square Chapel Trust had ambitious plans which were going to take a long time to realise.

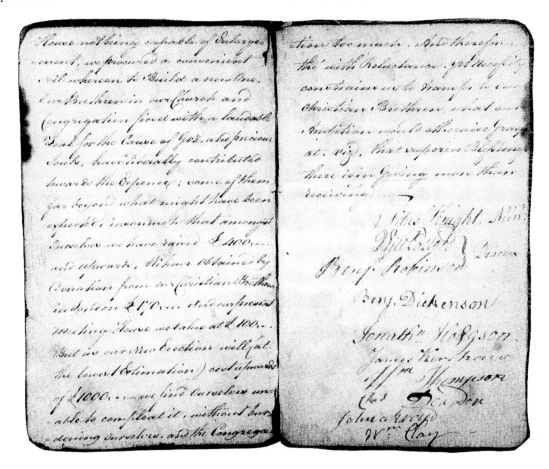

The chapel in 1772 and BELOW *Pages from Square Chapel's membership book 1772 showing signatures of founder members*

Building work has only been possible as funding became available and with the help of grants and exceptional generosity from the growing number of its supporters. It now serves as Halifax's principal Arts Centre and has a full programme of almost weekly concerts.

The Orchestra of Square Chapel started life in 1997 as a group of friends based in West Yorkshire who all felt the lack of a good-quality local chamber orchestra. Plenty of good symphonic and choral music-making was going on, as well as high-quality chamber music, but there were few opportunities to perform or listen to small-scale orchestral works. The project took off when Lawrence Killian agreed to conduct, and offered the use of Elland Church of England School for rehearsal. Members were drawn from several other local orchestras. The aims were clear from the outset – to perform small-scale orches-

tral music from a range of periods to the highest possible standard.

By choosing works which are highly rewarding for the performers as well as the audience, the orchestra seeks to draw in amateur and semi-professional players of high calibre and to perform to a professional standard.

Conductor Lawrence Killian has a special interest in 20th century works, and this is reflected in the orchestra's choice of repertoire.

In June 1998 the Orchestra took up residence in the Square Chapel, Halifax. This flourishing arts centre offered the fight surroundings for small-scale classical concerts, with excellent acoustics and a uniquely intimate atmosphere. In the early twentieth century Square Chapel had its own orchestra, the 'Square Orchestra', and today's orchestra is proud to continue the tradition of music-making in Halifax.

RIGHT: Lindsay string quartet play at the chapel during restoration, 1989
BELOW: the orchestra in 1998

University Music

Music at the University of Bradford

From its inception, the University of Bradford has always been keen to emphasise the importance of the Arts as part of its overall educational provision and although not offering formal degree programmes in Music, music-making in a wide range of styles is an important and vibrant part of University life. In addition, specialist research into musical sound has spread the name of Bradford around the globe, and new courses are preparing students for careers in the digital music business.

The University of Bradford appoints a professional Fellow in Music to initiate a wealth of musical activities that cater for all students and staff, and for the local community. The Fellow's appointment lasts for four years, and each new Fellow brings new skills to the post – all are conductors and instrumentalists, some are musicologists, some composers. This, and the changing University population, means that music-making at the University is never dull, never static in its emphasis, always exciting and always challenging.

University Choir and Orchestra perform in Bradford Cathedral

Thus, there are numerous opportunities to become involved in music-making at Bradford, accommodating all interests and tastes and levels of experience, for both the listener and the performer.

At the heart of the main campus is the impressive Tasmin Little Music Centre, named after the British violinist who is an Honorary Graduate of the University. The Centre has a rehearsal/concert hall, fully equipped practice room available 15 hours a day, and a common room. A programme of workshops allows student musicians direct access to professional expertise. Tuition is available on most instruments including voice and piano. Subsidies in the form of studentships and part studentships are available for those actively involved in University music making.

The University has an Orchestra with a membership of about 80 – although new members are always welcome. The Orchestra tackles large scale symphonic works ranging from Mozart to Mahler and beyond; they gave the British amateur premiere of Philip Glass's *Low Symphony*. Recent performances have included *Peter and the Wolf*, Wagner's *Die Meistersinger Overture*, Rachmaninov's Second Piano Concerto, Saint-Saens' *Dance Macabre*, and Sibelius' Second Symphony.

The University Orchestra has been supplemented since 1996 by a String Orchestra of between 25 and 30 players, which has gone from strength to strength since its inception. Their repertoire has included Tchaikovsky's *Serenade for Strings* and three of Bach's Brandenburg Concertos as well as *Adagio for Strings* by Samuel Barber and works by Rossini.

There are three other instrumental groups – Bradford University Jazz Ensemble, concentrating on big band music with occasional improvisation sessions; a Recorder Group with a wide repertoire spanning six centuries; and a highly popular Wind Orchestra. The Wind Orchestra consists of a mixture of wind, brass and percussion players, performing a range of music from the traditional Military Band programme through the Brass Band repertoire and orchestral transcriptions, to original wind music such as works by Horowitz and David Bedford. On occasion the Wind Orchestra performs in conjunction with the String Orchestra.

As well as these instrumental groups, the University boasts a Chorus and a Chamber Choir. The Chorus consists of staff, students and singers from outside the University – no audition is necessary! – who enjoy singing in a large vocal group. They perform major works from the choral repertoire (with lighter interludes), and give two concerts a year. Recent concerts have included Puccini's *Messa di Gloria*, *Requiems* by Fauré and Mozart, Carl Orff's *Carmina Burana*, and music by Borodin. The Chamber Choir is a much smaller group, performing music from the Renaissance through to contemporary and light popular music; they have a busy singing programme at home and abroad.

Apart from regular concerts by the University's own groups, the Music Centre promotes a season of professional performances known as 'Music for Lunch'. This free weekly series is very popular with students and with the wider public and features an amazing variety of musical styles from baroque to modern folk. All concerts take place in the Alhambra Studio, close to the University Campus.

The Bradford Computing Organ

At the University of Bradford, one of the oldest and most traditional of instruments, the organ, is wedded to the latest computing technology in an innovative musical creation, the Bradford Computing Organ. This is based on the 'Bradford System' of sound synthesis, designed and developed by Dr Peter Comerford and his colleagues in the Microcomputer Music Research Unit (MMRU) which is part of the Department of Computing and Mathematics. The success of this system world-wide has made the name of Bradford synonymous with impressive musical sound quality.

This system is unique in the way in which it uses additive synthesis to build up sound from basic sonic elements called sinewaves. This gives it great flexibility in changing complex sound to suit different acoustic environments and to accommodate the requirements of individual users. Altering sound becomes a matter of changing computer data rather than re-wiring circuits or applying filters or modifying wood and metal. In fact an organ or other instrument specification becomes a data file, which can be loaded into the system in much the same way as programs are loaded into a PC.

Research into the digital creation of musical sound began at Bradford in 1974, and the results have become increasingly sophisticated since then. The most recent generation of the system, known

OPPOSITE The Bradford Computing Organ in St Anne's Cathedral, Leeds

as Bradford Enhanced Synthesis Technology (BEST), allows every sinewave component (or partial) in each waveform to have independent, separately controllable amplitude and frequency patterns (or profiles) during its start period. What happens during the start period of a musical sound has a profound effect upon the perception of the sound as a whole.

The sounds are defined and altered (re-drawn) using a graphical user interface called Envelope Studio, which was written by one of the MMRU team Dr Nick Briggs.

The Bradford System has no 'characteristic sound' – the sounds it produces depend on how it is set up, and this depends on the skills and preferences of the person 'voicing' the instrument. The choices made will also be influenced by the acoustic of the building in which the instrument is heard, as noted above. For example, a large reverberant building will 'elongate' the starting transient portion of the sound, and may need brighter-sounding stops than a small building. It is reasons like this which make it so important to be able to adjust the details of the sound synthesis structure, rather than just rely on a recorded sample, to create a musically satisfying sound in whatever conditions the instrument is sounding.

The system is modular, so by using a number of modules together it is possible to create a large degree of ensemble with many independent sources sounding together – an important consideration for producing satisfying organ tone.

The research and development work has been supported by funding from the University, the British Technology Group and the Engineering and Physical Sciences Research Council. BEST system hardware was engineered for production by Wyvern Classical Organs of Bideford.

The MMRU use BEST as a tool in its research into the nature of musical instrument sound. Its work covers a number of different areas, including synthesis system hardware architectures, synthesis software algorithms, and musical psychoacoustics. This work falls on the boundary between arts and sciences – technology is used to explore musical sounds and, in the process, to create new musical entities.

The work also has commercial spin-off – there are a number of companies which use 'the Bradford system' to make instruments in different styles for sale across the world – and about 2,500 have been installed to date. The majority of these simulate classical or theatre organs, but some are used as piano, harpsichord and a range of other instru-ments. Six British Cathedrals have Bradford Organs (more than any other make of electronic organ) and in 1999 a Bradford organ was installed in Oxford University's Sheldonian Theatre.

The MMRU has been closely involved in liaison with and technical assistance to industry over the years, and has also undertaken contracts to provide sound specifications for commercial organs to provide funds for further research. For example, they were commissioned to set up and voice the sound data for the organ at the Sheldonian Theatre. This is an unique instrument,

The new case for the Bradford Organ in St Anne's Church, Strathpeffer

with multiple specifications based on the styles of specific historical instruments – the Willis organ at Salisbury Cathedral, the Father Smith organ at Pembroke College in Cambridge, and the great Cavaille-Coll at the Basilica of Ste Clotilde in Paris. The aim of this project has been not to copy these organs but to interpret their varied characters through a different medium in a different acoustic. A fourth specification, in the Baroque style familiar to J S Bach, is to be added at a future date. The Sheldonian instrument was installed by J Wood and Sons Ltd of Bradford.

More commonly, the organ voicer using a Bradford system is free to produce a specification voiced within a general style but to the requirement of a particular church or hall, rather than modelled on a specific instrument in a different building.

Courses on Computers and Music

The University's Department of Electronic Imaging and Media Communications has been running undergraduate courses and carrying out research in the field of digital media since 1991. Throughout this period it has run a final year course on Computers and Music. In the early years this examined ways in which computers could synthesise sounds – concentrating in particular on a program called CSound, which was written in the USA by Barry Vercoe in 1986.

Today the course looks at more user-friendly applications and capitalises on the major developments in music technology that have taken place in recent years. Many students produce music in the popular dance music genres, using synthesisers and samplers to produce their sounds, and software sequencers to organise them into finished pieces. These sequencing packages can also score and print out musical compositions with just a few clicks of the mouse. Others produce music in more traditional styles, recording acoustic instruments, but replacing traditional tape-based audio recorders with computers, which can offer many advantages in terms of recording quality and flexibility.

Students in the department also look at other aspects of computers and music including games soundtracks – in the UK the computer games business now turns over more than the music industry. They also study the role of the World Wide Web in music – in particular the MP3 phenomenon, which is causing headaches for the

The organ case in Witney Parish Church

music industry at present, as it enables anyone with a PC to download high-quality music files, often infringing copyright in the process. There is also a legitimate and exciting side to MP3 – it enables musicians without a recording contract to make their music available to the world via the Web.

The Department has two small digital studios – every student learns the basics, but only those who wish to concentrate on music take the final year course. Every year there is an enjoyable day when students present their compositions to their colleagues – no hits yet, but students and their tutors live in hopes!

So, from traditional music making in a wide range of styles, to technology used to produce impressive organ sounds around the world, and digital techniques to train the modern composers of tomorrow, the University of Bradford is justly known for its unique and exciting contribution to the music of Yorkshire.

The Department of Music at the University of Huddersfield

The Music Department of Huddersfield University is now the largest music department in any UK University. It has some 330 students, nearly 50 post-graduates and more than 70 teaching staff, 12 of them full-time. As the largest music department in the university sector it has earned for itself a recognition for excellence in both the quality of its teaching and its research.

The department was founded in 1948 as Huddersfield School of Music, becoming a department of Huddersfield Polytechnic in 1970 and of the University of Huddersfield in 1992. The history of the department and its rise to the prominence it now enjoys is long and complex and has, we understand, never been properly recorded. It owes its development to the energy, enthusiasm and foresight of a host of Heads of Departments, teachers and performers who have dedicated the large part of their working life to the department.

KEITH JARVIS, *Senior Lecturer in Organ Studies since 1976, writes:*

In 1966, the Huddersfield School of Music moved to purpose-built accommodation on the College of Technology campus in Queensgate. When the College attained Polytechnic status in 1970 it developed an undergraduate honours course based around free composition, performance and musicology. All degree teaching was concentrated at Queensgate and the former Milton Congregational Church; for many years, additional nearby accommodation had to be rented.

Huddersfield School of Music 1962-3

Meanwhile, the former Technical College had moved to another part of the town and its traditional music courses were based in the college's Highfields annexe. The two institutions shared many of the same staff.

The concept of a combined School of Music providing courses across the whole age-range from 14 upwards became increasingly difficult to sustain, since the funding arrangements for non-advanced courses (O and A Levels, External Diploma) and others classified as 'Advanced' (Degree and Postgraduate studies) were different, causing problems for both institutions. Although after 1973, all full-time staff were the responsibility of the Education Committee, this did not resolve the costs of accommodation and equipment.

Patrick Forbes, who in 1965 had succeeded Wyndham G Williams as Head of the music department, retired in 1977, to be succeeded in 1979 by Arthur Jacobs. By this time, the non-advanced Technical College courses (under H Sterndale Hurst) were increasingly separated from those at the Polytechnic and ultimately the two departments became independent of each other, though with some continuing staff liaison.

At the same time the Youth Orchestras – from their inception an integral part of the School of Music – also achieved administrative independence under Harold Newcombe, eventually moving to the former Oastler College premises above the (now former) Co-Op building.

During this difficult transition period the Polytechnic provided major funding for the restoration St Paul's Hall and the installation of a new concert organ. This most sensitive restoration and the superb quality of the organ (placed at the front of the hall) have brought national and international recognition to the institution. It is a major venue for Huddersfield music-making, and is heavily used by the community as well as by the Department of Music.

Almost all applicants for the University's Music Courses are auditioned or interviewed. Two 'A' levels or equivalent are normally required and one of these should be Music. The most popular undergraduate course is B Mus Hons which requires students to take musicology and one or two other subject areas (chosen from composition, electro-acoustic music and performance). The curriculum includes music awareness, harmony analysis and IT skills. The large number of options

St Paul's Concert Hall

Huddersfield is able to offer enables students to personalise their courses and play to their strengths.

The facilities include St Paul's Hall, a separate recital hall, eight 'state of the art' electro-acoustic studios, around 48 practice rooms and in excess of 80 pianos for rehearsal and performance.

Today, the Department has an outstanding reputation for the quality of its graduate and postgraduate courses: many of its former students have made their name in the music profession. The seeds planted in 1948 have borne striking fruit.

A more personal view of the department's history is given by RODNEY BASS, *who started life in the department as a student and later became one of its teaching staff.*

In September 1951 I became a student at the music department at Huddersfield 'Tech'. I was fifteen years old, and my only real claim to any sort of ability was that I played the clarinet fairly well. Not well-qualified in other respects, the chance of

qualifications but with some sort of musical talent either real or imagined (or invented by someone who sent them there). Fortunately I knew some of the students who were already there and senior to me, and so I did have some inkling as to what lay in store. George Brown from Golcar, a very fine violinist, was already installed there as was Darrell Wade, another fine violinist, and John Forester, who was just as good a viola player. All three of these young people went on to become professional players or teachers in later years: George is still well known in the town and has numerous very successful ex-pupils to his name.

The varied accommodation available to the music department was barely adequate to its needs. What might be regarded as the main body of it comprised the rooms which gave on to the balcony of what had been the Sunday School of Milton church: lessons in other subjects were held in the Technical College's adjacent 'Old Building'. The painting and decorating department occupied the ground floor of the church building, and the music department had a series of practice-rooms on the floor below that, in a sort of semi-basement. As far as individual instrumental lessons were concerned these small rooms were ideal, or they would have been had they possessed even the most rudimentary form of sound insulation – though come to think of it, I have yet to experience practice-rooms which do have adequate sound insulation.

We had no suitable place for large groups to rehearse except the large hall in the Old Building, the gymnasium, and one of the classrooms on the first floor of the former St Paul's school, also situated nearby. This particular room although quite large enough to accommodate the choir had the once-familiar glass partitions which could be drawn back in order to form an even larger hall. 'Why didn't we draw these partitions back?', you might well ask. Well, the answer is that the other parts of the same floor were occupied by other departments. To me at the time all these difficulties were not apparent; it was quite normal for things to be like this. All the schools that I had ever been in were built in this way and after all it was not long since the end of the war, with its 'make do and mend' mentality.

The head of the department was Mr Wintersgill, and Mr Freyhan was, I believe, his deputy. The other two full-time members of staff were, if I remember correctly, Mrs Eugénie

becoming a music student at the 'Tech' seemed the best way forward for me. Fortunately my parents were fully supportive of this idea, and so I found myself in Milton Hall on that September day in 1951.

I believe that I am right in saying that Huddersfield Tech was the very first college of its kind to offer a music course. Partly because of this the organisers were very flexible in the timetable that individuals could follow. The largest proportion of students were very much like myself – former secondary modem students with no academic

Everest and Mr Kruzynski. Mrs Everest taught singing, and Mr Kruzynski the piano. Other instrumental lessons were given by part-time lecturers. I had clarinet lessons from Mr Ronald Birkbeck, and piano lessons from Mr Kruzynski. The violin was taught by Neville Mortimer and the viola by Mrs Kaye, the widow of Arthur Willie Kaye, the well-known and well-respected Huddersfield violin teacher who was active in pre-war years and who had produced some distinguished players including Laurance Turner, leader of the Hallé Orchestra and Reginald Stead, leader of the BBC Northern Orchestra. There were at that time very few players of orchestral wind instruments in the department; when such players did eventually appear, teachers were found for them on an 'ad hoc' basis. There was a college orchestra, which held its rehearsals in the gymnasium next to the Commercial Department, where typing classes took place. We knew that they were typing classes because we could hear the specially recorded music, often Strauss waltzes played at a strict tempo of sixty beats per minute, or thereabouts, and played in a very particularly detached style designed, I presume, to keep the tyro typists typing at a regular speed; all this of course on top of the rhythmic crashes of the mechanical typewriters in use at that time.

In addition to our musical studies we also pursued other academic subjects – sometimes, I might add, without actually catching them. Everyone did English Language and English Literature and a foreign language. Classes in these subjects were provided by the appropriate departments within the college and we roamed about the various buildings from class to class. In these non-music classes we met students doing other courses, so there was a considerable intermingling of students within the college. For the boys, the course even included one period of 'gym' per week – much to the disgust of some of the members of the music fraternity! Several of the not very energetic members of this class conspired to miss these weekly workouts, but I must admit that I rather enjoyed them.

At the end of my first year, Mr Wintersgill left the college, and Mr Freyhan took up the reins of leadership. So far as I was concerned, things seemed to be continuing much as before and I found life very enjoyable. I was making good progress with my clarinet playing, and my general education was progressing satisfactorily if not spectacularly. At the beginning of my third year I was surprised to learn that Mr Freyhan had left, and just then there seemed to be no official head of the department. Mrs Everest was holding things together, but I did sense that the future of the place might be in some doubt. After some days Mr Wyndham G Williams arrived and things took a turn for the better. Mr Williams ('Taffy' to everyone behind his back) had been music adviser to the Huddersfield Education Authority since 1948: he knew the 'ins and outs' of the place very well and was an ideal person for the job.

He quickly set about the business of getting things on an even keel, and everyone seemed to

Below left. the Audiophonic workshop Right, the percussion studio.

The famous organ in St Paul's Concert Hall

behind St Paul's School, and we were able to play cricket during breaks and in the evenings. Generally speaking, the department was drawn together into a solid unit in a way that had not quite hap-pened before.

The well-established Huddersfield Youth Orchestra was now more or less drawn into the workings of the Technical College Music Department (or was it perhaps the other say round?), and so it was possible, for the first time, to tackle more challenging projects. Generally speaking, the size and musical standards of the department grew. The orchestra made annual visits to the Blackpool Music Competition and frequently won the orchestral class. During the summer of 1954 (I should think it must have been), the string section of the orchestra visited an international festival of music and dance at Passau in Bavaria where it made quite an impression. This was the very first time that most of us had ever been abroad and of course we travelled by train – the possibility of taking a coach with us was of course not practical in those days. However, after travelling for thirty-six hours we finally arrived in Passau where we had a very interesting time.

In those days National Service was still in force, and after finishing their courses all the male students went off into the services. When I had completed my four years of study I in my turn went off to join the army where I spent three years in the Coldstream Guards Band which certainly improved my general playing ability; during this time my contact with the department was limited to visits while home on leave, and during this time things there continued to grow. I imag-

sense a new feeling of optimism. His energy seemed to be boundless. For whatever reason, the results from the English Department had not been as good as desired. Taffy's response was typical of him – he took on the teaching of English himself. Similarly he took over the training in the gym personally – and woe betide anybody who had the nerve to miss any of his training sessions! Quite frequently during these sessions, out would come the boxing gloves, the class would be divided into pairs and everyone had to fight. On one occasion a cricket bag mysteriously arrived from somewhere full of cricket equipment along with a set of nets which were erected in the yard

ine that it was during this time that Harold Truscott was appointed to the full-time staff and through my visits I got to know him quite well. When I left the army in 1958, I did some clarinet teaching at the department in and among all my other playing and teaching assignments, and Harold and I would meet one evening a week to play together and talk. We gave the odd recital or so in the college, and he wrote a clarinet sonata of which we gave the first performance.

Expansion gathered pace (I think that it was probably around 1960 that Richard Steinitz, later to become world-famous as the founder of the Huddersfield Contemporary Music Festival, joined the staff). Of course it was not only the music department that was growing at that time: the rest of the Technical College had also been expanding and had become a 'College of Technology'. This led to a reconstruction of the campus: the old St Paul's school was demolished to make way for the extensions to the rest of the college. Once more the department was on the lookout for accommodation. There were plans, I imagine, at this time for a new music building for the department, but until this was eventually constructed it had to function elsewhere. For a while a semi-permanent home was found in what had been the YWCA building at the top of the town not far from the railway station.

A corollary of the Technical College's having become a College of Technology was that it now set a higher entry age for the student admissions than had the former Technical College. This resulted in the emergence of a separate technical college, which had its headquarters at Highfields. Ultimately (as Keith Jarvis has explained above) the split between the two colleges became absolute.

Perhaps it might not be out of place to mention some of the people who went on to better things in later years after leaving the old place. There are bound to be omissions of course (my memory is far from perfect) and anyone who feels left out must accept my assurance that such omissions have not been made out of malice. One of my old friends whom I knew at school before going to the 'Tech' was John Noble who went on to Leeds University and then to Doncaster, where I believe he became head of the music department at Doncaster Tech. I have already mentioned John Forester (viola),

Darrel Wade (violin), and George Brown (violin) who all made successful careers in the world of music. Dennis Bamforth went on to Aberystwyth University and then to Sale Grammar School where he became head of music. Michael Hirst went to London and became a successful freelance flute-player in the established orchestras. Richard Stoker went to the Royal Academy and later studied with Nadia Boulanger before becoming an established composer; for 24 years he was a Professor of Composition at the Royal Academy of Music. Val Taylor went to London where she studied the oboe with Janet Craxton. Alan Lockwood went on to play the flute in the BBC Northern Orchestra. Warwick Hill played the violin in the London Symphony Orchestra. John White became a member of the staff at the Royal College of Music, and Christina Clarke sang in the highest circles of the profession.

• *Later students who have made their mark in the profession (another unavoidably selective list) include the violinist Robert Taylor and the cellist Rayford Kitchen (both long-serving members of the Hallé Orchestra), the soprano Barbara Rodway, the organist and conductor Peter Seymour (a prominent figure in the musical life of York and its University) and, most recently, the percussionist Julian Warburton.* – EDITOR

Music in York

Though other towns in Yorkshire might lay claim to primacy as musical centres, the dispassionate observer must surely award pride of place to the ancient city of York, which was the county town of the three Ridings until the reorganisation brought about by the Local Government Act (1972). Both on account of the city's historic importance and the amazing diversity of its present musical life, it is therefore accorded (alone of the places mentioned in this book) a chapter to itself. For a detailed study of the subject the reader is referred to David Griffiths' fascinating book A Musical Place of the First Quality *(York Settlement Trust, 1990). Here, the treatment of the subject is unavoidably brief and selective.*

A definitive list of musical organisations currently active in York includes the following:

Choirs: York Musical Society, University of York Choir and Chamber Choir, Yorkshire Bach Choir, Micklegate Singers, Chapter House Choir, Ebor Singers, York Youth Choir, White Rose Singers – and, of course, the Minster Choir.

Orchestras: York Symphony Orchestra, Guildhall Orchestra, University of York Orchestra and Chamber Orchestra, Academy of St Olave's and York Chamber Orchestra.

Operatic Societies: York Opera, York Light Opera.

York is also a major centre for the performance of Early Music (as shown elsewhere in this book), the triennial presentation of Medieval Mystery Plays and is home to the British Music Society of York, which promotes chamber concerts of a distinctive character.

In addition, the city possesses an unrivalled wealth of concert venues. **York Minster**, apart from its staggering architecture, offers a generous acoustic especially appropriate for choral music. There is a variety of performing areas allowing audiences of between 200 and 3000. The **Sir Jack Lyons Concert Hall** in the University's Department of Music houses audiences up to 450 and has an acoustic notably sympathetic to chamber music. A particularly attractive feature of the **Central Hall**, also on the University campus (seating 1,100 is the proximity of all the audience to the performing area The **Barbican Centre**, a dual-purpose sports /concert hall accommodating 1,500 people is at its best for large orchestral forces. There is a proliferation of city centre churches of which **St Michael-le-Belfrey**, (where Guy Fawkes was baptised), with room for 650, is the most used. The medieval **Guildhall** holding 200, **Merchant Adventurers' Hall** (150) and classical **Assembly**

Rooms (200) are all of outstanding architectural beauty and interestingly varied acoustics; the Guildhall's clarity and warmth is particularly attractive.

York is, of course, one of England's most visited tourist centres. Nevertheless an outsider is bound to ask: 'in a relatively small city of 104,000 people where do all these organisations find their audiences?'

York Minster

York Minster, known in full as the Cathedral and Metropolitical Church of St Peter in York, is the seat of the Archbishop of York, who is the Anglican Primate of England. The Minster is the Mother Church of the Northern Province of the Church of England, as well as the Diocese of York.

In his *History of the English Church and People*, the Venerable Bede notes that in 627 St Paulinus appointed James the Deacon to found a school attached to the Cathedral in York. It would be fanciful to claim that there has been an unbroken history of a choir school since 627, but there has undoubtedly been an educational presence attached to the Minster, and the present school represents a continuation of the tradition established by St Paulinus.

At the heart of the Minster Choir's work is the

ABOVE inside York Minster

LEFT the Choir with Philip Moore and John Scott Whiteley. Photo courtesy of the Dean and Chapter

Philip Moore

singing of the daily services. Today's Choir sings eight services each week. Since 1997 there has been a treble line of girls, who rehearse and perform separately from the boys. Most of the services are sung either by the boys and men or the girls and men. All the Choristers attend the Minster School, a day preparatory school, and they have a daily practice at 8.15 each morning. The Songmen of the Choir are all professional singers and rehearse with the Choristers before each service.

The present Organist and Master of the Music is Philip Moore. He succeeded Dr Francis Jackson in 1982. As well as his work in the Minster, Philip Moore is active as a recitalist and composer. He also conducts the York Musical Society, a choir of one hundred and fifty voices. The Society has been conducted by many of his predecessors. Philip Moore's works are performed extensively both in this country as well as in the USA and Australia. In 1996 a CD of his choral and organ music was produced. The Assistant Organist is John Scott Whiteley and has worked at the Minster since 1975. He is a distinguished recitalist and scholar in his own right and has many solo recordings to his credit, both on the Minster Organ and on others in this country and abroad. Jonathan Wainwright is the Assistant Choir Trainer; his main brief is to train the Girl Choristers, a post he combines with a lectureship at the University of York. He is well known in academic circles for a variety of historical research projects that have been published and widely acclaimed. The current Organ Scholar is Robert Poyser. The Canon Precentor, Paul Ferguson, is also a trained musician, and so too is the Headmaster of the Minster School, Richard Shephard. His work as a composer and as a singer is well-known.

The Minster Choir has a large number of recordings to its credit. The latest, called *Masters of the Music*, is a recording of music by Philip Moore and his predecessors, many of whom were composers. There is also a recording of music by Samuel Sebastian Wesley, which contains several extended, unpublished and hitherto unrecorded works. In 1997 a recording of works by Dr Francis Jackson was made, to coincide with his 80th birthday.

As well as its work in the Minster, the Choir has toured extensively, both in England and abroad. Among its most memorable visits was one to Poland in 1992. There have also been trips to Belgium, France, Sweden and Denmark, in addition to four visits to the USA. The Choir frequently performs on Radio and Television and each term one or more sections of the Choir visit a variety of churches in the Diocese of York.

PHILIP MOORE

Yorkshire Baroque Soloists and Yorkshire Bach Choir

The founder and conductor of both these groups is Peter Seymour, Senior Lecturer in Music at the University.

Yorkshire Baroque Soloists was formed in 1973 to explore a repertoire from the 17th and 18th centuries for forces ranging from chamber to orchestral size. The ensemble is to be heard most often with the Yorkshire Bach Choir, which Seymour formed in 1979 to sing a repertoire ranging from Tudor to contemporary music including commissioned works by Duncan Druce, Christopher Fox and John Paynter. The choir concentrates, however, on music from the late 16th to early 19th centuries, both unaccompanied and with original instruments; a major part of its work has been to research performing styles in use at the time of composition but which are relevant to and appropriate for a modern audience.

Recent performances by the two groups have included Bach's Christmas Oratorio, Mozart's *Requiem* and C Minor Mass, Cantatas for the Feast of St Michael by Bach and Monteverdi's Vespers of 1610. Commercially released recordings have included Bach's Motets, the *Festal Mass at the Imperial Court in Vienna, 1648* and Mozart's *Requiem*. Purcell's *Dido and Aeneas* is due for release shortly.

The Soloists performed a programme for Channel 4 about Bach's work in Leipzig which, amongst other compositions, included Bach's *Ascension Oratorio*. In recent York Early Music Festivals, the BBC and West German Radio have recorded the group's performances of Handel's *Semele*, *Alexander's Feast*, Bach's *Cantatas for the Feast of St Michael*, Purcell's *Come ye Sons of Art*, *The Yorkshire Feast Song*, Blow's *Welcome Every Guest*, Clarke's *Music on the Death of Henry Purcell*, Haydn's *Theresienmesse*, Purcell's *Dioclesian* and a psalm sequence of music by Charpentier. In recent seasons the Soloists have performed programmes of Purcell's music on an Early Music University Network Tour and, with the Choir, recorded for the BBC a programme of music by Biber including his *Missa Alleluia*, scored for eight-part choir, eight soloists, six trumpets, timps, two cornetts, three trombones, strings and continuo. Other recordings have included a further BBC programme of music by Muffat and Biber. Earlier this season they performed a programme of Blow for West German Radio broadcast live by the European Broadcasting Union. In July 2000 they appeared in York Early Music Festival performing a programme of Schütz (*St John Passion, Seven Last Words, Resurrection History*) which was recorded by the BBC.

The Choir is a regular visitor to UK festivals including Swaledale and Ryedale as well as at York Early Music Festival and Northern Aldborough Festival, but it has also appeared in France, Germany and Czech Republic.

The 1999/2000 programme included Lutheran masses, motets and *St Matthew Passion* by J S Bach and programmes of Monteverdi, Carissimi, Charpentier, Byrd and Tallis. The coming season will include Bach's *B Minor Mass*, more Lutheran masses, music from Salzburg by Haydn and Mozart and programmes of music from the late 16th century and 17th England.

University Music Department

While it is true that the tradition of music-making in York is longstanding and venerable, it is also the case that by the 1960s that tradition had become somewhat ossified (see Griffiths, *op cit*, p 192). In 1963, however, a remarkable transformation was about to take place. In that year, the University of York was founded and in 1964 Wilfrid Mellers became the first full Professor of Music in any of the 'new' universities – a position he was to hold until 1981.

Mellers, though no mean musicologist himself, insisted that *performance* and *composition* should be at the heart of a university music course, rejecting the somewhat dry academic approach which had long characterised such courses. He attracted staff of the highest quality, including a number of leading composers (at present, no fewer than seven are in residence). The department's graduate and postgraduate courses, with notable specialisations

in electro-acoustic, ethnic and early music, and jazz, have won international recognition.

But no less important than the department's achievements in its own right is the profound impact it has had on concert-giving and music-making in the city – nothing less than the transformation alluded to above.

First of all, the Department has not only founded many of the organisations listed above (notably Peter Seymour's Yorkshire Bach Choir and Yorkshire Baroque Soloists) but it has also provided a steady stream of singers and instrumentalists who have played a significant part in enriching already-existing amateur societies. Its own ensembles (including, for instance, its 250-strong choral society) have given the city an unparalleled diversity of concerts.

Most striking of all, however is the year-round concert series which it promotes (now between 40 and 50 in a season). These cover orchestral, choral and chamber genres, featuring leading professional orchestras and international artists as well as highly talented student ensembles, alongside jazz, non-Western music, electronic music and so on.

Shortly after the founding of the university, Richard Middleton, one of its first postgraduates, asserted that 'musically at least ... the city has little to offer' (quoted in Griffiths, *op cit*). Today, nothing could be further from the truth.

PETER SEYMOUR

Early Music

INTRODUCTION

The broad thrust of this book relates to music of all genres and its seeming magnetic attraction to the towns and villages of the West Riding. Theories abound why this should be so, but how could any of these apply to music as early as 1700, 1600 or even earlier?

Impossible? Think again. Early music, as it has become known, and certainly its more recent revival since around 1960 has a concentration in the area which requires explanation, if indeed it wasn't spawned in the county. There are quite a number of instrument makers, amateur and professional consorts operating throughout the region, and a lot of early music is played and taught. York and Beverley have their own Early Music Centres and Festivals and in commercial terms, the centre of the early music universe is The Early Music Shop, which has its base in Bradford.

The Early Music Shop was formed almost by accident. A fairly large education order was received by its parent firm, J Wood & Sons Ltd, some time around 1963, which contained, amongst other items, a soprano shawm. Not surprisingly, the firm had no idea what this was, made enquiries, and on a visit to Frankfurt International Music Messe, which in itself was only in embryo at that time, ordered a shawm along with several other early instruments quite speculatively along with a couple of sets of recorders. What was then perhaps careless speculation became justified when local enthusiasts gathered around the new stock like 'bears round a honey pot'. The stock was quickly sold, replaced, and the stock widened with further speculative abandon. This stock then became the subject of The Early Music Shop's first catalogue – just a duplicated sheet with a few cutout photographs.

At the same time, David Munrow was just beginning to establish himself, firstly as presenter of BBC's 'Pied Piper' and then as a compiler of music for the series *Wives of Henry VIII* starring Keith Michel and Glenda Jackson, a series which rapidly became nationwide compulsive viewing – perhaps the first of the BBC's successful costume drama productions. The series had authentic music played throughout on original instruments, and suddenly the early music revival was born. Shortly afterwards, the BBC had to issue an internal memo saying that the BBC output of early music was reaching saturation point and the interest in early music had to be limited. Presenters were rationed to the amount of early music for which time was available.

David Munrow in fact became a good friend of the shop and visited many times to purchase instruments and music. On one memorable occasion, when David lost his entire collection of instruments in a theft in central London, he shot up to Bradford and was re-equipped overnight.

David was an incredibly talented performer and raconteur on all subjects relating to early music. He was a gifted presenter for the BBC with a natural articulate delivery which commanded attention. This, accompanied by virtuosic playing on a huge variety of instruments, made him in demand for lecture recitals and broadcasting. His untimely death in 1976 was a tragic loss to the entire early music movement. Amazingly, no-one has risen sufficiently to follow in his footsteps, although many of the players who formed his band of musicians continue as performers in their own right and have carved individual careers in the early music field – James Bowman, John Turner, Christopher Hogwood and Oliver Brookes to name a few.

Early in the shop's history, the founder, Richard Wood, hadn't found an acceptable title for the shop and sat down with David Munrow to devise one. One fear was that the term 'early music' might incorrectly give the impression of the music being suitable only for children, but the title nevertheless stuck and the term 'early music' was registered on a nationwide basis. Even the magazine *Early Music* had to write for permission to use the name.

The growth in early music in England at that time became spectacular, although it must be said that it had had a more sedate earlier upbringing in

the enthusiasm shown in the subject by Arnold Dolmetsch and the Haslemere Festival. Another story.

In Germany too, the movement had begun much earlier and Dolmetsch's equivalents on the Continent were Professor Peter Harland and Otto Steinkopf. The recorder maker, Moeck Verlag, produced early instruments with Otto Steinkopf almost uniquely in the 1950s, along with other pioneers

LEFT *The York Waits*
BELOW *David Munrow*

such as Rainer Weber, and followed later by Gunter Korber in Berlin. These small German factories produced most of the world's only available early woodwind instruments, and with the explosion of interest in England, the supply soon fell far short of demand. Fresh sources had to be found, and Richard Wood sought these from as far afield as East Germany, Romania, and a handful of very small-time makers in and around southern Germany.

Supply still outstripped demand throughout the 1970s to the extent that the firm began making their own instruments – crumhorns, racketts, cornamuse, dulcians – in a very small way in a workshop in the firm's attic. The attic then became two floors of the shop, the catalogues became more comprehensive, more ambitious, and the firm's clientele soon covered the entire globe, with agents in most countries of the world.

At the same time, the firm gathered together a handful of the country's leading makers and held the first Exhibition of Early Musical Instruments in the Royal College of Music, London, an exhibition which was ultimately to grow into the London International Exhibition of Early Music with exhibitors from all over the globe. The exhibition, now an annual event, is attended by upwards of 100 exhibitors.

York Early Music Foundation

For many years, St Margaret's Church in Walmgate, York lay neglected, used only as a props store by York Theatre Royal. Now, thanks to a grant from the National Lottery through the Arts Council of England, York Early Music Foundation has brought this magnificent Grade I listed building back to life.

The vision was to create the National Centre for Early Music – a focal point for the study and enjoyment of early music – and to revive this neglected corner of central York. The project restored one of York's most important churches, creating a concert venue and purpose-built rehearsal and recording facilities, as well as establishing a garden for all to enjoy and appreciate. The Centre acts as a vital cultural force for the whole city of York, and for the future development of early music both in this country and throughout Europe.

The York Early Music Festival

At the time of its inception in 1977, the York Early Music Festival was a pioneer in the field. Its role is to promote historically informed performance of early music. Now established as Britain's premier festival of early music, it draws in audiences from all over the world and has contributed much to the acceptance of historically informed performance as a popular feature of British musical life. Its audience has expanded from a network of enthusiasts to include people interested in all kinds of music and a range of cultural activities. A profusion of fringe events has sprung up around the Festival including lectures, young artists' concerts, walks, talks and related educational projects.

The York festival has an increasingly strong international dimension with many of the visitors coming to the annual festival travelling from America, Canada, Australia and Japan. Guest artists include musicians from non-Western traditions such as Tibet, India and North Africa as well as the Americas, reflecting the increasing awareness that performers of Western 'early music' have much to learn from the performance practice of other musical cultures.

Artists

Each year, the festival chooses to focus on a particular theme. Leading soloists and ensembles from every field of early music have been engaged over the years to perform in York, including notably Emma Kirkby, Nigel North, Anthony Rooley, Melvyn Tan, Stephen Varcoe, the Academy of Ancient Musicke, Musica Antiqua of Köln, the Choir of King's College Cambridge, Ton Koopman, Yorkshire Bach Choir and the Rose Consort of Viols – and many, many more, too numerous to mention.

The theme for the 2000 festival was J S Bach and the theme for 2001 is the music of Northern Italy and the 500th anniversary of the birth of the Italian music printer Petrucci.

The York Waits – Renaissance City Band

The York Waits are an early music band, specialising in the wind instruments of the Renaissance, who have been a popular concert attraction in Yorkshire and around the country since 1977. In that time there have been only two changes in membership.

The band is unusual in that it seeks to recreate not just a distant repertoire of music but a specific group of historic musicians – the original York Waits, who were paid and liveried by the city authorities from the Middle Ages until 1836, the year of reforms in local government.

Naturally, over such a long period the size, repertoire and duties of the original waits of York would have varied enormously. Today's band sets

St Margaret's Church, Walmgate

out to recreate how the group might have sounded and looked in the early 16th century. This gives them the opportunity to play some of the finest secular music of the renaissance, with special emphasis on Franco-Flemish composers such as Jacob Obrecht and Josquin des Pres.

The York Waits perform in carefully recreated historical clothes, including bright red livery coats and chains of office copied from original waits' chains that survive.

The waits are also a product of the wave of enthusiasm in the early 1970s for the rediscovery and reconstruction of the instruments of the Renaissance. The same movement also led to the establishment of the Early Music Shop in Bradford.

The emergence of many specialist makers of early instruments at this time enabled the Waits to equip themselves with ensembles of renaissance recorders, flutes, crumhorns and curtals, plus re-creations of early bagpipes and hurdy gurdies.

But the quintessential sound of the waits of old and of today's York Waits is the loud shawm and sackbut ensemble – the shawm being a double reed instrument constructed in two main sizes and the sackbut being the early trombone.

The sound of this ensemble would have been familiar to renaissance townspeople throughout Europe and the original waits would have deployed it for the ceremonial and processional functions which were an important part of their duties as civic employees.

In addition to giving concerts, today's Waits also perform such ceremonial duties. For example, in July 2000 the band played from the top of Micklegate Bar in York to greet the Queen as she arrived in the city, just as the waits of earlier centuries heralded a succession of monarchs.

One member of The York Waits, Dr James Merryweather, has researched the history of the original band and published the results in his book *York Music*. Here he sums up the duties of the original group and perhaps the origin of their name:

'The waits played the music for all civic ceremonies: mayor making, sheriffs ridings, grand processions, banquets and dances, as well as occasionally accompanying the choir at the minster. At night they perambulated the streets, keeping watch and playing to mark

The York Waits

the hours. The night watch was a relic of waits' original duties: the name 'wait' may have been derived from the watchman's association with the 'wayte', 'wayte-pipe' or shawm, the main instrument of the waits before 1600.'

Today's York Waits are Tim Bayley, Anthony Barton, James Merryweather, William Marshall, Ian Richardson and Roger Richardson. They have issued several recordings and played overseas on many occasions, most recently in Belgium, Norway and, in the run up to Christmas 1999, the USA.

Brass Bands

INTRODUCTION

There are many apocryphal stories of early brass bands, like the oft-told one of the band which, in accordance with tradition, was about to celebrate a contest victory by marching down the village Street playing *The Victors Return*, or perhaps *See, the Conquering Hero*. Unfortunately, the train home was delayed, and it was about two in the morning when our heroes arrived. Ever-thoughtful, they took off their boots and played in stocking-feet, so as not to wake the inhabitants. Then there's the one about the committee man who arrived late to a meeting. The Chairman explained that they were discussing the purchase of a new chandelier: 'Well', said the latecomer, 'Who's ba'an ta play it if we get one?'

Unlike bandsmen of today, early bandsmen were uneducated and unsophisticated, and there

may well be a grain of truth in some of these tales. The brass band movement was nurtured in the mid-nineteenth century – an off-shoot of the Industrial Revolution, when people from agricultural regions flocked to the towns, helping create an environment where bands (and choirs) flourished. Most bands were formed in the vicinity of a mill or group of mills. The members, working men who lived and worked in appalling conditions, would get together after work to make music, as a kind of antidote to the more unsavoury aspects of their lives. Some wealthier members of the community were willing to subscribe towards the cost of instruments and music – maybe even towards the purchase of a uniform.

Early Days

Though the history of amateur bands can be traced back to the close of the eighteenth century, the all-brass band didn't appear until the 1830s, and was rare until the 1850s. The first generation of amateur bands had relied on clarinets, flutes, and the aptly-named 'serpent', as early brass instruments (except the trombone) had a restricted range of notes – equivalent to those of a bugle. Horns and trumpets, which were found in early bands, had no valves, and were unable to play conventional melodies.

The appearance of the ophicleide family – which included the keyed bugle (invented in 1815) – heralded new possibilities for the brasses, but it was through the invention of the valve, around 1820, and the work of instrument makers such as Adolphe Sax that the brass band as we know it became a reality.

Brass instruments had many advantages for

factory workers. They were relatively cheap to buy and easy to play, and the group of three valves (or the slide of the trombone) could easily be manipulated, even by the rough and malformed hands of manual workers. The cornet was preferred to the trumpet and the tenor saxhorn to the French horn, and the combination of comets, various sizes of saxhorns, and tubas, meant that players could easily transfer from one instrument to another.

Thus, if a band needed a euphonium player but had a spare cornetist, it was relatively easy to change over. This would obviously not be possible with a violin and cello, or clarinet and bassoon in the orchestra.

The all-brass band flourished initially in York and the East Riding, but by the early 1850s the West Riding had become the main stronghold. Leeds was an important centre in the early years of the decade, but by the mid-50s the influence of a number of West Riding mill-owners was having a significant effect. These included John Foster in Queensbury, Titus Salt in Saltaire, Jonas Brook in Meltham and Lister Marriner in Keighley, each of

whom was able to offer employment to good players, supply up-to-date instruments, and provide uniforms, rehearsal facilities, music, and high calibre band trainers. Thus, Black Dike (old spelling), Saltaire, Meltham and Marriner's bands became, for a time, the dominating bands in the district and further afield.

Another stimulus emerged from 1859 with the re-formation of the Volunteer Force, a part-time army assembled to counter the threat of invasion from France. Many local bands benefited from this, being funded either entirely or partially by the Force. Amongst the more successful volunteer bands in the district was one in Halifax, but Dewsbury, Saltaire and Marriners were amongst those who, for a time, were attached to the Volunteers.

The mid-nineteenth century also saw the development of railways. It was a great advantage to a band to be located close to a railway station, and the railways were significant in the development of the contest, ease of access by a number of bands being essential.

The Brass Band Contest

Success was generally measured in terms of contest results, and as bands increased in numbers, so did contests. These were to become of paramount importance to bands; they not only provided the stimulus to play well, they were a source of income to the better bands, and provided entertainment for a large number of people, crowds of 10,000 or more not being unusual, even at local contests. Virtually all were held outdoors; Manningham Park Bradford and Roundhay Park Leeds were amongst the many popular venues in Yorkshire.

Mention must be made here of the so-called 'temperance bands'. Contrary to popular belief, these were neither funded by nor attached to any temperance organisation. By the 1870s many bands had become populated with addicted drinkers, and money earned through band work was immediately spent in the local pub. Bad behaviour and hooliganism became their hall-marks. However, not all bandsmen approved, and in some cases the more sober-minded members of a band broke loose

and formed a separate band which, because of the social habits of its members, became known as the temperance band. Friction – even hatred – often existed between the old and the new, and behaviour at contests sank to even lower depths.

One Yorkshire village which had two such bands was Wyke, near Bradford. Wyke Old Band had been formed in the 1840s, whilst Wyke Temperance came into being in the early 50s, becoming all brass in 1859. There were no real problems as long as the 'Old' was doing well in contests, but as their rivals improved and contest results started going the other way, the trouble started. The 'Old' was supported by publicans and the beer-drinkers of Wyke; the supporters of the 'Temps' were fewer in number and less vociferous. Legend has it that on their return from a contest, whichever band had won paraded from the station into the village playing its own particular march. The villagers would listen to see which tune was

being played, and would immediately know whether their favourites or the opposition had been successful.

Supporters of both bands regularly assembled on a bridge under which the winning band would march, and on the occasions on which Wyke Temperance Band were successful, unruliness from the opposite camp could be expected. One slightly humorous story concerns a supporter of the 'Old' uttering some obscenities, and stating that he hoped the bridge would collapse as the 'Temps' marched under it, losing sight of the fact that he was himself on the bridge, and would have gone down with it.

Though neither band exists today, Wyke Temperance outlived the Old, surviving into the twentieth century. Like many other non-sponsored bands, it survived largely through the efforts of its ladies' committee, a group which had nothing to do with the administration of the band but which, by means of jumble sales, sales of work, Christmas draws and the like, provided much of the money which the band needed for its existence.

Though by the end of the nineteenth century there were literally hundreds of contests each year, the principal one was that held annually each September at Belle Vue, Manchester. It is interesting to see how the better Yorkshire bands fared between 1853 (the date of the first one) and 1900.

	1sts	2nds	3rds	4ths
Black Dike Mills	10	4	4	1
Meltham Mills	4	4	1	1
Wyke Temperance	3	3	2	1
Leeds Railway Foundry	2	1	–	–
Dewsbury	1	8	2	1
Halifax Rifle Volunteers	2	–	–	–

The Great Conductors
The domination of Black Dike was due to its longevity. Other bands came and went, whilst the band from Queensbury was (and still is) always at the forefront. Nevertheless, the first great milestone was achieved when Meltham won at Belle Vue three times in succession (1876-78). They were then barred for two years, and Black Dike followed immediately with its first hat-trick (1879-81). The winning conductor in the years 1876-1880 was John Gladney, a clarinetist in the Hallé Orchestra, who became known as 'the father of the brass band'. He was the senior member of a trio of conductors known as 'The Great Triumvirate'.

The middle member of this group, and the only Yorkshireman, was Milnsbridge-born Edwin Swift, a self-taught musician who worked full-time in a woollen mill before cutting loose and earning his living through conducting and adjudicating. He is reported to have said, 'I'm a weaver by trade and a musician by chance!'

The other member of the Triumvirate was Alexander Owen, a gifted comet player, brought up in an orphanage near Manchester, but later coming under the influence of John Gladney. Owen played solo cornet with Meltham during the period of their hat-trick, and in 1881 succeeded Gladney as professional conductor of Black Dike.

During the 1890s the leading conductors, in particular Gladney, began taking their skills, and the gospel of the brass band, into other regions – Scotland, Wales, the Midlands and the South.

They were able to do this because of the further development of the railways, as well as the great improvements taking place in road travel.

More about Contests
We've seen how the brass band was cradled in Yorkshire. From here it spread north into Durham and west into Lancashire, and from thence south into Staffordshire. Lancashire – like Yorkshire, dominated by textiles – also spawned many good bands, and to this day, the bands of the two counties have their own particular brand of the Wars of the Roses.

All these contests needed organising, and the chief entrepreneur of the early ones was Enderby Jackson, born in Hull in 1827. He became a professional musician, but also an indefatigable worker on behalf of amateur bands. He composed and arranged music for them and organised many contests. His *coup de grace* came in 1860 when, in an attempt to create enthusiasm in London for these working men's musical ensembles, he organised a contest at the Crystal Palace. No fewer that 172 entries were received for the two-day event, and though not all of them attended, it was one of the most spectacular events in the history of brass bands. Twelve platforms were erected in various parts of the grounds, and bands drew lots to determine on which platform and in what order they would play. The better bands from each group competed in the grand finals, where the ultimate winner was Black Dike, and the runner-up Saltaire. No mean triumph for West Yorkshire!

Another Yorkshire band, Bramley Old, gained a certain notoriety at this contest. The success of the occasion was in no small measure due to Jackson's astuteness in obtaining free travel on the railways for competing bands. When a rival company set up a band contest on the day preceding the Crystal Palace event, Jackson decreed that bands were not to play anywhere in London in the run-up to his contest, otherwise the travel concession would be withdrawn. Undeterred, Bramley appeared at the rival event, and then at Crystal Palace. Playing in the preliminary round, they qualified for the final. However, thay were not allowed to play in this, had their travel warrants rescinded, and were ordered by Jackson to 'clear off'. This didn't worry the Bramleyites, as the organisers of the other event covered their travel costs and gave them appearance money, so they returned home having had a unique adventure in the capital, a good night out, and were able to take home presents for their families.

Despite the enormous success of the 1860 Crystal Palace contest, the enthusiasm of southerners for this distinctly northern pastime was shortlived, and the northern bands found it

BLACK DYKE JUNIOR BAND 1910   HAIGH

increasingly irksome travelling to London when there was a perfectly good contest in Manchester. From an estimated audience of 29,000 in 1860, figures slumped dramatically, and the first series of Crystal Palace contests ran for only four years.

Leeds Forge Band

Before leaving the nineteenth century I must mention one more Yorkshire band – Leeds Forge, which had a short but spectacular career, counting both Owen and Swift amongst its conductors, and winning many prizes. The owner of the Forge and benefactor of the band was Samson Fox, a highly successful industrialist, great supporter of the Arts, and one time Mayor of Harrogate.

One of Fox's most charitable acts was to donate £30,000 towards the building costs of the Royal College of Music in London. Naturally, he took his band to play at the laying of the foundation stone. Sadly, following a change of management in 1892, the band was closed down.

Into the Twentieth Century

Belle Vue remained the Mecca of the brass band contest, and in 1898 John Henry Iles, a Bristol businessman, visited it. An amateur musician him-

self, he was very impressed with what he heard, and amongst many other initiatives which he undertook, he founded the National Brass Band Championships, in 1900. These took place at the Crystal Palace until it was destroyed by fire in 1936. After a brief spell at Alexandra Palace and an enforced suspension during the War they were moved to the Royal Albert Hall. To this day, bands from all over Britain converge on this splendid venue each October, to compete for the title of 'National Brass Band Champions of Great Britain'. It is the brass band equivalent of the FA Cup Final.

The 1890s had been the peak years for many social activities, not least for brass bands. But with a new century there came many alternative leisure pursuits – a growing interest in sport, the rise in popularity of ballroom dancing, the coming of jazz, the gramophone and, later, the 'wireless'. Bands suffered from a further affliction – their music had become old-fashioned. A largely Victorian repertoire and outlook could be accepted to a degree by the Edwardians – even up to the onset of the Great War, but in the post-war years it was distinctly unwelcome, and brass bands became less and less popular.

Having cradled and pioneered the development of brass bands, Yorkshire became a less dominating region in the early part of the twentieth century, though Black Dyke (this spelling is more common after the turn of the century) remained all-powerful east of the Pennines, whilst Besses o' th' Barn led the field in the west. An unhealthy rivalry had developed between these two bands, particularly when, in 1888, 'Besses' lured Alex Owen away from 'Dike'. He had been professional conductor of both bands for a number of years, but now he defected and made 'Besses' his principal band. However, John Gladney, the senior member of the Triumvirate, returned to his former post and remained with Black Dyke until he retired from banding in 1907.

Perhaps I should explain that for the top men, brass band conducting really had become a profession, as each regularly conducted five or six bands in a single contest. Not surprisingly, most of the prizes went their way! They also made special arrangements of musical selections for their bands, and were heavily involved in adjudicating.

During the 1890s the better bands had been spreading their wings and developing a concert repertoire, playing to large audiences in parks, and even giving some indoor concerts. In 1906 'Dyke' and 'Besses' spread their particular wings still further by travelling overseas, the former undertaking a five-month tour of America and Canada, whilst Besses went even further with the first of its two so-called world tours on which, during a period of almost a year and a half, it visited not only America and Canada, but also Hawaii, the Fiji Islands, Australia and New Zealand – a mammoth undertaking for a group of working men. The members of Black Dyke worked in the mills owned by their sponsor, and would be granted time off work for the tour. The Lancastrians did not enjoy this luxury; they simply gave up their jobs in the hope that they'd be able to find alternative employment on their return.

New Developments

Though unique to the time, these tours were symptomatic that brass bands were achieving more recognition as musical rather than merely social forces than had been the case in Victorian times. Not only were conductors becoming famous, some leading players also built fine reputations. Trombonists had always had links with orchestras; now cornetists, who were able to interchange with the trumpet, also had similar opportunities, and it was not unknown for brass band players to become fully fledged orchestral instrumentalists. There has been a steady stream of such players from Black Dyke alone, and amongst former principal cornet players who moved into orchestras were John Paley and Ceres Jackson from the early days, and more recently, Harold Jackson, Willie Lang and Maurice Murphy. (Lang and Murphy were both to become principal trumpet players with the LSO, no less).

But to return to the bands. Changing musical tastes were now reflected in changing repertoire, with old dances such as the waltz, the polka and the quadrilles being replaced by the modern waltz (played much slower), the fox-trot and the lancers. Operatic selections in concerts gave way to extracts from musical comedy – *The Arcadians, The Geisha, Chu Chin Chow* &c., and programmes

featured the star players of the band in solos and duets.

New bands from further afield were coming into the limelight – Fodens Motor Works in Sandbach, Cheshire, and St Hilda's Colliery in South Shields. New conductors also appeared to take the place of the Triumvirate, though Owen conducted 'Besses' until his death in 1920. The new generation of conductors included two Lancastrians, William Rimmer and William Halliwell (each of whom became professional conductors of Black Dyke and other Yorkshire bands) and the most famous brass band family of all times – the Mortimers.

The Mortimer Family

Fred Mortimer was bandmaster of Hebden Bridge Band, and as such, when he played the cornet, he held it in one hand and directed the band with the other. Under his guidance Hebden Bridge made good progress, and he was able to persuade Rimmer, and later, Halliwell to become its professional conductor. Towards the end of the Mortimer era at Hebden Bridge the band had a few years of glory at Belle Vue, winning third prize under Rimmer in 1909 and fifth under Halliwell in the following year. It went on to win the competition in 1911, but by then the Mortimers had moved south, where Fred had become bandmaster of Luton Red Cross Band. (This name had nothing to do with the Red Cross as we know it today).

At the time of the move there were four children in the family, two of them destined to achieve great fame in the brass band world. The younger of the two, Alex, was to become one of the finest euphonium players of all time and a leading conductor, taking Black Dyke to victory in the National Championships of 1950 before crossing the Pennines and building the CWS (Manchester) band into one of the finest bands of that era. His elder brother was the legendary Harry Mortimer – a name respected throughout the musical world. He founded the modern style of cornet playing, became principal trumpet player of both the Hallé and Liverpool Philharmonic Orchestras, and was by far the most successful brass band conductor of his generation. He was also in charge of brass and military band broadcasts at the BBC

Harry Mortimer

during the vintage years from the mid 1940s to the late 1950s, when ten or more band broadcasts per week was not unusual, and anything fewer than seven was considered poor. (There is now only one regular band broadcast per week – 'Listen to the Band'.)

However, this is moving on rather too quickly. Halliwell was already professional conductor at Luton, and it was through his influence that the Mortimers moved south. I referred earlier to Gladney and company taking their expertise to other parts of the country and thereby spreading the gospel of the brass band. Here was a twentieth century example of the same process, for between them, Halliwell and Fred Mortimer brought the band in Luton up to such a high standard that by 1920 it was figuring in the prizes at the Nationals, and in 1923 became the National Champion Brass

Crossley Carpet Works Band of Halifax, in the early 1960s. Fodens had, in fact, become the working base for the Mortimers. In 1925 they left Luton and moved to Sandbach where, between them, they were to make Fodens Motor Works Band the band of the decade in the 1930s.

Yet More about Contests

From 1900 there were two major annual contests, the well-established Belle Vue September contest, later to become known as the British Open Brass Band Championships, and the Iles-inspired Nationals at Crystal Palace. To win both in the same year has always been regarded as a special achievement, and is even more rare than a hat-trick at either single event. Black Dyke were the first of only five bands to do this 'double', and they did it in 1902. (They were to do it again in 1972, 1976 and 1977).

The most notable event in the early years of the twentieth century happened in 1913, when Iles introduced the specially-composed 'test piece' into the Nationals. It replaced the 'Selection' (a collection of excerpts from opera, oratorio, or from the works of a particular composer) which had been the staple diet at contests almost from the beginning. This led to the growth of a large repertoire of so-called 'original works' – invariably used as test pieces at today's contests, but also greatly enhancing the brass band's concert repertoire.

1914 and Beyond

The Great War took a terrible toll in the injury and death of hundreds of thousands of young men. As brass banding at that time was virtually 100 per cent male-dominated, the war had a devastating effect on bands. Hundreds of bands folded – many forever. Those which survived struggled owing to shortage of players and money, worn-out instruments, and another slump in popularity.

Between the two World Wars the fortunes of bands were mixed. They were, of course, badly hit by the effects of the General Strike of 1926 and the Slump of the 1930s. Unemployment and poverty faced many band members. Things were brighter for the better bands, however. This was the heyday of the park bandstand concert, and in addition to local engagements, the 'crack' bands were able to accept week-long Summer engagements, giving twice-daily concerts in places as far apart as Dunfermline and Eastbourne, and

Band of Great Britain. This was, and remains, the only time that a band from the South of England has won the title. There were, by now, three Mortimer sons, Harry and Alex having being joined by Rex. He was the least successful instrumentalist of the trio, but became a well-respected conductor, directing operations at Fodens for a number of years, and conducting several other bands, including the successful but short-lived

Imperial Metals – which won the Belle Vue contest in 1970 and 1971. Grimethorpe Colliery Band had been formed in 1918, but had to wait many years before achieving its present status as winners of all the major championships, stars of *Brassed Off* and with a reputation as a concert band second to none.

But the band which above all others came to the fore during those difficult mid-war years was Brighouse and Rastrick. With a history going back well into the nineteenth century as Brighouse and Rastrick Temperance Brass and Reed Band, it first hit the headlines as Brighouse and Rastrick Band in 1929, when it performed a 'double' of a different kind from the one described above. Since 1886 there had been a 'July' contest at Belle Vue, open to bands which were not quite in the top league. The winner was invited to take its place with the best in the land in the following September. To win both in the same year would be the equivalent of a first division football club winning the League Championship in its first year with the big guns. That is what Brighouse did in 1929. The only other band ever to achieve this was Batley Old, back in 1890. To prove that it was no mere 'flash in the pan' Brighouse went on to secure a hat-trick of wins at Belle Vue in the years 1932-1934 and then, being barred for a year, returned to win again in 1936. 'B & R' has remained a leading band ever since, proudly and rightly boasting that is the only non-sponsored band in the country to have stayed at the top all these years.

Scarborough and Southport.

This was also the age of the 78 rpm gramophone recording and again, the better bands produced hundreds of these. The less-illustrious ones had no such luxuries, and survived with great difficulty. Then, as now, better players gravitated to better bands, often amidst accusations of poaching and underhand practices used to prise them away from the very bands which had nurtured them.

New names began to appear in the prize-lists at the major contests. These included King Cross (Halifax), Sowerby Bridge and Rothwell Temperance, as well as a number of colliery bands, including South Elmsall Frickley Colliery (now Carlton Main), which won the 1922 Belle Vue September contest. New bands emerged, including Yorkshire Copper Works, formed in Leeds in 1936, and later to achieve fame as Yorkshire

Another Yorkshire band which made a serious bid for glory was Slaithwaite ('Slawit'), based near Huddersfield. This band came near to equalling Brighouse's success of 1929 almost a decade later, by winning the July contest in 1937, coming second in the September, and going on to win it in 1938. However, history was to intervene at this point, as Slaithwaite, like hundreds of other bands, was decimated by the call-up of players needed to fight in World War II. Although still in existence, and having enjoyed a measure of success in the post-war years, Slaithwaite Band has never regained its former glory.

1939 and Beyond

As had been the case in the years 1914-1918, bands again faced hardships – often extinction – during what was, for many people, the second world war in living memory. There were few contests and few engagements, apart from concerts organised to raise funds for the 'war effort'. A number of Home Guard ('Dad's Army') bands were formed, and these helped keep the brass band flag flying.

Though it is difficult to make comparisons at this distance in time, I'd say the brass band was closer to extinction in the late 1940s than it had been in the early 1920s. But despite all, it survived. The National Championships, suspended during the time of both wars, were reinstated in 1945, with the redoubtable J H Iles at the helm. By now he owned Belle Vue and organised the contests there. In connection with the Nationals, he instigated a series of regional qualifying contests, the 'Area Contests', through which all aspirants were tested before being allowed to compete in the finals later in the year. Iles designated eight centres for these preliminaries, with four sections or divisions in each. Thus, the humble village band could aspire to becoming, for example, 'Fourth Section National Champions, and there was an attainable target for hundreds of bands throughout England, Scotland and Wales. This series has remained much the same to this day, except that, as in the case of the football leagues, we now have five sections, not four.

This network of contests probably did more than anything else to preserve the brass band. A few years later another significant point was reached. The post-war years saw the birth of the instrumental teaching service in a number of schools and the formation of school bands. This was to make fundamental changes in the social structure of brass bands, because players were no longer restricted to members of the working classes as they had been from the 1830s, nor were they restricted to members of the male sex. There are few bands today which don't contain members of both sexes and in fact, in Lancashire, girls are to

be found in Besses Boys Band, and there are boys in the ranks of Trinity Girls! Doctors, lawyers, bank managers and other professional people are also now found sitting alongside students and members of working-class families in many of our bands.

Individual school bands led to the formation of area bands for school children, and it wasn't long before we had a Yorkshire Schools Brass Band, funded by a number of Local Authorities. This in turn led to the formation of the National Youth Brass Band of Great Britain in 1952. There's a Yorkshire connection here, because the NYBB's first course was held at Thornton Grammar School, Bradford, attracting about 100 young players from all over Britain. It was founded by Dr Denis Wright, a fine musician and one who,

SOWERBY BRIDGE PRIZE BAND. 1934.

WINNERS OF THE
HOLMFIRTH CHALLENGE TROPHY. SCARBOROUGH TROPHY & MEDALS. 'COURIER & GUARDIAN' ROSE BOWL.
ALSO
WHOLESALE MARKET TROPHY. LEICESTER DURING 1933

though he could not play a brass instrument, had an enormous impact on the brass band movement between the 1930s and his death in 1967. In addition to conducting and adjudicating, he had composed a number of original works, and transcribed or arranged literally hundreds of pieces from the orchestral repertoire, and of popular music of the times. The NYBB has become one of the flagships of the movement, meeting twice each year for residential courses, performing in major concert halls under leading conductors and with leading soloists, and helping many of its members on the road to stardom either within or beyond the field of brass bands.

Returning to the main stream of bands – in the

same way that Victorian music had been unacceptable in post-1918 Britain, the music of the 1920s and 1930s needed modernising by the 1950s. Harry Mortimer had now become the movement's most dominating personality. He had been the professional conductor of several leading

bands, taking them consistently into the prizes at major contests, but he had also, since the early 1940s, championed massed band concerts. These had been part of the spectacle at the conclusion of the old Crystal Palace contests, but had not been taken seriously from a musical point of view. Mortimer used a smaller number of bands, usually three or four, a more sophisticated repertoire, and often invited high-profile orchestral conductors such as Sir Henry Wood, Sir Adrian Boult, Sir Thomas Beecham, Sir John Barbirolli and Sir Malcolm Sargent to appear as guest conductors. Many of the transcriptions of popular classics made by Denis Wright were bread and butter to them, and the fact that they lent their name to these events helped establish a new credibility for the brass band. 1952, the year of the founding of the NYBB also saw the birth of another legendary group, for this was the year in which Harry Mortimer founded his 'Men o' Brass', a combination of three of his bands, Fairey's, Foden's, and Morris Motors. With this large group he undertook concerts, concert tours, and made recordings on a regular basis, introducing new repertoire and a new style of playing. He concentrated on good-quality programme music, and began what was to be a revolution in the popular side of brass band repertoire.

On the more serious musical front, as we've already seen, J H Iles sowed the seed of the 'original' repertoire in 1913 when he used the first of such works as test piece for the Nationals. Incidentally, this was *Labour and Love*, a tone poem by Percy Fletcher, well known as a conductor and composer of light orchestral music. Other early original works were written by minor composers such as Hubert Bath, Cyril Jenkins, Henry Geehl, Thomas Keighley and, indeed, Denis Wright. In the late 1920s and early 1930s Iles took this process to a new level by commissioning Holst, Elgar, Ireland, Bantock, Bliss and Howells to join the ranks of composers of brass band music. This further increased the credibility of bands, though in reality to only a limited degree. The War, along with financial problems experienced by Iles, put a stop to all this, as well as creating the problems already discussed.

Towards the Modern Era

As we've seen, problems were encountered in abundance and gradually solved, but when, in 1958, the elderly but highly regarded Ralph Vaughan Williams composed his *Variations* for Brass Band as test piece for the Nationals, we can now look back and see that the progress of the brass band was back on course. On the lighter side, the 1960s saw the start of a series of compositions and arrangements by Gordon Langford, who wrote for the BBC Concert Orchestra, and regularly appeared on such programmes as 'Friday Night is Music Night'. Many others have followed in his footsteps. Another BBC man, Gilbert Vinter, helped bridge the gap between traditional brass band test pieces of the pre-1960s and the later and far more modem works which were to appear after his death in 1969.

Eric Ball, the most prolific of all composers for brass band, helped bridge another gap – that between mainstream brass bands and the Salvation Army, which has had its own band movement since the late 1870s whilst Frank Wright, a former

Australian Champion cornet player, and an important figure in the post-war Nationals, made a series of masterly transcriptions of a group of overtures by Berlioz and Wagner, which have become standard repertoire both in concert and contest.

Thus, by 1970 the scene was set for the veritable explosion which has taken place in brass band activities during the last 30 years. With the exception of the huge tours undertaken by 'Besses' and Black Dyke in the early years of the nineteenth century, brass bands did little overseas travelling until after 1945, when visits to Holland and Belgium became fairly common. Later, Switzerland, Norway, France, Germany, Denmark, Sweden and even Finland became targets for bands' touring activities – usually as part of their Summer holidays.

From the 1970s, as long-haul travel became more common: we find bands visiting Australia, Canada, America and even Russia, Japan and Korea. Overseas tours by bands have ignited interest in these far-off countries, and the Nationals at the Royal Albert Hall have become a focal point for the gathering of brass band fans from all over the world. There are now well-established annual European Brass Band Championships, and there have been several so-called World Championships, though none has so far become established on a regular basis.

On the home front, bands have appeared in the Henry Wood Proms and at many other prestigious music festivals, and have attracted new works from leading modern composers. The contest has ceased to be the only or even the principal activity of most bands, though it does remain an important aspect of banding.

In the popular music scene, Black Dyke recorded for Paul McCartney, and Grimethorpe had a very successful partnership with Peter Skellern (a former member of the NYBB, incidentally), whilst Brighouse and Rastrick achieved world-wide fame with conductor Derek Broadbent's chart-busting arrangement of *Floral Dance*. Grimethorpe has also had a long-standing connection with the distinguished orchestral trumpet player and conductor, Elgar Howarth, who took the brass band into the world of the 'avant garde', commissioning composers such as Harrison Birtwistle to write music which introduced bands to a new kind of audience. More recently, Grimethorpe (since the closure of the

pits, which affected so many bands, now known as RJB Grimethorpe Colliery Band) hit the world with its populist film *Brassed Off* – which has led directly to tours of Japan and Australia, and the Williams Fairey Band, from Stockport, has built up an association with 'Acid Brass'.

On the educational front, the schools instrumental service has continued to support bands, feeding them with new talent, though it has taken a knock in recent years with cut-backs in government funding. However, it survives, and has led to the instigation of courses for band people in higher education. In 1976 I helped start a course in band musicianship at Salford College of Technology. This began as a two-year diploma course; the college, now part of the University of Salford, currently offers a BA (Hons) degree, as well as the opportunity to study for higher degrees such as the MA and PhD. Many other colleges and universities have followed in Salford's wake, amongst them Huddersfield University, which offers brass band options in its music courses, and Barnsley College which, like Salford, offers courses in band musicianship, these validated by Sheffield University.

Conclusion

These and many other factors all add up to put the brass band movement on a more professional footing than hitherto. Though still basically amateur, it is organised more professionally, and the technical and musical facilities of leading bands would have been inconceivable only a few years ago. Bands have benefited, and continue to benefit, from grants from the National Lottery, which enable them to buy new instruments, build new bandrooms, or help them organise educational functions. The quality of female players has increased dramatically in recent years, and now most bands have ladies in their ranks. We also have a composite band, the 'All Star Girls of Brass', which has broadcast, recorded, and undertaken high-profile concerts. Since the closure of Belle Vue, Manchester, the September contest (the 'British Open') has been housed in Manchester's Free Trade Hall and the new Bridgewater Hall, but is now firmly established in the magnificent Symphony Hall in Birmingham. Amongst developments in the contest field, so-called 'Entertainment' contests have become popular. In these, bands play a programme lasting around 20 minutes to demonstrate their versatility and presentational skills rather than their ability to interpret a set test piece. These have become very popular with audiences, and have encouraged bands to introduce new ideas into their concert performances.

It must not be thought, however, that everything in the brass band garden is rosy. Many of the lesser bands still struggle for survival, hit by cuts in school instrumental services, and the loss of many players who leave home to go to far-off colleges and universities. There's an uncomfortable gap between what I call the élite bands – some of which are able to attract high fees and lucrative sponsorship – and the rest; there's a dearth of broadcasts and television appearances, and local council cutbacks have dramatically reduced the number of paid engagements available to bands. But still, new contests appear, the professionalism in bands leads to wider initiatives being explored, and all in all, I'm very optimistic about the future of brass bands in the twenty-first century. It is a great national heritage, worthy of the whole-hearted support of the nation which gave birth to it and which, collectively, has derived so much pleasure from it.

One final word, and returning to the subject of contesting. It is always good to see a new name in the limelight, and we've certainly seen this during the last few years. It is even better (from the point of view of this article) to record that the band concerned is located in the heart of the West Riding – in Huddersfield, to be precise. It was formerly the Hammonds Sauce Works Band, but following a change in sponsorship is now Yorkshire Building Society Band. Under its young Australian-born conductor, David King, it has taken the band world by storm. It has been European Champions four times (1996, 1997, 1999 and 2000), British Open Champions twice (1998 and 1999) and All England Masters Champions (a relatively new contest, held in Cambridge) twice – in 1999 and 2000.

ROY NEWSOME

Roy Newsome was born into a brass band family, his father and paternal grandfather both having been bandsmen, as was also his maternal great-grandfather. He was born in Elland, Yorkshire, in 1930. Starting his musical career on the piano at the age of six, he acquired his first brass instrument — a comet — when, at the age of 10, he joined Elland Silver Band. Over the next few years he played with several bands, but following National Service, decided to concentrate on playing the organ. However, at the age of 21 he succeeded his father as conductor of Elland Silver Band. This really appealed to him, and after leading the band to the National Fourth Section title in 1958 he launched into a more concentrated course of musical studies and successfully completed examinations for the diplomas of ARCM and FRCO, and for the degree of Bachelor of Music and qualified as a school teacher.

In 1961 he left Elland Silver Band to become musical director of Slaithwaite Band, and this eventually brought him to the attention of Black Dyke Mills Band, where he served as bandmaster/resident conductor from 1966-1970, and from 1972-1977. During this period the band averaged 60 concerts per year, broadcast regularly, toured overseas and made some 30 LPs. It also won six National and six British Open titles. Following this, he became the professional conductor of Besses o' th' Barn, then Williams Fairey and finally of Sun Life (Stanshawe) bands, collecting a further three British Open titles and one at the Nationals, as well as leading his bands to a number of BBC Band of the Year successes.

In 1976 he became a senior lecturer at Salford, pioneering higher education courses in Band Musicianship, and in 1984 was appointed Music Director of the National Youth Brass Band of Great Britain. He has had a distinguished career in both roles, retiring from the full-time appointment at Salford in 1989, but continuing to the present time in a part-time capacity, and fulfilling his role with the NYBB. until the present time. He will relinquish this position at the end of 2000, and will be succeeded by Elgar Howarth.

Amongst other activities in the brass band world, he has adjudicated at virtually every major brass band contest in the world, has about 100 published musical compositions and arrangements, and has written three books about bands. He is President of the National Association of Brass Band Conductors and an executive member of the Association of Brass Band Adjudicators. Amongst the awards he has received are the Iles Silver Medal of the Worshipful Company of Musicians and the All England Masters Dedicated Service Award.

Black Dyke Mills Band circa 1865

Black Dyke Band

In 1815 a brass and reed band was founded by Peter Wharton in the Yorkshire village of Queenhead – later to become Queensbury. John Foster, apart from being the founder of Black Dyke Mills, played french horn in this band. It has been said on many occasions that Black Dyke was formed from it; however this is not strictly true, since 'Peter Wharton's band went out of existence through loss of members'. In 1833 a new band was formed named Queenshead Band, which may well have contained players from the former band. It is reported that 'this Band reached its zenith from 1838 to 1843, at which time it consisted of 18 musicians'. However it is recorded in the *Halifax Courier* of the 15th September 1855 that:

'Queenshead Band, formed early in the century by residents, came into difficulties. John Foster & Son, having lately become acquainted with the depressed state of the band determined to make an effort themselves to raise it up again. Accordingly they have purchased from that eminent maker Mr Joseph Higham, of Manchester, a new set of instruments which have this week been delivered to the band, which in future is to be denominated Black Dyke Mills Band. A new and talented leader, as well as sev-

eral performers, have been added to the band which now comprises 18 musicians. Messrs Fosters have provided for them a comfortable room in which they will meet for practising.'

Thus the Black Dyke Band was formed. Most of its musicians both lived in Queensbury and worked at the mill, so a close link between the band and the community was formed which remains to this day. The band has always been at the forefront of Brass Band activity, making one of the earliest Brass Band recordings in 1904 and embarking on a five-month tour of Canada and the United States in 1906, on which it played in over 200 concerts and travelled over 13,000 miles. Since then the band has toured many different countries, including Germany, Austria, Italy, Switzerland, Russia, Belgium, Sierra Leone, and Spain, returning to Canada in 1972. In 1988 the band took part in the Bicentennial Celebrations in Australia; it also had a sellout tour in Japan. 1995 saw a return to Wiesbaden in Germany to play at the Rheingau Music Festival. The band has also had successful concert and masterclass tours in Denmark, Northern Ireland, Sweden and Switzerland.

A remarkable event took place on the evening of June 29th 1906, when the band embarked on one of its most spectacular tours, crossing the Atlantic ocean to visit Canada and the United States. To help our younger readers to appreciate the enormity of this project it has to be borne in mind that there were no aeroplanes, motor cars were in their infancy, and North America really was the other side of the world; and the nearest railway station to the bandroom was over a mile away at the bottom of a long steep hill (Queensbury is 1,100 feet above sea level). The band would have been transported there by a local man, Bartle Chatburn, in his uncovered horse-drawn 'wagonettes'.

Quite often at concerts even today, some ninety-odd years later, relatives of players who were in the band around this time, tell stories handed down through the family of the 'tour'. Some have distant recollections that a relative could have played in the band, but are not too sure, so here is the complete list of members: *Conductor* John Gladney; *Manager* Henry Drake, *Financial Secretary* Arthur B Pryce, *Soprano Comets* Thomas Scatliffe, Harold Coates; *Principal Cornet* Ceres Jackson; *Solo Comets* Louis Allison, Harry Bower (*Bandmaster*), Thomas Bottomley;

Ripieno Cornet Ernest Ambler; *Comets* Sam Midgley, Wilson Farrar; *Flugel Horns* Frank Bramfit, Willie Jeffrey; *Tenor Horns* Harry Charnock, Edgar Coates, Wilfred Jackson, Charles Pearson; *Trombones* Fred Bower, Harold Laycock, Mark William Ambler; *Bass Trombone* Harry Craven; *Baritones* Joe Jackson, Alfred Gray; *Euphoniums* Harry Waddington, Joe Ambler, John Arthur Wood; *Eb Bass* Alfred Bower, Harry Firth, Arthur Greenwood; *Bb Bass* Alfred Ingham; *Drums* George Ambler and Sam Cowgill Briggs.

This report coming from the *Halifax Courier and Guardian* (30th June 1906)

'The famous Black Dike Band left England last evening for a lengthy tour in Canada and the States and as may be imagined they received from their numerous friends and admirers a most enthusiastic send off tram the village of Queensbury. Since its formation in 1855 the band has met with wonderful success and are the winners of over £8,000 in prizes so that it was only natural that upon their first voyage across the Atlantic they should have a farewell at once hearty and encouraging. Nor was this confined to the bandsmen's immediate friends,

BELOW an early Black Dyke Band from a postcard in the collection of ROY NEWSOME

Black Dike Mills Band,   Quee...

for the whole of the village of Queensbury assembled this morning to show their respect, while the members at the firm of Messrs John Foster and Son Ltd, who take such an interest in the welfare of the instrumentalists, and [by] whose kindness the tour was made possible, were none the less cordial in wishing the men "Bon Voyage". During the interval at the mill for breakfast [in those days the mill started work very early, and after three hours' work would stop for breakfast at around 9.00 am] the band assembled at the Albert Memorial in the village and played selections. They then departed by train from Queensbury Station for Bradford.'

The following excerpts come from a comprehensive diary of the whole tour compiled by one of the euphonium players, John Arthur Wood.

Friday June 29th 1906
We played a few tunes outside the Exchange Station, amidst a very large crowd of people, we were then entertained to a light lunch in the Great Northern Hotel, by Major F C Foster. We then pushed our way through the crowd, amidst loud cheering, onto the platform, where we caught the 11.10 am train for Liverpool, arriving there at 1.20 pm. We had no time to spare at Liverpool so went straight onto the ship, *Empress of Ireland*, a new ship 14,500 tonnage, which is her maiden voyage. We had a look around her and considered her to be a floating palace. About 5.20 pm we went onto the first class deck and played *Hearts of Oak, Rule Britannia, Lead Kindly Light*. And just as the anchor was weighed we played *Auld Lang Syne*, amidst cheers on the decks, and handkerchiefs waving. Never shall I forget that sight, leaving my country and home – there was scarcely a dry eye in the Band. We had a beautiful dinner and then went on deck, we passed the Isle of Man, about 11.05 pm.

Saturday June 30th 1906
Arriving at Inoville in the North of Ireland, about 6.20 am where we waited for the mails till 1.30 pm, thus losing already 6 hours. We lost sight of land about 6.30 at night and it was a beautiful night on the sea.

John Gladney, Professional conductor 1888-1908

Sunday July 1st
A beautiful morning, at 10 am a Service was held in the 1st Class Saloon, at which 8 of the band played for the Service, I being one of the 8. After Service all the Band played the *Hallelujah Chorus*. The Service was the most solemn Service I have ever seen, the Captain read all the lessons and prayers which were mostly for the safety of people on the sea. The rest of the day was spent sitting on deck in quietness … '

Monday July 2nd
We awoke to find we were in a very heavy fog, the vessel was only going slow, and the fog horn was blown every minute, after dinner (lunch) the fog cleared and it was a nice afternoon but rather cold. At night we gave a concert in the 3rd Class Saloon, which was packed almost to suffocation, the concert was much enjoyed by all the passengers, there was no collection.

Tuesday July 3rd
A very nice day all day but rather cold, we played games on deck, one was a kind of Hop Scotch, with long sticks. At night we gave a Concert in the 2nd Class Saloon for the benefit

of the Sailors Orphans, the collection amounted to £9/15/8d [in terms of a mill-worker's wage of the time, the value in 2000 would be approximately £1,600.00].

In the formative years, competitions played a major part in the brass band calendar. It seems that their popularity was due to the fact that at this time there were no 'holidays with pay' for a majority of workers and no personnel transport: consequently a day out using the rapidly expanding railway system proved extremely popular. There had been 'contests' of sorts as early as 1818, but the one that seemed to have a little more prestige than had been experienced previously was held at Burton Constable near Hull in 1845 and was hosted by the Lord of the Manor, Sir Clifford Constable.

There were only five bands competing. What is more interesting is the fact that this was the first contest for eighteen-year-old Enderby Jackson, who went on to become the great band entrepreneur of the 1850s and 1860s. In 1851 Jackson attended the Great Exhibition, where it is reported that he met James Melling of Stalybridge and Tallis Trimnell of Chesterfield, accomplished musicians and brass band enthusiasts. Much discussion took place between the three regarding the interest shown in brass band contests, after which they went their various ways. Not long after this meeting James Melling went into partnership with Jennison of Belle Vue Gardens in Manchester and they put on the first 'British Open' contest in 1853. Jackson always maintained that Melling and Jennison had stolen his idea.

However, undeterred, Jackson organised his first contest at the Hull Zoological Gardens in June 1856. He had special arrangements with the North Eastern and Midland Railway companies which enabled him to offer attractive low fares. According to *The Hull Packet* there was an audience of 14,000 and 'the gardens are very densely peopled in every direction'. To make the affair even more impressive the competing bands on leaving the train 'parade in full blowing order to the gardens'. This was the first contest that Black Dyke Band attended: the main test piece was Jackson's *Yorkshire Waltzes* plus an 'own choice' item. Twenty-one bands had entered, but only fourteen put in an appearance: two of these 'modestly withdrew their pretensions when they saw with whom they had to contend'. The report in *The Hull Packet* continues:

'Of No 1 (Buslingthorpe, conducted by

William Hesling in an overture of his own), the less is said the better – the intonation was particularly defective. No 2 (Leeds Joppa, conducted by R Smith) passed very well through its various performances. No 3 (BLACK DIKE MILLS, conducted by Samuel Longbottom) was superior to No 2 and its performances were better in style than either of its predecessors. No 4 (Huddersfield, conducted by W Drake) was moderate. No 5 (Gamthorpe, conducted by A Jessop) and No 6 (Bridlington & Quay, conducted by J B Acey) were better than No 4 in the tone of the introduction, but were different in time. No 7 (Smith's Leeds Band, conducted by R Smith) was a very fine band; indeed we have rarely, if ever, heard a finer private band. Eventually Black Dyke was awarded second prize, the value in cash was £5.00 [equal to ten weeks' wages of a mill-worker]

Black Dyke had won its first contest in June 1857 at Halifax, bringing home prize money of £10.00. Its first major success was in 1860 at the Crystal Palace, on the 10th and 11th July. This, said *The Daily Telegraph*, ' [was] the first "Contest of Brass Bands" ever held in the South of England'. Because of the number of bands involved, the contest was held over two days: 72 bands had entered for the first day's competition and 98 for the second. With this tremendous number it was impossible to carry out the sound plan that had been adopted previously of having a set piece for all and a second item chosen by the individual bands. It was therefore decided to allow each band to play once, in a test piece of its own choice.

The contest itself was divided into two 'rounds'. It rather looks as if there had been a kind of involuntary preliminary also: the number of bands that actually appeared on the opening day had diminished to about 44. Six platforms had been erected, with three judges in charge of each, the band had its definite allotments, so that eliminations could proceed simultaneously. At each platform two bands were chosen to play before the whole of the judges in the next stage for the final award.

The twelve bands selected to appear in this final part of the contest were: Black Dyke, Saltaire, Cyfarthfa, Darlington, Dewsbury, Deighton, Witney, Accrington, Stanhope, Chesterfield, Stalybridge and Holmfirth. Black Dyke was awarded first prize and Saltaire were declared run-

ners-up. The second day's contest followed the same pattern as the first, but because of their success on the first day Black Dyke and Saltaire were excluded. As a result of being awarded first prize Black Dyke was presented with £40 cash, a silver cup valued at £20 and a Bass valued at £36/15/0d.

September 1862 saw Black Dyke celebrate the first of its many triumphs at the September contest held at that time in Belle Vue Gardens, Manchester, known as 'The Open', or to give it its correct title 'The British Open Championship of Great Britain' (a contest now held in Symphony Hall Birmingham). While Black Dyke have not entered every 'British Open' contest, they have been British Open Champions twenty-seven times (at least once in every decade except the 1920s and 1940s). Since 1945 Black Dyke Band have also won the 'National

Championships' fifteen times.

In 1866 a local man, Phineas Bower, joined Black Dyke on tenor horn; a few months later in 1867 the band's solo euphonium player was taken ill and the position was offered to Phineas, which he accepted. His first contest was at Hull on July 20th 1868 where the band gained third prize. It was at the British Open at Belle Vue on September 8th of the same year, however, that he scored his first individual success. He was awarded the euphonium prize of £23/2/0d [the average weekly wage of a mill-worker at that time was between 18/- (90p) and £1/1/0d (£1.05p)]. Conducted by Samuel Longbottom the band took first prize in 1870; this consisted of £30 in money, a Bb Bass valued at £27 and a silver medal. At the same contest the prize of a euphonium valued at £19/19/0d was awarded to Phineas Bower. In

The Crystal Palace Thousand Guinea Trophy and BELOW *the Band in 1928 with the trophy.* RIGHT *jug detailing the £2011/9 /0d prize moneys won between 1856-1882*

*Black Dyke Band
at Niagara Falls,
February 2000 –
94 years after the
Band first visited
there*

1873 again at the 'Open' the band was awarded prizes and instruments to the value of £93/18/0d. The euphonium and trombone prizes were both awarded to Phineas Bower!. At the start of the test piece – *Dinorah* by Meyerbeer – Phineas was playing the euphonium and when it came to the trombone solo he picked up a valve trombone and played the part. As a result he was awarded both instrument prizes. This was a unique feat and clearly demonstrated the amazing skill of Phineas Bower. When the contest authorities discovered that the adjudicators had awarded two medals to one person they tried to persuade him to forego one of them, 'but Phineas bluntly refused to do so'. This was the last time that valve trombones were allowed at the 'Open' and also the last time that a player received two 'specials'. It was in 1873, also, that 'modern' contesting band of twenty five players became definitely established. Previous to this time the number of players allowed was nineteen.

Black Dyke Band has made over 50 recordings, with former Prime Minister Edward Heath as guest conductor on one, whilst Paul McCartney and Wings broke new ground with the band with another. In 1996 they won The Music Industries' Association Award for the Best CD in the orchestral category, with their recording of Sir William Walton's Music, featuring the Shakespearean actor Robert Portal. In February 1999 the album that the Band recorded with Evelyn Glennie was nominated in the 'Crossover Classical Section' for a 'Grammy Award' in Los Angeles, followed in the next month by an Oscar nomination for the best song in a film – *That'll Do* from the film *Babe 2*

(the vocalist was Peter Gabriel).

The band has enjoyed success with other recording artists including 'Torry Amos' and the well-known group 'Beautiful South'. It also provides the background music to the popular UK Television programme *Groundforce* and in October 1999 its CD *Groundforce* was released with music by Jim Parker. The latest record release is entitled *Façade* and features the music of Sir William Walton with Lady Walton MBE and Richard Baker OBE, TD taking part. In addition to touring and recording, the musical life of the band has included television shows, films, broadcasts, concerts at music festivals, universities, The Proms, *Fanfare into Europe*, *Songs of Praise*, covering the whole musical spectrum, appearing with Lesley Garrett, Elton John, Evelyn Glennie, James Morrison, Phil Smith, Rod Franks, Ian Bousfield and many more.

In October 1993 Black Dyke Band made an historic appearance as the first British Brass Band to perform at the Carnegie Hall, New York; also in October 1994 it became the first Brass Band ever to perform at The Royal College of Music. It has subsequently appeared as guest of the London Symphony Orchestra Brass ensemble at the Barbican, performed composer masterclass sessions for The Society of Promotion for New Music and engaged to perform before His Royal Highness the Duke of Edinburgh.

Over the years the Black Dyke Band has produced an abundance of famous instrumentalists; in the formative years players such as Ceres Jackson, John Paley and Harold Pinches, were recognised as the very best. In recent decades, Rowland Jones, the euphonium player, who had a wonderful voice,

Black Dyke Band in Durham Cathedral, February 2000

went on to become Principal Tenor at Sadlers Wells. It has to be said that his training in the brass band, particularly in sight-reading, was a tremendous advantage. Jack Pinches was solo trombone for Black Dyke at 16 years of age; he went on to become principal trombone in the BBC Symphony Orchestra.

Two former principal comets at Black Dyke, William Lang and Maurice Murphy, achieved the position of principal trumpet at The London Symphony Orchestra. William retired in 1995 and Maurice, said by many people to be the greatest cornet player ever, holds the position currently. His co-principal is Rod Franks, another former cornet player with Black Dyke.

The band enjoys 'full house' audiences at concerts and music festivals and is much sought-after. It was invited to take part in the Bermuda Festival in February 2000, playing to capacity audiences and receiving standing ovations, flying on from Bermuda to Canada for another Black Dyke 'Gala Concert' in Toronto and the same reception from an audience, many of whose numbers had travelled thousands of miles for the occasion. In concluding his report on the Toronto concert, William Littler, the columnist and music critic of the well-respected *Toronto Star*, observed: '...But if the band had

played no more than the fanfare from Strauss's *Festmusik der Stadt Wien*, it would have slackened my jaw. Virtuosity of this order takes the breath away...'

In recognition of its continued success, services to music in general and the region in particular, the Band was awarded the Honorary Freedom of the City by the City of Bradford in 1976. It was granted charitable status in 1997 which will ensure a sound structure for years to come: it is now known as Black Dyke Band (1855). Although a registered charity itself the band has a prolific record for fundraising concerts for a wide range of needy causes. The Band has a Society of Friends with members (Pondashers) throughout the United Kingdom and worldwide; membership is open to anyone of any age.

• The band logo of the stag's head and Latin quotation ('*act justly and fear nothing*') is taken from the armorial bearings granted in 1857 to John Foster, founder of the band. This was particularly apt when in 1999 the band was invited to the 'Oscars' ceremony in America: to much worldwide surprise and delight, the band declined the invitation because it already had a concert booked on the same date in Bournemouth.

Brighouse and Rastrick Band

The world-famous Brighouse and Rastrick Band – renowned International Concert Performers, winners of All-England, National, British Open, European and World Championships, Gold and Silver Disc award-winning recording artists and radio and television broadcasters – is undoubtedly the best and most consistent 'public subscription band' in the world. It was formed in the last century by the people of Brighouse and Rastrick who donated funds to establish the band, which today still continues to be supported through public subscriptions and its own fundraising efforts.

Its amateur members pride themselves on being financially independent, yet they are still regarded as one of the 'élite' on both contest and concert platform.

B&R officially celebrated its centenary in 1981. Until the 1920s it could be described as just another band, but steady progress culminated in 1929 when it won both the July and September Contests at Belle Vue Manchester, a feat not equalled since.

The band won the British Open Championship (September), again in 1932-33-34, was barred in 1935 but regained it in 1936. It has continued to feature in the prize list ever since, but had to wait until 1978 to win the 'Open' again.

After the Second World War, the National Brass Band Championships of Great Britain began, B&R winning this title for the first time in 1946. The World Championships were introduced in 1968: B&R became the first winner, and in retaining the title in 1969, was the only band to win this short-lived contest more than once.

They were National Champions in 1973 and 1980; runners-up in 1981 but the following day carried off the top prize at the European Championship. The band was National Champion Band of Great Britain again in 1997 and once again European Champions, bringing this title back to Brighouse in early May 1998. Two weeks later the success increased further with the addition of the All England Masters making a totally unique 'triple' – English, British and European Champions all at the same time. The band retained the National title in October 1998, was runner-up in 1999 and fourth in 2000.

The All-England Masters Brass Band Championships was established in 1989 and quickly gained prestige, attracting entries from the top bands in England. Brighouse and Rastrick held this title in 1993 and 1998 and was runner-up in 1999. In 1968 it was BBC Band of the Year and in 1975 Granada Television Band of the Year.

B&R has always been a prolific prize-winner at the Whit Friday Quick Step March Contests in

The Brighouse and Rastrick Band.
Photo ALAN WILLIAMSON, Oldham

Saddleworth. Records show it has won more prizes than any other band – over 400 since 1910 – and has been Saddleworth Whit Friday Champions many times.

In 1977 for nine weeks the band was at number two in the British 'pop' charts with its recording of *The Floral Dance*. Held off the top by Paul McCartney, it still achieved sales of over a million, earning both Gold and Silver discs.

The band moved into its purpose-built headquarters, 'West Ridings', in 1995, and looks forward to making its mark on the new century. Today, with countless radio, TV broadcasts and recordings to its credit, the band is kept very busy giving concert performances both nationally and internationally.

It is true to say that no other public subscription band has held such high status for as long as the Brighouse and Rastrick Band.

The Bradford Metropolitan Concert Band

The BMCB was formed in April 1975 under its original name 'The Bradford Metropolitan Military Band'. Its founders – Ken Hall (current Musical Director and Life Vice-President), the late Ken Dinsdale and the late Harry Coleman – all had a wide experience in civilian and army bands. They felt that the time was right to introduce a military band incorporating woodwind and brass instruments as an alternative to the straightforward brass bands for which the area is world-famous. An advertisement was placed in the *Telegraph & Argus* and the first rehearsal, which took place at Fairweather Green WMC on the 6th of April 1975, was attended by nearly 40

musicians. The first concert given by the band was at the same club only three months later in July.

A year later the band gave its first broadcast and in the same year, 1976, made its first appearance at the National Festival of Concert Bands in Solihull, gaining a Merit Award. In 1979 the band was awarded first place in Deportment and second place in the Music Programme Competition at the National Festival which again was held at Solihull. Since 1980 the band's calendar of events has not had the space for festival entries owing to its full list of concert dates.

In recent years the band has been involved in Pantomime with 'Drama Unlimited' and has also given concerts further afield – in, for example York, Blackpool and St Annes. The band has to thank a short but distinguished list of Presidents for their support. The first President was the late Bert Parish who was for many years conductor of the Bradford City Police Band. Mr Parish was succeeded for a short but splendid term by another former Bradford policeman – Bert Simpson.

The current President is Basil Walsh who is well known to all in the musical fraternity as a former Musical Director of the Bradford Catholic Players.

The Bradford Youth Concert Band

This band was formed in the early days of the Bradford Metro Concert Band and was originally titled the Bradford Metropolitan Military Junior Band. Its first conductor, Mr William O'Connell, was appointed in June, 1975; two years later he was succeeded by Mr Robert Hardy. In 1978 the band entered its first competition at the Robertshaw Festival; later that year it took part in the Horsforth and Wharfedale Festivals.

A learner band, designated the Bradford Metro Junior Band, was formed in 1979 under the direction of Mr Eric Parker, a former flautist in the senior band. Afterwards he took over the Youth Band which shortly was given its present title.

The band has been very successful in competition throughout the years and looks forward to continuing this success under its present Musical Director, Mr Winston Sutcliffe, who took up the reins in 1999 when Mr Parker's business commitments brought about his resignation.

Friendly Band (Sowerby Bridge)

Many of the bands which exist in the area today can trace their origin well back into the last century, and beyond, and one of these is The Friendly Band (Sowerby Bridge). which dates back to 1868.

One of the founder members Mr O Hartley, who was described as the father of the band, died in 1922. He often used to tell the story of how four or five of the founder members set off and walked from Sowerby Bridge to Huddersfield. They each bought, using their own money, an instrument. The idea was to play at Church Anniversary Services and local fetes.

The name 'Friendly Subscription Prize Band' is taken from the area of Friendly in Sowerby Bridge, where the hand is based. The name was later changed to the 'Friendly Band' and, in the early 1960s the Sowerby Bridge part was added to the name giving it the full title of Friendly Band (Sowerby Bridge), as it remains to the present day.

The band started in a small way, but in time it was able to take a room near the White Horse public house. Later it moved to a small house in Water Hill Lane, then to a room in the Friendly Inn. In 1891 a square wooden bandroom was built in Water Hill Lane, the deeds still being in the possession of the band. The band had to leave the small house in Water Hill because the bandsman who owned it was getting married. He wanted to live there with his new bride. Later, he had to sell his instrument to buy a crib!

At the time of the First World War the band was reduced to only four playing members, but in the 1920s the ambition to have a new bandroom was realised. The site of the present Friendly Snooker Club was acquired, and a building to accommodate 300 people was built at a cost of £1,400. Such a low figure was only possible because of all the voluntary labour. The band stayed at these premises, at Tuel Lane top, until 1933 when owing to financial difficulties, smaller premises had to be found. After leaving the Concert Hall, the members used each other's homes in which

to practice, and anywhere else they could find.

In 1936 the band moved to a wooden bandroom, opposite the Friendly Inn. This was a temporary move – which lasted until January 1985, almost 50 years! This temporary bandroom was acquired for the sum of 15 guineas, which was payable on a hire purchase scheme. It had no running water, or toilets: in fact the gentlemen's urinal was made from an old trombone plumed

through the bandroom floor. The ladies had to make do with nearby bushes.

In 1985 the band purchased an old plastics factory and converted this into a superb bandroom, this time with running water arid properly plumbed toilets. This bandroom is once again situated in Water Hill Lane, just yards from where the band first started.

The band is currently in the Third Section, nationally. Rehearsals are held every Tuesday and Friday evenings and a very well attended learners' class is held every Thursday evenings. The junior band rehearses on Sunday mornings. The senior band is under the musical direction of Mr Graham Hooper, an ex bass-player of Brighouse and Rastrick, whilst the junior band is directed by Ms Carol Caton, the Solo Euphonium of the Senior Band.

The band is proud of its name: proud to be a friendly hand and a family band, with quite a few members of the same family being involved together – a band which is totally without sponsorship, free of subscriptions and fiercely independent.

Yorkshire Building Society Bands

At the turn of the twentieth century in the Yorkshire village of Saltaire, a brass hand was formed and operated for many years representing Salts Mill.

In 1947 Hammonds Sauce Company Limited adopted the band and changed its name to the Hammonds Sauce Works Band. Thus the Company for the first time sponsored a brass band and played an important part in strengthening the brass band movement in Britain. Shortly afterwards, through interest shown by many younger players, the Company introduced a Junior Band to give concerts and enter contests as a separate entity. Under the direction of the late Mr Gersham Collinson the Junior Band went from strength to strength and became formidable contest opposition.

In 1974 it was decided that with the advent of a large number of younger players, they should be formed into the Junior Band – and the previous Junior Band became known as Hammonds Sauce Band 'B'. At the beginning of 1979 Band 'B' changed its name again. Over a period of many years the Hawley family had given tremendous service and support to the brass movement – in particular the then Group Chairman and Band President, Mr Horace R Hawley and the late Mr H W Hawley, the founder of bands at Hammonds Sauce Company Limited. To honour their contribution to banding both in Britain and abroad Band 'B'

changed its name to The Hawley Band.

The late 70s proved a memorable period in the band's fortunes as it succeeded in winning a series of contests. These included Yorkshire Area Champions, Fourth Section, in 1977; Champion Band of Great Britain, Fourth Section (also 1977); Qualifiers for the National Finals, Third Section (1979); First Prize Winners in Pontins Contests; and several victories in entertainment contests.

The Hammonds Sauce Works Band, under the direction of Gersham Collinson, won promotion to the Championship Section in 1956, a status it has retained ever since. Over the years the band has been a proven favourite with band followers for the quality, style and variety of its music playing, which also proved popular with radio and television audiences – highlighted in 1969 when the band won the

RIGHT The Yorkshire Building Society Concert Brass Band during rehearsal and ABOVE band members at Bradford City's Valley Parade Ground before a local derby with Huddersfield.

Yorkshire Area Championship Section and was awarded the title of BBC 'Band of the Year'.

In the early 1990s the Hammonds Sauce Company underwent several changes of ownership, and this eventually led to the decision to stop sponsoring the bands. There was an emotionally charged farewell concert in the intimate surroundings of the Dobcross Band Room, when, under the baton of Geoffrey Witham (Musical Director of the band, with exception of a four-year break, since 1965), the 33-year association with Hammonds came to an end.

Fortunately the Yorkshire Building Society came to the rescue and agreed to sponsor all three bands: the Hammonds Sauce Works Band, The Hawley Band and The Junior Band. The sponsorship deal came at a time when, because of the recession, many traditional works and colliery bands were struggling to survive. Name changes were agreed and the bands became The Yorkshire Building Society Brass Band, The Yorkshire Building Society Concert Brass and The Yorkshire Building Society Junior Brass Band; and all three have flourished under the new patronage.

The Yorkshire Building Society Brass Band, under its young Australian-born conductor, David King, has taken the banding world by storm. Since the inception of this partnership the band has held the title Champion Band of Europe in 1996, 1997, 1999 and 2000 and was awarded the coveted title British Open Champions in January 1998 and again in 1999. In addition the band won the All England Masters title in May 1999 and May 2000 and the prestigious *Brass Band World* magazine CD of the year in both 1996 and 1997 for *Cry of the Celts* and was runner-up in 1999 with *Vitae Lux*.

The Yorkshire Building Society Concert Brass, under the musical direction of Brian Broadbent, himself a Freeman of the City of Bradford and a player with Black Dyke Band for some 27 years, the band has climbed the UK rankings from Fourth to Third to Second Section, and in January 1999 to the First Section, achieving third place on three occasions in the National Brass Band Championships Finals in London and Birmingham en route. Owing to its achievements the band fulfils many concert engagements with professionalism and an extremely varied repertoire – anything from classical masterpieces and medleys to modern-day masters, including Glenn Miller and Frank Sinatra. Concert Brass plays pop and jazz and the ever-popular modern musicals.

The band has a loyal following of music lovers and has enjoyed the position of representing the City of

Bradford in its twinning with the town of Hamm in Germany for many years. Several reciprocal visits have taken place with the Hamm Music School, with the relationship becoming even more poignant following the Bradford City fire disaster. The gift of friendship in the form of a statue in memory of those who lost their lives in the fire, presented by the people of Hamm, now stands in the Centenary Square outside the City Hall.

On special occasions or for big matches the band entertains football supporters at Bradford City's Valley Parade ground before the games and has become somewhat of a lucky mascot, since Bradford wins most of the games the band plays at, perhaps the most important to date being the last match of the 1999/2000 season against Liverpool which Bradford won 1-0 to stay in the Premier League.

The Yorkshire Building Society Junior Brass Band is under the musical direction of Stuart Derrick, himself a euphonium player with the Yorkshire Building Society Band. It encourages young or less experienced players to develop their skills and hopefully process through the bands to become top-level players. The band has given many concerts, having performed in local cancer hospices, sheltered housing complexes and nursing homes as well as village galas and the like.

ABOVE the band at the City Technology Centre in Bradford where it rehearses.
TOP Hammonds Junior Band before its name change to the Hawley Band, in 1979.

Wilsden Band

A village band and a family band!

Wilsden Band has always had strong associations with village families. Some of these links have continued to the present day. Today the band has 30 players, of which 10 are fathers/sons,

mother/daughter, uncle/nephew and brothers. The youngest player, Thomas Holt, is 11 years old, and the oldest player, Stanley Florence, is 72 years young. Of the original band reformed in 1981 just two members remain – band secretary Dennis Renshaw (who also plays Eb Bass) and his son Matthew on first trombone.

The Past

Originally, mention was made of a band in Wilsden in W Cudworth's book *Round about Bradford* which was published in 1876. So the present band has its origins over 100 years ago. In those days the band was very much an integral part of village life. Christmas would see the band marching and playing carols in and around Wilsden. They would finish the day at the local Bulmer's Cider factory — no doubt full of Christmas cheer! Whitsuntide dances were held in the village and the band was very much a part of these until a fire destroyed the dance hall and all the instruments in 1927. £10,000 of damage was reported, £200 of which was the cost of instruments and music. The band continued until 1956. then 'wound up'.

At a meeting in November of that year a decision was taken to sell off the instruments and invest the money in case another band was formed.

The *Bingley Guardian* at that time stated:

'The decision to disband was not taken lightly and there are many people in Wilsden and many old bandsmen too who remember with pleasure the Whit Walks led by the band. Prominent among them is Mr Edgar Tetley who played tenor horn with the band for some 50 years. He has seen many ups and downs and was one of those who with the late Norman Clarkson, former Bingley Councillor, tried to reform the band as a youth group towards the end of the war...'

The Present

After an absence of 25 years the band was reformed In 1981, with support from the Village Society amidst a resurgence of community spirit, a small group of people got together and started it up again. From an initial group of 10 stalwarts the popularity of the band has grown and it now numbers 30 players. The band has in the last 20 years performed on over 350 occasions. In addition to the present membership. another 80 players have played with us and moved on. As well as appearing at many events in the Wilsden area, the band has played further afield – at Harrogate, Chester, Scarborough, Whitby and Morecambe. We were delighted to restore the old tradition in the village of marching in front of the procession at the annual gala.

The band is financially self-supporting, not receiving any moneys from sponsorship. However we have created a Friends Association of supporters with over 100 members, which provides some financial support. We hold our annual 'Friends Concert', which plays to a packed house of over 150 people! We are particularly proud of our Christmas charity efforts. Proceeds from our Christmas collections are donated to charity. In six years we have raised over £4,000 for such charities as the Guide Dogs Association, Imperial Cancer Research, Spina Bifida and Multiple Sclerosis.

Youth Policy

Because of constant losses of promising players to other bands and university, a Youth Policy was introduced in 1990. This has proved successful in that several players have made progress through to the Senior band. There are close links with Parkside Cullingworth, Wilsden First and Lady Lane Park, Bingley.

Queensbury Music Centre

Queensbury Music Centre is the parent organisation which since 1969 has been promoting brass-playing among the young people of Queensbury and the surrounding area. It has developed the award-winning Queensbury Band, Pennine Brass, a succession of Junior Bands and latterly the Queensbury Brass Ensemble, during its many years of activity.

Originally it was formed by Mr James Shepherd (at that time a West Riding peripatetic brass-tutor) from the young players he taught, and developed into a Youth Band in 1969, supported by a parents' fund-raising committee. After outstanding successes in the Youth Sections of the competitive world of brass bands, it entered the senior arena in 1976, and then worked its way up through the sections, achieving Championship status in 1988. Now the band was in competition with the 'giants' of the brass band world. The band travelled widely, performing for appreciative audiences in concert halls as well as on contest platforms, led by our conductors, chiefly Jack Haigh, Andrew Owenson, Ian Craddock and Brian Dyson. This successful period led to many players receiving invitations from the 'big-name' bands to join their ranks, and they moved on to continue their brass-playing in wider circles.

Many organisations at times like these are obliged to close down, but not so Queensbury! Owning our own premises and most of our equipment enabled us to survive this period, and successfully make the transition to a less traditional style of brass group. Our remaining players formed themselves into the Queensbury Brass Ensemble, still performing with great skill, but in a more informal style. This group still rehearses twice a week, and performs at a variety of functions, parties, dinners, receptions, weddings etc. as well as formal functions. The Brass Ensemble is the main fund-raising group of the Music Centre, shouldering responsibility for the expenses of the organisation. Unlike the players of most groups of their standard, the players receive none of the

money raised themselves. Such is their loyalty! All goes to maintaining the Music Centre, and fulfilling its aims.

Throughout the years of its history, the Music Centre has trained and developed Junior Band groups. It has always hoped to provide facilities

for the musical training of young people. The present Junior Band was formed in 1991 under the leadership of Mrs Eleanor Wood, a playing-member since 1970, a qualified teacher and horn player who completed her training at the Birmingham School of Music. The players rehearse under her leadership on Saturday mornings at the Bandroom, and also perform concerts in the local area. Young players are always welcome, and details are available on 01274 637006. For the keenest players, much is on offer: training in group performance skills, opportunities for solo work, a friendly family-orientated atmosphere and progress to leadership in the sections of the band. Many of our present players have received their five years' loyalty awards. Two will soon achieve their tenth year award, and two players have now been promoted to membership of the Brass Ensemble, performing alongside the adult members at all engagements.

We are always ready to welcome new and former players. Should you find that the pressures of membership of a contesting band no longer fit in with your work or family life, but yet you enjoy performing to a high standard, perhaps membership of our Brass Ensemble would be ideal for you. So the opportunities are here – the rest is up to you!

Drighlington Band

The Drighlington Band is based in the village of that name which is situated on the southern fringe of Leeds and Bradford. The organisation comprises three groups – Senior Band, Youth Band and Learners Group. For most of its 25 years the organisation has been entirely self-supporting except for a six-year period of sponsorship from Yorkshire Electricity between 1991 and 1997.

In 1976 Wyn and Ken Crossland, brass band enthusiasts from Drighlington, decided the village should have its own band. A meeting was organised and six young people attended. One of them, Michael Archer, has led the bands for many years and still plays solo cornet with the senior band. From these humble beginnings the Drighlington Junior Band was formed, its first conductor being Cecil Smaje.

At their peak in the 1980s and early 1990s, by then under the baton of Eric Dews, they achieved great success becoming Yorkshire Champions three times (1985, 1986 and 1991) and representing their county in London at the National Finals, where they twice gained a creditable third place. After their success in 1986 they appeared on Yorkshire Television's 'Sounds Good' pro-gramme and they were given a civic reception in recognition of their achievements. Tours abroad have included trips to Germany, France and Italy. The band still provides a valuable service to the local community by supporting many fund-raising events. Eric stayed with the band until 1991. Their current conductor is Terry Jackson.

The Learners' Group provides free weekly tuition and free loan of instruments to all levels of novice. Over the years scores of local children have passed through, many of them moving into the junior and sometimes the senior band – three members of the current senior band started in the learners' group.

Such was the success of the junior band that in 1983 a Senior Band was formed with many of its members being elevated from the junior ranks. Cohn Hardy was appointed as conductor. Starting off in Section 4 the band won acclaim in contesting both locally and further afield. Under Cohn's guidance they became Pontins Champions in successive years and successive sections – Section 4 in 1986, Section 3 in 1987 and Section 2 in 1988. At national level they represented Yorkshire in the London Finals in 1985 (Section 4), 1986 (Section 4), 1987 (Section 3) and 1990 (Section 2) and became National Champions in 1986 and 1987.

In 1991 the band moved up to the Championship Section where they remained until 1999. Throughout the 1990s they made regular appearances in the Grand Shield. Tony Whitaker took over the baton in 1994 when Cohn retired and subsequently in 1999 Mark Bentham was appointed as Musical Director. Success followed when they won the Milton Keynes 2000 Contest and then qualified in March 2000 to represent Yorkshire once more in the First Section of the National Finals. The band has travelled widely and toured Austria in 1991.

Over the years the music of the bands has been featured on both radio and television. Their third CD 'Titanic Brass' has just been released and they have also made five cassette recordings.

BELOW
Drighlington
Band and RIGHT
the youth section

Pennine Brass

Pennine Brass was formed in March 1999 by John Lockwood (Chair), Bruce Jones (Secretary), Mike Pearson (Treasurer), Paul Fligg (Musical Director), Martin Leech, Ken Booth, Ruth Milnes, Sue Jones and Karen Jazwinski. These founder members were quickly joined by a number of close banding colleagues, resulting in the band's first performance on the 8th of May at a house-warming party in Halifax, followed later that month by its first competition at the Slaithwaite March Contest. The band went on to perform 32 times in its first year, culminating in being crowned Northern Open Champions (Section B) in November 1999.

The band's objects are:
• To educate the public in the Musical Arts, and primarily that of the brass band movement;

• To develop public appreciation of the brass band movement by the presentation of concerts and other activities;

• To develop the musicians within the band by involving them in other musical experiences in addition to those traditional to brass band and providing a widening portfolio of services, both musical and non-musical.

Based in Huddersfield the band was formed from a position of zero assets; however, difficulties in matters such as instruments, rehearsal venues, players, music and uniforms, to name a few, were surmounted by a mixture of player generosity, a determined and dedicated management team, dynamic musical direction and unrivalled player commitment. The band's first uniforms were actually purchased by the players at the time and immediately donated to the band. Despite its humble financial status the band gave a substantial percentage of its first Christmas collections to selected charities.

Following the loss of its first Musical Director, Paul Fligg in August 1999 owing to work com-

mitments, the band was delighted to appoint Ian Porthouse (ex-principal cornet with YBS, Black Dyke, Desford, BNFL and Tredegar Bands) as his replacement. This gave the band a fresh impetus and helped greatly in the recruitment of the few missing players required to complete the team.

Given a Second Section grading in early 1999 by the Yorkshire Area Contest Committee the

band went from strength to strength and eight months after formation tasted its first contest success at the renowned 'Northern Open'. This was despite having to borrow all the required percussion equipment from another local band, and one of the Bass players announcing at the pre-contest rehearsal that his already less than adequate instrument was falling to pieces.

This initial success was consolidated in 2000 by a third placing at the Rochdale Contest, victory at the Yorkshire Area qualifying competition, a number of top 10 positions and several Best Second Section Band prizes at the Whit Friday marches, second place at the inaugural Brighouse March competition and other notable results in local hymn tune and march competitions. The band rounded off a memorable first 18 months with a deserved second place in the Millennium Second Section National Finals at the Royal Albert Hall in October 2000, following which it gained promotion to the First Section.

Sellers International Band

It is fitting that the famous engineering firm of Sellers, makers of the textile machinery that has kept many of the Huddersfield mills turning since 1912, should be associated with this enterprising young band. All forms of human enterprise need to update and adapt to changing circumstances in order to survive and succeed in a world where competition is the order of the day. Sellers have proudly supported this bold and remarkably successful newcomer to the established, and very competitive, brass band world since Remembrance Day 1987.

The 'Huddersfield Tecol Band' was formed in January 1986 by Phillip McCann, who at the time was Head of Brass Music at the Huddersfield Polytech College. He formed the band from a group of 26 students augmented by two more experienced players. In late February the band entered the Yorkshire Area Competition, Section Three, and won! This was capped by coming sixth in the National Finals in London. July of the following year saw the Tecol Band spending the college vacation in Valencia, Spain.

The Tecol Band's first Charity Concert at Huddersfield Town Hall was in September 1987, when it shared the stage with the Huddersfield Choral Society Youth Choir. Further recognition came in the form of a thoroughly practical partnership with Sellers & Co (Huddersfield) Limited, which provided the now renamed Sellers College Brass with a permanent home encompassing a new bandroom, uniforms, transport and all musical requisites. This was the first of the name changes which featured Sellers' involvement in the living tradition of amateur music making.

On St Valentine's Day 1988, Sellers College Brass made the national press for being unable to play at a concert in Milton Keynes. The coach boot jack was jammed and a disappointed band returned north unheard! The May Grand Shield Contest, held in Manchester, gave the musicians the chance to make up for it by achieving second and qualifying for the prestigious British Open in the Autumn.

Manchester's Free Trade Hall may be considered the Valhalla of Northern music making. To enter a competition here is to dare to stand up to be judged by, and amongst, the giants. To achieve 17th place at first try was a brave start, which has been bettered every subsequent year. By contrast, the band played to Christmas shoppers in the streets of nearby Halifax and the first major Sellers charity concert raised £6,240 for the Mayor of Kirklees.

In February 1990 the band played to a packed Town Hall at the next Mayor's Charity Concert; it raised £9,164 for Guide Dogs for the Blind. In May 1990, Sellers College Brass made its debut at the All England Masters Competition held in Cambridge. In September 1990, the band travelled to Belgium, home of the Brussels Conservatoire of Music, to give concerts to international audiences. The members had barely time to return

Launch of the Sellers & Co (Huddersfield) Limited sponsorship, 11 November 1987.
Photo FRASER PHOTOGRAPHY

Phillip McCann and the Huddersfield Tecol Band, February 1986
Photo RON MASSEY

home to Huddersfield, let alone draw breath, before they participated in the Brass Bands Championship Section at the Royal Albert Hall where they were placed third. 1990 continued as it had begun, a year to remember, with the Sellers Engineering Band joining Kathryn Stott for the world premiere of a composition for piano and brass by Bill Connor.

In May 1991 a charity event saw the band playing with four Gilbert and Sullivan societies in aid of the Huddersfield Royal Infirmary Breast Clinic Appeal. Towards the end of 1991, the band went to the Durham coalfield to compete in the Spennymoor Entertainment Contest and in the face of hot competition came eighth.

In February 1992 Sellers Band went to play at the first 'Brintons' Charity Concert in Kidderminster Town Hall. May that year saw the band take third place in the Swiss Open Contest in Berne, when the solo prize was won by Thomas Ruedi, their euphonium player. Late 1992 saw the band once again playing at concerts in Belgium. Sellers Engineering now expanded its sponsorship by offering Music Scholarships for students reading music at Huddersfield University; the first competition was jointly won by Claire Shepherd and David Holling.

At the Yorkshire Area contest held in Bradford in March 1993, the band suffered a rare setback. Conducted by Major Peter Parkes, played what many thought to be the most outstanding performance in its history; but to the surprise of everyone, the adjudicator placed it fifth. The judge's word was final!

In May the band participated in the annual Whit Friday Marches for the first time, when it proved as popular in procession as in concert and competition. July saw the Royal Northern College of Music provide the venue for the World Premier of Rodney Newton's composition *Variations for Percussion and Brass* played by Evelyn Glennie accompanied by the Sellers Band at the 'Hearing Concern' Concert which raised over £5,000. In August, the band returned to Worcestershire for the Three Choirs Festival held that year in Worcester Cathedral. A Christmas Concert at Dewsbury Town Hall raised £2,684 for Cancer Research, another example of the valuable contribution made by the band in supporting the voluntary sector.

In July 1994 the band played for the Women's Institute Conference at the huge NEC in Birmingham. The band capped this, in September, by accompanying The Huddersfield Choral

Society with Patrick Stewart and Thelma Barlow at the Gala Opening Night of Huddersfield's new Lawrence Batley Theatre. The next major event was in the Royal Albert Hall, to accompany 1,000 male voices in the Yorkshire Cancer Research Concert in November 1994. Soon after, the band once again joined The Huddersfield Choral Society in a Christmas edition of the BBC's *Songs of Praise*. On Christmas Eve the band, with Honley Ladies Choir as guests, was featured in Radio 2's *Listen to the Band*.

The April 1995 *Come Sing A Messiah* concert in Leeds Town Hall raised £8,000 for 'Breakthrough Breast Cancer', another notable event for Sellers Band which had come second in the 1995 Yorkshire Championship. The band subsequently accompanied the Rugby League Centenary Commemorative Service in August held in Huddersfield, the birthplace of the game, with The Huddersfield Choral Society, Honley Male Voice Choir and Colin Welland. Another 1995 Centenary, that of the National Trust, was marked by the band's appearance at Fountains Abbey. This was subsequently the feature of another BBC TV *Songs of Praise*.

A triumphal return to the Swiss Open Contest,

LEFT *Sellers International Band outside the offices of Sellers Travel Limited, May 2000.* Photo FRASER PHOTOGRAPHY

BELOW LEFT *The Sellers International Youth Band with their Musical Director, David Essex (centre).* Photo FRASER PHOTOGRAPHY

RIGHT *at The Alfred McAlpine Stadium, Huddersfield*

BELOW *a recording session with Brian Kay and The Huddersfield Choral Society.* Photo FRASER PHOTOGRAPHY

ABOVE *Yorkshire Day, Huddersfield Town Hall 1998. Photo* GREAVES PHOTOGRAPHERS.

BELOW *David Armitage, Chairman of Sellers International Limited presents the Huddersfield & District Army Veterans Association representatives Walter Downs, Charles Russell and George Noble with a cheque for £5000.* Photo THE HUDDERSFIELD DAILY EXAMINER

May 1996, was rewarded by the band taking second place and Peter Roberts, soprano cornet, winning the solo prize. A fortnight later, the band beat all its Yorkshire rivals by coming fourth in the All England Masters Contest at Cambridge.

Sellers International Band celebrated its tenth birthday on the 23rd June 1996 in style. By then, Phillip McCann, who had been with the band since its inception in 1986 and who was recognised as one of the leading lights of the brass band movement, had been replaced by Alan Morrison. The programme to mark the tenth anniversary, despite being described as 'for easy listening', was technically demanding for both soloists and all sections of the band. They responded well to the direction of conductor Alan Morrison, and Frank

Renton, Musical Adviser to Sellers International Ltd, with the verve and unity which speak of dedication to, and pleasure in, great achievements. The band's good friends from the Honley Male Voice Choir 'sang their hearts out', particularly when offering their conductor Alan Jenkins' own arrangement of hits from *Les Misérables*. To cap it all, this memorable occasion raised a sum in excess of £10,000 for the Huddersfield Royal Infirmary Breast Clinic Appeal.

In 1998 the band received Lottery funding, through the Arts Council, that enabled a Youth Band to be formed. There are now over thirty youngsters who willingly accept the disciplines and challenges imposed by working up to the standard of one of the best bands in the land. In December 1998, under the leadership of David Essex, the Youth Band made its concert debut at Dewsbury Town Hall. The youngsters were accorded applause as rapturous as that given to their more experienced seniors.

Once again, the Huddersfield Choral Society called upon Sellers Band to accompany them at its Christmas Concert held at the Town Hall on 10th December 1999. This thoroughly delightful Christmas celebration, in which the audience participated as is usual at Christmas Concerts, was recorded for broadcast by BBC Radio 2 on Christmas Eve.

On 6th June 2000, the Sellers Band took part in a 'Brass Night at the Proms' Concert at Wembley Conference Centre attended by more than 2000 Women's Institute members and the evening ended with a wonderful rendition of *Jerusalem* and *Land of Hope and Glory*. The band was applauded long and loud but, on the following morning at the beginning of the Triennial Conference, this normally smooth-running and stoutly apolitical event hit the news when the Prime Minister of the day, an unexpected guest, made an overtly political speech. The delegates of all that is best in rural Britain quietly and effectively evinced their distaste for what was thought to be an abuse of their hospitality. What a change from the previous night!

During its short but illustrious existence the Sellers International Band has made fifteen CDs and cassettes, accompanied on some by those mentioned in this brief history. In the last year, three concerts, each raising on average £5,500, brought the band's total contribution to charitable causes to over £150,000.

Holme Silver Band

Holme Silver Band was founded in the 1860s. Descendants from people living at that time are still linked with the band today. Now based in a purpose-built bandroom in the heart of the Holme Valley in Holmbridge near Holmfirth, the band is going from strength to strength.

In the last ten years it has had many contest successes, becoming in 1999 Yorkshire Area Champions in its section and, later, clear winners at the National Finals to gain the title of Second Section National Champions of Great Britain 1999. This brought the band promotion into the First Section from January 1st 2000. Other successes include winning the Pilkington Contest in four out of the last six years. Whit Friday, one of the biggest Brass Band events of the year with nearly 100 bands competing at over 50 different contests in one day, usually proves to be a good day out for the band. In July 2000, Holme Silver Band won the Mosley March contest for the second year running.

Holme Silver, as well as competing, has a busy concert schedule, with engagements which include weddings, funerals and galas; in recent years the band has led the parade at the Wakefield Remembrance Day Service. As it has no major sponsorship arrangement, funds must be raised to pay the conductor's fees and to maintain the upkeep of instruments and the bandroom. One of the best ways of raising money is to go out busking on Christmas Day and Boxing Day: everybody loves the sound of a brass band at Christmas.

The band has also had its ten minutes of fame, appearing on *Last of the Summer Wine* several times and twice on the *Sooty Show*. In November 1999 Holme played at two memorial services for the late Bill Owen, one in Holmfirth and the other at Broadcasting House in London. The band made a couple of records with Bill Owen, one of which was called *Compo Has Gone and Lost his Wellies*. In 1998 the band joined New Mill Male Voice choir to record The Holmfirth Anthem, a CD of Yorkshire music.

Holme Band is composed of 25 brass players and three percussionists. There are three married couples who play in the band and two sets of brothers. The oldest player is over 50 and the youngest is 15. Several of the players have been with the band for nearly 25 years including the principal cornet player, Darren Rank, and the bulk of the members have been there for ten years. For the last four years the band has been conducted by Mr Duncan Beckley, a well-respected figure in the brass band world.

Recently a Junior Band has been formed so that Holme Silver Band can keep the tradition of the brass band movement alive long into the future.

Hebden Bridge Junior Band

Hebden Bridge Junior Band was formed by its present Musical Director Brian Haydn Robinson on October 19th 1971. The band's first public performance was given by eight players in December of that year. Since that time the band has grown to its present strength of about 40 players.

Hebden Bridge Junior Band is totally self-sufficient with no sponsorship; all income is derived from engagement fees and collections, with the occasional small grant from local Councils. The band performs in a wide variety of settings, from formal concerts to shopping centres, marches, garden parties, weddings, civic parades, etc.

The Band is managed by a Committee of parents with officers elected annually. Membership is open to children from Hebden Bridge and surrounding areas. Rehearsals take place at the Holme Street Arts Centre in Hebden Bridge on Monday and Thursday evenings at 6 30 pm, with a 'B Band' and learner classes taking place before the main rehearsal. Children may come into the Band as learners from the age of seven and have to leave by their 19th birthday. Although the Junior Band does not have formal links to other local Bands a number of past members now hold key positions in adult bands and orchestras locally, nationally and in the armed forces.

As well as performing locally, Junior Band has

toured extensively, performing in Switz-erland Austria, Germany, Denmark, France, the USA and, more recently, in Norway and Italy. The band prides itself on having an extremely wide reper-toire which includes traditional pieces for brass band, as well as modern music, arrangements of classical pieces and music from the shows.

The band's Musical Director is Brian Haydn Robinson, who began his musical career in the Black Dyke Mills Junior Band before moving to the National Youth Orchestra of Great Britain. He later studied at the Royal College of Music in London. In 1957 he joined the Band of H M Irish Guards. After completing his military service he worked as a professional trumpet player in dance bands and in concert and theatre orchestras. He worked for many years as a peripatetic brass instructor with the former West Riding County Council, then for Calderdale Education Authority. He is now a freelance teacher of brass in a number of schools in Calderdale and Bradford.

Marsden Band

The band we know today as Marsden Band was established in 1889. Little is known of its early his-tory, except that at some time it established its own bandroom on Oliver Lane in the village centre.

The band moved into its present headquarters on Marsden Lane, Marsden in 1931. For many years after that it was to suffer a chequered history: its membership was unstable and for the most part it aspired to performing no more than the tradi-tional functions of a village band.

In 1961, however, it entered the famous Belle Vue Contest at Manchester and won first prize in the senior trophy section at the spring festival, but this appears to have been an isolated success. A determined effort was made to celebrate its cente-nary in 1989: £10,000 was raised for the purchase of four new bass instruments. Unfortunately, the momentum gained by the centenary soon petered out, and, with its best players defecting to higher section bands, the fortunes of Marsden Band sank to an all-time low. Nevertheless, in 1990 it entered the Yorkshire Area Contest, and though having only 16 performers on stage, put up a creditable show.

From then onwards, steadily the band started to improve, and get back up to full strength. The turning point came in 1997 when the band won

first prize in the area contest at Bradford – the prize was an invitation to play at the finals at Symphony Hall, Birmingham. Here it was placed fourth out of 20 bands. A string of contest suc-cesses followed with the band being placed first on many occasions.

The band was promoted to the Second Section in 1998, and straightaway gained third place in the Yorkshire Area Contest. It has appeared on TV in 1998, in the series *Where the Heart is*, filmed in Slaithwaite. 1999 brought further success: it gained second prize in the Rochdale contest at the end of January, and was placed sixth in the Yorkshire Area Contest in February. With that result the band gained promotion into the first section in January 2000.

The band's conductor, Alan Widdop, started playing baritone at the age of five. He then went on to trombone playing with Blackburn Valley, Hebden Bridge, Lockwood, Besses and National Youth Brass Band. By the age of 17 he had become a full-time instrumentalist. He spent six years with Black Dyke Mills Band, followed by five years with Versatile Brass.

He left Versatile Brass to become a teacher and a freelance player with bands such as the Sid Lawrence Orchestra, the BBC National Dance Orchestra and the New Squadronaires. He subse-quently took up conducting and has been associ-ated with the Whitworth Vale, Goodshaw and Rochdale bands. His most notable achievement has been to take Marsden Band from the Fourth Section to the First.

Hepworth Band

The Band takes its name from the village of Hepworth (mentioned in the Domesday Book), which is about two miles from Holmfirth high in the Pennine foothills near Huddersfield. Long before the Holme Valley became famous through *Last of the Summer Wine* on TV, there was a strong tradition of brass bands, and Hepworth is among the oldest in England, having been founded in 1882. The Band still has strong local links, and many local people still help to pay for its upkeep. The 1990s saw one of the most successful periods in the Band's history. Hepworth represented Yorkshire at the National Brass Band Championships in London in 1991 and 1992. In 1995 and 1996 the band took the titles at the Northern Open Championships and the Greater Manchester Police Championships, and was runner-up at the Pontins Championships. Success continued in 1997 with wins at the Buxton Festival and Easingwold March Contest and again runner-up at Pontins. In 1998 the Band retained the Easingwold title, won the Holmfirth Contest, was runner-up at the Tameside Championships and regained the title at the Northern Open Championships. It suc-cessfully defended this in 1999. The band's con-

sistency on the contest platform was rewarded in 1999 with promotion to the Championship Section, where Hepworth now competes against Britain's premier bands.

As well as having gained such an impressive contesting record, Hepworth is equally at home on the concert stage. The band has established a good relationship with the local community and performs regularly at engagements in the Huddersfield area. The band also performs further afield in Championship Brass Concert Series in Leeds, Bradford and Burnley, and in Regent's Park, London, for the Royal Parks Commission. The band has recently recorded *Carnival*, its first CD, following on from its earlier recordings *Marching with Hepworth* and *A Century of Brass*. Hepworth's Musical Director is Norman Law.

Lofthouse Youth 2000 Brass Band

Lofthouse Youth 2000 was brought to life in 1999 by an enthusiastic group of parents, to enable players of all ages and abilities to develop as musicians and to perform for the benefit of the community, both near and far afield.

As a result, the band now provides a varied brass banding experience to anyone regardless of age, and a service to the public in the form of entertainment, whether it is a formal concert, parade, gala, wedding party etc.

It is our aim to keep brass banding alive through the youth of today. We hope to appeal to all the family as ages range from eight years old to grandads. We also intend to have some fun along the way.

Weekly rehearsals take place at Lofthouse Methodist Chapel on Saturday mornings from 10 00 am – 12 00 noon (unless we have an engagement), where you are always welcome to come along and listen and have a cup of tea.

Funding

As we have no financial backing from any other organisation, funds are generated from weekly subscriptions, performances and public donations. We also have a very active social committee who make sure life is never dull and organise many successful social/fund raising events.

Huddersfield Youth Brass Ensemble Association

The Association was formed as an independent charity in 1990, when the Huddersfield Music Centre decided to dispense with the Junior Brass Ensemble. The Huddersfield Youth Brass Ensemble, however, had been in existence since about 1960 when it was created by Mr Edgar Whitham as the brass band of the Huddersfield Youth Orchestras.

The Ensemble has undertaken many educational tours of Europe and North America where it has been a very successful ambassador for Britain and the town of Huddersfield. Its most recent concert tour was in August 2000 when it visited Denmark as guest of the Horsens Garde Brass Band.

The HYBEA has evolved to the point where it can now provide a varied brass banding experience to anyone regardless of age, and a service to the public in the form of entertainment, whether a festival concert, parade, gala, wedding, party or whatever.

The HYBEA provides subsidised lessons, and the Junior Ensemble offers a group environment where the youngest members are encouraged to play for the first time. As they improve the children are encouraged to join the Youth Brass Ensemble where they will encounter more challenging music and perform more often to a much wider audience. Included in the Ensemble's busy annual schedule are regular appearances at Ilkley Carnival and the Huddersfield Civic Remembrance Day Parade.

Members of both youth bands are encouraged to further their musical education by passing practical and theory examinations. Both young bands are directed by Mr Alan Jazwinski, and music lessons are provided by resident tutor Miss Kerry McEwan.

The Huddersfield Brass, the senior band of the Association, is composed predominantly of current and ex-members of the Youth Brass Ensemble from whom it was originally formed, although some new members have been recruited from outside the Association. Since starting to compete in 1992, it has achieved notable success and has climbed swiftly in national gradings from the Fourth to the Second Section. In 2000 it achieved third place in the Second Section of the Yorkshire Area Championship.

Ripponden Carriers Brass Band

Ripponden Carriers Brass Band has quite a long history. It was originally formed in the late 1800s in the village of Krumlin, near Barkisland; taking its name from the nearby river, it called itself the Blackburn Valley Band.

In the 1960s, lack of interest and shortage of players brought about the band's closure, its instruments being loaned to Queensbury Music Centre; but in the 1970s it reformed as Ryburn & Blackburn Valley Band, with practice rooms in Ripponden. This enabled young people living in the Ryburn Valley of Calderdale playing in their school band a chance to continue their playing after they left school.

Subsequently the band renamed itself as Ripponden Village Brass Band so that outsiders knew exactly where we were from; about ten years ago it became Ripponden Carriers Brass Band when we were fortunate to gain sponsorship from Ripponden Express Carriers.

Players pay a weekly subscription towards the band's running costs, but, as with other bands, most of our income is earned from concerts and other events in the local community and anywhere else we are invited to play. Players like to travel to new venues and we have appeared regularly at Scarborough, Blackpool, Granary Wharf (Leeds), Burnley and elsewhere. We also give concerts in the area covered by the Huddersfield Brass Band Association, of which we are members. Each year

the band receives a small grant from Ripponden Parish Council.

The band also enters two or three contests each year, including the Yorkshire Area Contest in Bradford. Each year we give at least one concert

for charity – this year it was for the *Halifax Evening Courier's* 'Macmillan Nurses Appeal'.

The band is conducted by Gordon Milnes. In July, 1999, it was awarded a Lottery Grant for the purchase of a complete set of new instruments, which meant that the original instruments could be passed on to the thriving Junior Band and Learners' Class who are taught free of charge by two band members, Jack Heap and Peter Simons.

The Senior Band practises on Tuesday and Thursday, and the Juniors on Monday and Wednesday.

Rothwell Temperance Band

The present Rothwell Temperance Band was formed in 1985 from a group of juniors, as an off-shoot from the senior band. In 1989, with a full complement of players and new instruments, it was able to enter competitions. In 1991 they qualified for the National Finals and gained second place. Next came promotion to the Third Section. In 1994 it won the Yorkshire Championship and went on to compete in the National Finals in London gaining second place. In 1995 it once again won the Third Section, Yorkshire Area Championships, and yet again came second at the National Finals. It was promoted to the Second Section in 1996.

In March 1996 the band gained first place, playing first out of 14 bands. This was a marvellous achievement for the band.

In 1997 it was promoted to the First Section and once again qualified for the National Finals. The band gained fifth place having been drawn the dreaded number one. It was extremely pleased with their performance, this being their first year in the First Section.

In 1998 the band, once again, won the Yorkshire Area First Section and qualified for the National Finals. Success continued in 1998 with a third place at the Pontins Championships and a superb win in November at the Malton Entertainment Contest. At this contest the band was able to beat three Championship Section bands which was a great achievement.

1999 was an incredible year for the band. In February, after promotion to the Championship Section, the band again qualified for the National Finals and represented Yorkshire at the Royal Albert Hall in October. This was something that the band thought would be impossible to achieve in such a short space of time, but as a result of hard work and dedication it achieved the ultimate success.

In October 2000 the band travelled to Lucerne in Switzerland to compete in the Swiss Open Brass Band Championships in what proved to be a fantastic weekend both playing-wise and socially. After a memorable performance of Lalo's *Le Roi d'Ys* Overture, the band walked away with the title of Swiss Open Champions, becoming only the second English band to do so.

The band's conductor is David Roberts, who started his playing career with the Rothwell Temperance Band, progressing through the junior band to become the principal cornet player at the age of 14. In 1984 he left the band to study music at Manger Folkehogskule, Norway. On his return he joined the Yorkshire Imperial Band and the National Youth Band of Great Britain, and won the Best Instrumentalist Award at the North of England Solo Championships. In 1990 he moved to the Black Dyke Mills Band and won the

Rothwell Temperance Band

Rothwell Temperance Band Achievements since 1994

1994

Yorkshire Area Championships Third Section – Winners

Malton Entertainments Contest – Winners

Cleethorpes Entertainments Contest – Winners

National Brass Band Championships, Wembley – Second

1995

Yorkshire Area Championships Third Section – Winners

Pogson Bray Contest, Dewsbury – Winners

National Brass Band Championships, Wembley – Second

Malton Entertainments Contest – Winners

Cleethorpes Entertainments Contest – Winners

1996

Yorkshire Area Championships Second Section – Winners

Northwest Association Contest – Second

1997

Chesterfield Entertainments Contest – Winners

Cleethorpes Entertainments Contest – Winners

National Brass Band Championships, Birmingham – Fifth

1998

Yorkshire Area Championships First Section – Winners

Malton Entertainments Contest – Winners

Pontins Brass Band Championships – Third

1999

Yorkshire Area Championships, Championship Section – Third

Royal Albert Hall, National Brass Band Championships – Sixth

2000

Swiss Open – Winners

European, British Open and National Championships. In 1995 he took part in that band's wonderful grand slam year.

David is a brass teacher at Leeds Grammar School and also Bradford Grammar School, and recently became a cornet tutor with the National Youth Brass Band of Great Britain. He began conducting in 1993 with the RTB and has guided the band to no fewer than 15 victories.

Linthwaite Band

The village of Linthwaite is situated three miles from Huddersfield on the A62 Huddersfield to Oldham road. The present-day bandroom is located within a few hundred yards of where the band was first formed nearly 150 years ago. The band has had its own bandroom for the last 40 years. Prior to that it had rented rooms in clubs and public houses within the district.

The band is one of the oldest brass bands in the country. It was founded in 1852 at Upper Clough, Linthwaite by the Baxters, Mellors, Swifts and Haighs, and Mr Henry Swift was appointed as leader and bandmaster. The first engagement was on the 8th April 1854 under the leadership of Joseph Armitage and the band comprised 20 players.

In 1853 a young local boy called Edwin Swift joined the band. He was ten years old at the time, and as he was such a naturally talented musician, he made great progress and was soon in great demand to perform at venues about the district. In 1855 at the age of thirteen years, he was appointed solo cornet player and conductor, and so began a long and illustrious partnership, which lasted to his death on the 9th February 1904.

During this time Edwin Swift became one of the most famous and sought-after band teachers and professional conductors of the movement. When the band was formed, bandsmen had to buy all their own instruments and music, the instruments being of all shapes and makes.

In order that the band could be formed into a contesting band, in 1867 an appeal for funds was made to the public. This resulted in a few up-to-date instruments being purchased, and in the early part of 1868 the band became the regimental band of the 34th West Riding Yorkshire Volunteers. Colonel Bradbury presented it with a few additional new instruments and the contesting band was achieved.

Under Edwin Swift's careful training the band progressed and competed at its first contest at Belle Vue, Manchester in the September Championships, 1868. It was unsuccessful at the event, but between 1869 and 1891 appeared in the prizes 16 times, winning first prize in 1874. In 1877 the band won first prize in Edinburgh and was awarded what was then the highest cash prize ever given at a contest – £60.00.

During the late 19th and early 20th centuries, Linthwaite Band was one of the top brass bands in the country, and has always had a reputation for giving satisfaction at engagements, both in performances and presentation. Probably the most bizarre engagement ever accepted was to perform at the celebration to mark the completion of 'Titanic Mill', Linthwaite. Bandsmen were hoisted up to the top of the mill chimney in a large bucket, and gave a short concert on a 'stage' constructed across the top.

The policy of the band is to train and promote the talents of young players, and this is shown in the long history of contest successes and the numerous players who have moved on to top-flight bands. This has been brought about by the dedication and patience of the bandmaster/tutors who have been associated with the band, and the efforts of loyal supporters. The band has always been self-supporting, does not have club facilities and does not receive any sponsorship.

The latest contest success was achieved in June 2000 when the band won the Ripon Festival Entertainment Contest, held in the magnificent Cathedral.

Festivals

The Haydn Wood Music Festival

Haydn Wood was born on 25 March 1882, at the Lewisham Hotel, Station Road, Slaithwaite. He was one of three sons of Mr & Mrs Clement Wood, who all grew up to be distinguished musicians.

At the age of 15 he won a scholarship which took him to the Royal College of Music in London, where he studied the violin. After his marriage to Miss Dorothy Court, the soprano vocalist, the couple toured the country for 13 years, appearing in theatres and on the concert platform. It was at this time that he turned to composing and wrote ballads, choral works and orchestral suites. During the 1914-18 war he composed the ballad for which he is perhaps best known, *Roses of Picardy*. He died on 11 March 1959, but his music, as with all works of art, lives on.

In the following year, the Colne Valley Urban District Council, wishing to commemorate Slaithwaite's most famous musical son, arranged a Musical Festival named after him, which became an annual event. For many years the competition was held at Colne Valley High School (opened in 1956); not unnaturally, most of the competitors came from the school, the ruling being that the festival should be open to children between the ages of 9 and 18 and residing in the council district. The first festival had 15 classes and attracted 141 entries. Our present accompanist came second in the 12-14 Piano Solo Class and the Piano Duet Class!

The rules have changed slightly over the years, notably following local government reorganisation in 1973 when the Colne Valley UDC became part of Kirklees Metropolitan Council. The festival is now open to 'young people up to the age of 21' who live in Kirklees and Calderdale. However, the Haydn Wood Trophy still remains to be won by the competitor with the highest mark who lives in the former urban district.

This year the festival has 41 classes. Over the years, many trophies have been donated, and there is now a wonderful array of silverware for the young people to win.

The Holmfirth Music Festival

Holmfirth Musical Festival was founded in 1946 by Leslie Kendall-Green, father of our current president, Gwynneth Kendall-Green. He had come up with the idea of of launching an annual festival which would enable local children to show off their musical talents. Taking his young daughter with him, he visited musical festivals in various districts. The information and knowledge thereby gathered was carefully noted, and Holmfirth Musical Festival was born.

The first festival was held in the Sunday School at Lane Chapel; nowadays it takes place in Holmfirth Civic Hall. To set a high standard, the committee felt that it should make it a rule to engage only the best adjudicators available, and the practice has continued to this day. Since then the committee has received many generous donations of trophies and prize money and is deeply grateful to all who support the festival in this way.

Over the years the festival has grown, and new classes have been introduced. We now have 35 classes which offer a wide choice for choirs, solo vocalists and the pianoforte and other instruments. This year we have introduced a Family Class which is open to at least two generations of the same family performing a programme of entertainment and musical content for six minutes. Some classes have test pieces; others give freedom of choice.

In 1995, the festival held a most successful 50th anniversary celebration, the proceeds going to the Malcolm Sargent Cancer Fund for Children. In 1998 we were able to run two masterclasses thanks to a £2,500 lottery grant from the Arts Council of England's Arts for Everyone scheme.

It is most gratifying to see a wide range of musical talent pass through the festival. We have a hard-working and dedicated committee and pride ourselves on being a friendly and welcoming festival. Throughout the year the committee holds numerous social functions to raise money; more recently we have approached local business people to sponsor a class in local business people to sponsor a class in return for an advertisement in the programme. With such a nucleus of enthusiasm for the task in hand we hope that the festival will continue for many years to come.

Huddersfield Contemporary Music Festival

In its early years, the Huddersfield Contemporary Music Festival was regarded with some astonishment by the national media, surprised that such an important national showcase of new music could be located in a relatively small West Yorkshire mill town, some disbelieving that it was even possible outside London. Now, nearly twenty-five years after its tentative beginnings in 1978, the Festival has become a widely-applauded star of the national cultural calendar, and it is also the musical event which, more than any other, earns Yorkshire an international reputation.

During the 1980s, the Contemporary Music Festival notched up a succession of impressive achievements, but the 1990s have been even more a decade of progressive growth, during which the Festival extended its venues, including the newly-opened Lawrence Batley Theatre in 1994, and more than doubled its audience and budget. At the twenty-first Festival in 1998, a series of spectacular programmes drew so many people that even the Town Hall was repeatedly sold out.

Richard Steinitz, Artistic Director. Photo PAUL HERMANN, Profile Photo Agency.

15-26 November 2000

Besides those who make an annual pilgrimage from London, from elsewhere in Britain, and a significant number of overseas visitors, there is now an encouragingly large local public, aware that standards of performance are among the best in the world and eager to extend their musical experience beyond the increasingly routine fare of other concert series. Recent statistics show that over half the audience live in West Yorkshire, many more coming from the wider northern catchment area.

Financial resources have been built up through energetic fundraising, persuasive lobbying, the development of collaborations and international partnerships and through recognition that the Huddersfield Festival is an effective shop window in which to invest. A clear attraction is the sheer variety of the programme, which includes concerts, opera, dance, film, installations, multimedia and an imaginative education programme. From a first budget in 1978 of under £3,000, by 1999 the 22nd Festival presented some 73 events across twelve days, in which world-famous composers, ambitious concerts and many other genres rubbed shoulders, with an overall budget of £483,000.

Unique factors have contributed to the Festival's success. One is the productive relationship between the Festival – as an autonomous enterprise – and its principal mentor and host organisation, the University of Huddersfield, with its highly regarded Music Department. Further associations exist with Kirklees Cultural Services and Yorkshire Arts, the regional arts board, from whom the idea of the Festival originally emanated. Another advantage is afforded by Huddersfield's fine venues, which are exceptional for a town of its size. Close to the Town Hall, with its splendid Victorian interior and excellent acoustics, is St Paul's Church, handsomely converted in 1981 into an atmospheric medium-sized concert hall, from which many Festival events are broadcast. Equally close is the Lawrence Batley Theatre, an even more remark-able transformation behind its elegant Georgian facade, whose completion in 1994 owed much to a new cultural

impetus in Kirklees which the Festival itself helped to generate.

Over the years, the Festival has brought to Huddersfield just about all of the world's leading living composers. Stockhausen and his family have been involved as performers on two occasions. The first was in 1988, when Huddersfield Sports Hall was decked out as an indoor park complete with shrubs, trees, candle-lit processions, six performing ensembles and several hundred of the public wandering amongst the foliage for the first UK performance of Stockhausen's *Sternklang*. The music critic of *The Times* even brought his dog! In 1992, the Sports Hall was used again for the UK premiere of Gerald Grisey's *Le Noir de l'Etoile* performed by Les Percussions de Strasbourg, which incorporated a pulsar signal beamed directly from outer space into the hall via Jodrell Bank. The audience sat concentrically around a sand-covered arena under canvas sails. That same

The UK premiere of Gorecki's Beatus Vir *(1993). Photo* HUDDERSFIELD EXAMINER

year, Iannis Xenakis made one of his three visits to the Festival for several extraordinary performances and projects which included a theatrical compilation of pieces in the Town Hall, based on the story of Faust, with the breathtaking spectacle of trapeze artists swinging from the stucco roof.

Of course, the majority of the Festival events are concerts, many of them in St Paul's Hall. In this agreeable setting, many of the world's lead-

L-R *John Cage, Olivier Messiaen, Pierre Boulez at the 1989 festival.* Photo SELWYN GREEN

ing ensembles have performed: the London Sinfonietta on numerous occasions, Asko from Holland, whose performances of Ligeti in 1993 in the composer's presence were especially brilliant, Klangforum Wein from Austria, Avanti from Finland, ArrayMusic from Canada, a traditional instrumental ensemble from the Central Conservatory in Beijing, the Tokyo International Music Ensemble, artists from Africa and India, and Germany's Recherche and Ensemble Modern, probably the most prestigious of all new music ensembles who made their British debut here in 1986, conducted by Heinz Holliger, and returned in 2000 to contribute to an important German Retrospective.

Remembered by Festival regulars with special affection is John Cage, whose benign, if iconoclastic *joie de vivre* cast its spell over the whole Festival during his ten-day stay in 1989, just three years before his death. At this Festival, Pierre Boulez and Olivier Messiaen were also distinguished guests, and the warm reunion after many years of these one-time avant-garde associates was captured in a historic photograph.

Another visitor fondly recalled was Alfred

Schnittke, whom the Festival presented on stage with a candle-lit birthday cake after a powerfully dramatic and moving portrait concert given by Huddersfield Choral Society and the English Northern Philharmonia, conducted by Gennadi Rozhdestvensky on the composer's 56th birthday, 24th November 1990. Alas, eight years later, Schnittke would be dead, drained by a stressful and difficult professional life in pre-glasnost Russia. Also in Huddersfield on that occasion was Sofia Gubaidulina, now Russia's leading composer, whom the Festival has featured three times and of whom it has presented more than ten UK and world premieres. Four years before, in 1986 there was no indication of whether Gubaidulina would be allowed to accept the Festival's invitation and travel from Moscow, until she actually arrived.

Even from its early years the Festival has continued to receive an astonishing series of press accolades. 'Who needs Vienna when you've got Huddersfield?' proclaimed *The Observer* in 1997. 'Centre of the musical universe' announced *The Independent on Sunday* a year later; whilst, in 1994, the then Heritage Secretary, Stephen Dorrell, famously advised people to take a cultural weekend-break in Huddersfield during the Contemporary Music Festival in preference to Paris. In praising the 'actively provincial approach we have in Britain' in contrast to the 'centralised metropolitan culture of the French', he neatly overlooked France's equivalent new music Festival in Strasbourg, which enjoys six times as much subsidy!

One of the most interesting reviews was in 1984 from David Cairns, then music critic of *The Sunday Times*, who chose to observe the Festival's first extended educational and participatory programme in preference to the professional concerts which in that year followed afterwards. His comment that 'in spite of weather like the end of the world...the effect of the few days in Huddersfield has been to fill me with optimism for the future' encouraged the Festival to continue working with different sectors of the community every year in an astonishing range of memorable and innovative projects. Alas, the 'brutal and crassly short-sighted education cuts' which David Cairns had already deplored in 1984, have continued to damage musical and cultural education throughout Britain even more seriously. Over the years, the Festival's varied and original educational schemes have provided a valuable antidote.

Not surprisingly, the Contemporary Music Festival has become a model for others in Europe and Scandinavia. In the UK, it has won important awards including the Prudential Award for Music in 1992, a British Gas/Arts Council 'Working for Cities Award' in 1994 and the Royal Philharmonic Society's Award for concert series in 1999. The education programme won the Sainsbury's Award for Arts Education in 1991 and the RPS Education Award (sponsored by Classic FM) in 1999, making the Festival the only institution to have won two RPS Awards at once. Richard Steinitz, founder of the Festival and its Artistic Director since 1978, was made an OBE for services to music in the Queen's Birthday Honours in 1995. He received the biennial Lesley Boosey Award in 1992 and was made an honorary member of the Royal Philharmonic Society in 1999, one hundred and eighty-second in a line of recipients dating back to Carl Maria von Weber.

Steinitz's inquisitive and undogmatic approach, detailed knowledge of and contacts with composers and musicians from all over the world, have kept successive Festivals varied and interesting. For several years he planned and organised the whole operation virtually alone, whilst holding a full-time teaching job at what in 1992 would become the University of Huddersfield. As the Festival has grown, however, it has gradually established a strong administrative team headed by a General Manager, including an Education Director and a technical team recruited for the Festival period itself, whose task is to deliver some of the most complex technical challenges undertaken by any festival in Britain.

Whilst the interaction between music and technology becomes ever more intricate, new music also speaks through its own powerfully direct and compelling voice, resonant with the concerns and sensibilities of our own time. Essentially, the Festival's brief is to represent the work of composers living today, biased perhaps in favour of British and European culture, but also embracing global and ancient musical traditions. Each Festival weaves a counterpoint of specific themes, some indigenous, some international, some purely acoustic, others theatrical or multi-dimensional, celebrating the highest professional achievement as well as

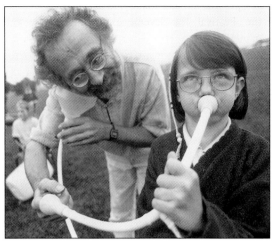

Instrument maker Kevin Renton helps a pupil from Newsome J and I school

providing opportunities for newcomers, young people and amateurs. To attend virtually everything in one twelve-day Festival is, indeed, a heady experience! Yet many people return from far afield to Huddersfield to do exactly that every year. Such is the magnetism of music as it emerges newly incandescent from the crucible of creative fire. Such is the Contemporary Music Festival's unrivalled reputation.

The Kronos Quartet with Foday Musa Suso (1993)

The Leeds International Pianoforte Competition

It was the desire of a Leeds piano teacher forty years ago to encourage young pianists that led to Yorkshire becoming home to one of the world's most prestigious piano competitions. Now known the world over as the 'Leeds', the Leeds International Pianoforte Competition was the brainchild of Fanny Waterman in 1961.

Fanny Waterman already had a growing reputa-

Fanny Waterman OBE

tion as one the country's leading private piano teachers, and had enjoyed a successful career as a soloist. Born in Leeds on March 22 1920, Dr Waterman showed musical talent at an early age. Her father, Myer Waterman, a Russian Jew who emigrated to England to work as a jeweller, paid for his daughter to travel to London for private lessons with Tobias Matthay when she was 17. She began public performances and in 1941 opened the concert season in Leeds, with the Leeds Symphony Orchestra. Later that year she won a scholarship to the Royal College of Music where she studied under Cyril Smith. In 1944 she married Geoffrey de Keyser and her concert career was curtailed with the arrival of her first child in 1950. She then concentrated on teaching.

By the early 1960s she felt young pianists needed a goal to give them a competitive edge with foreign players. 'There is a necessity for a young musician to enter and win a competition to become established on the international music map', she explained in *The Times* (July 20 1998). 'With the breakdown half a century ago of the patronage system which fostered great soloists of previous generations, and the disappearance of great impresarios willing to nurture from their own resources outstanding young talent, the competition ladder remains for most the only fair alternative.'

The challenge was how to fund and organise such an event in a northern industrial city. It was not certain that a major international music competition outside London would succeed. But Dr Waterman – awarded an OBE in 1971 for her services to music – enlisted the help of her friend Marion Thorpe, at that time Countess of Harewood. They jointly founded the Leeds Competition in 1961, which is now one of the world's top such competitions alongside Moscow and Warsaw. The competition, held normally every three years, was born through Fanny Waterman's passion, gritty determination and the enthusiastic support of well-connected and generous friends. She gained sponsorship from local businesses, Leeds City Council and the Arts Council of Great Britain, and the support of the University of Leeds. Patrons have included Princess Mary, sister of King George VI, and the Duchess of Kent. The current patron is Dame Janet Baker.

The first competition, like subsequent ones, was held in the Great Hall of the University of Leeds and had a budget of £8,000. Applicants under 30 from around the world were invited. The winner received £1,000 and jurors gave their services free. The jurors included notables such as the great Soviet pianist Jakob Flier, John Pritchard (the then musical director of the Royal Liverpool Philharmonic Orchestra), Sir Arthur Bliss (Master of the Queen's Music) and Clifford Curzon. The second competition, in 1966, which attracted 91 entrants from 35 countries, caught the interest of the media. BBC Radio recorded the semi-finals and broadcast a live transmission from the finals, and the documentary Great Expectations was also filmed: it later won an international award.

Not all the contests have run smoothly. In 1978, for example, the competition got off to a shaky start. An air traffic controllers' dispute hit flights into London, and only 68 of the 95 entrants arrived in Leeds the day before the competition was due to start. The competition would not be such a success without the goodwill of local people. The contest forges links between young foreigners and Leeds families, who offer their pianos – ranging from fine Steinways to modest uprights – for competitors to practise on. The competition now has its own Friends Organisation which recently donated £30,000 towards the cost of accommodating the competitors during the 2000 competition.

The competition has just been held for the thirteenth time: it has come a long way from the old days. It is now one of the most important international arts events in Yorkshire, and one of the most prestigious in the UK. Its principal sponsor is the Halifax plc, one of the country's largest banks and mortgage providers. There is also wide financial support from other local, national and international organisations, as well as from individuals. Woods, the famous Yorkshire music store, for instance, lends over a dozen pianos for the competitors to practise on. Says Dr Waterman: 'Mounting an important competition is now an expensive operation, and the expenditure cannot

be recouped at the box office. Sponsorship is essential – it is our lifeblood.' Run from 6-23 September, the 2000 competition had a budget of £550,000, prizes worth £57,800 and a record number of entries – 298 – from applicants in 45 countries all over the world.

'The calibre of national and international engagements offered to the Leeds prizewinners is as great as ever and sets us apart from many other competitions', states Fanny Waterman. This year the Leeds had over 120 engagements to offer the winners. 'We always hope', she continues, 'that a young pianist will emerge with a touch that proclaims a master – with a fine technique, beauty of tone, musical understanding, judgment and integrity, rhythmic vitality, passion and that indefinable inspiration, artistry and magic.'

The 2000 competition consisted of four stages. In the first, all competitors played from memory and combined set works from the Baroque and

ABOVE Sir Simon Rattle conducts the City of Birmingham Symphony Orchestra in the 1996 finals. BELOW Ilya Itin, the 1996 winner, with the competition's current patron, Dame Janet Baker

Classical eras with pieces of their own choice. 33 competitors were admitted to the second stage: in this, recitals included works selected from the great Romantic repertoire. 12 went on to the semi-final – a free-choice recital of a maximum 75 minutes' duration, for which there were special prizes for the performance of a contemporary work and the music of Schubert. The six who competed in the final – televised by the BBC – chose from a list of the greatest piano concertos. They were accompanied by the City of Birmingham Symphony Orchestra conducted by Sir Simon Rattle, recently appointed as Music Director of the Berlin Philharmonic, appearing for the fifth time in the competition.

The Leeds Competition has played a crucial role in the careers of prizewinners. Many, including Radu Lupu, Murray Perahia, Andras Schiff and Mitsuko Uchida have become international stars. Michael Roll, who gave up his place to study medicine at the University of Leeds after his 1963 win, has since played around the world. Others have taken very different paths. Jean-Rodolphe Kars (a finalist in 1966), for example, abandoned the piano and took holy orders to become a Catholic priest; Aleksei Nasedkin (also 1966) later became a professor at the Moscow Conservatory.

While Leeds helps give winners a platform from which to launch a career, there is much more to becoming a successful artist than playing the piano. 'A music competition', argues Dr Waterman, 'is only one piece in the whole mosaic of artistic life. When a competition announces a winner, it merely says to the musical world: 'here is someone we think you ought to listen to.' Touring, as she points out, is lonely, and sometimes critics' comments can be unfavourable. Competitors are often young, in their 20s; they fall in love and marry. An unhappy marriage can play havoc with a career. 'I've seen first-prize competitors go up or come down depending on their personal lives', explains Dr Waterman (*Clavier*, January 1999). 'Succeeding in this profession takes being an artist in living as well as playing; it calls for treating everyone with the greatest respect and gratitude. After winning a competition, the artist realises that the competition of real life begins the next day.'

But the Leeds International Pianoforte Competition goes a long way to revealing artistic gifts. As the late Sir Clifford Curzon, writing to Dr Waterman in 1973, said: 'What greater or more touching pleasure is there in life than giving a young and beautiful talent a little lift in the direction only (for we can never reach them) of the stars.'

After a thrilling final, the first prize in the 2000 competition was awarded to Alessio Bax, a 22-year old Italian who gave an impressive and fluid interpretation of the Brahms Piano Concerto No 1 in D minor. The second prize was awarded to another Italian, 27-year old Davide Franceschetti, and the third prize to Severin von Eckardstein of Germany.

The Mrs Sunderland Musical Competition

In the UK, only two competitive festivals for amateurs in the performing arts can boast a longer unbroken record of promotion than Huddersfield MSMC. This festival is also unusual in that it began, in 1889, as a contest solely for solo singers and instrumentalists. Up till then, competition had always been among choirs (particularly in Wales), brass bands and sometimes orchestras.

But an account of this eponymous festival cannot be complete without the story of Mrs Susan Sunderland herself, to whom it can be considered to be a warm, and still living tribute (not a memorial, as many people venturing an opinion glibly state). The lady had another 17 years left to her when the festival was first mounted and she had herself given it her blessing. She attended, and presented the prizes at, several of the early contests.

Born on 30th April 1819, she lived in Brighouse all her life. Before she married Henry Sunderland, a former butcher in 1838, she was Susan Sykes, one of a large family of children. Her father, James, was a gardener; both her parents were musical. Because Susan, as a child, loved to sing, they saw to it that this quality was encouraged; and she was taught, initially by local blacksmith and Parish Church Choirmaster, Luke Settle, who clearly was ultimately responsible for the vocal qualities for which she became famous. Local teacher John Denham also fostered her musical knowledge; but ultimately she was taught by Dan Sugden of Halifax, who was actively associated with the Halifax Choral Society, and who, later, obtained engagements for her with the London-based Sacred Harmonic Society.

It is commonly asserted that she first sang in public in the early months of 1834 at Deighton, then a village between Brighouse and Huddersfield, at the age of 14. But evidence is quite clear that her first public appearance was on 22nd November 1833 (appropriately enough, St Cecilia's Day – patron Saint of Music). This was at an annual event known as the Rastrick Concert, held at the Red Lion Inn, Rastrick (no longer there, but identified as being opposite Rastrick Grammar School, and now a convalescent home.) It consisted of items from Handel's *Acis and Galatea*, from which 'Miss Sykes' took the soprano part in a trio and a duet; and a miscellany of glees and part songs, in which one of her fellow singers was 'Mr Dyson' – presumably her early teacher, local tenor John Denham.

Before long, and still in her teens, she was a soloist with the Halifax Choral Society, following which she was very much in demand at oratorio and glee concerts throughout the West Riding. She sang in London for the first time, for the Sacred Harmonic Society, in 1842, to enthusiastic acclaim. Altogether she sang in public in London on six occasions to considerable enthusiasm, and regret from the press that she lived in the North; they would like to have heard much more of her. During most of her professional career she was closely involved with the Huddersfield Choral Society, both as a member of the chorus and as a soloist.

The growth of the railway system enabled her to accept engagements much further afield, and she is recorded as performing at venues as far apart as from Hull to Belfast and Waterford, and apart from London, from Lincoln and Birmingham to Aberdeen. Clearly she was well-liked in Scotland, for she visited Glasgow and Aberdeen several times, singing with the local Choral Unions. Certainly by the time she last performed in Aberdeen the Choral Union's Committee was pre-pared to offer a fee nearly three times greater than what had been settled on for her first visit to the Granite City and considerably more than the other members of the soloists' ensemble. In April 1859, the Centenary of Handel's death, she was in Edinburgh at which were performed *Acis and Galatea*, *Samson* and *Judas Maccabaeus*, to consid-erable approval from the Scottish press. That year would, of course, be a busy year for Handel singers.

In 1858 she was invited to be one of 19 vocal soloists of international repute at the concert

which was part of the celebration marking the opening of Leeds Town Hall in the presence of Queen Victoria and the Prince Consort. She had been asked to sing the National Anthem (all three verses) – not uncommonly given as a solo concert item at that time (even in Europe). Perhaps as a

ABOVE the silver casket in which a testimonial marking her golden wedding was presented to Mrs Sunderland BELOW a young Susan Sykes

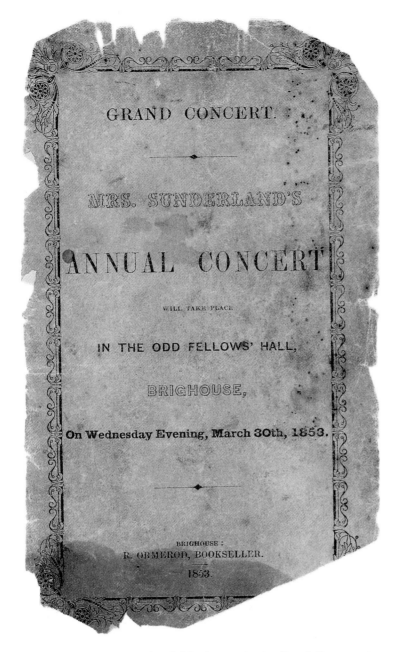

West Riding, she made her final appearances at two concerts in Huddersfield in June, giving the soprano solos in a performance of *Messiah* at the first one, and with other soloists, offering ballads at a 'sell-out' concert the following evening.

During the ensuing 24 years she lived a relatively quiet life, with a few favoured singing pupils. But in 1888 she and her husband would be celebrating their Golden Wedding (which in the 19th century must have been quite an unusual achievement). The occasion was considered sufficiently remarkable for a committee to be formed to plan a suitable celebration, which took the form of a 'Grand Complimentary Concert', with the presentation to Mrs Sunderland of a congratula-

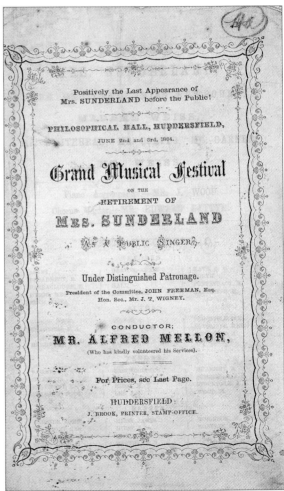

result of this she received a Royal Command to sing at one of the Queen's musical soirees at Buckingham Palace, an occasion she remembered with affection. Her recollection of the 'terrible Airs' adopted by the royal flunkeys almost duplicates the comment on these flunkeys vis-à-vis the humbler servants of the mere aristocracy in *A Book of Snobs* by Thackeray!

To universal regret and while still at the height of her powers, she chose to retire from the concert platform in 1864, at the age of 45. At a time when life expectancy was, generally, less that 50, this is perhaps not as surprising as it might at first seem. After a busy round of 'farewell' concerts in the

tory address and testimonial (contained in an impressive silver-gilt casket) in Brighouse Town Hall. The occasion was financed by subscription and the sale of tickets. Afterwards, surplus funds remained. After an initial idea that they should be passed to the RAM or the RCM to fund a bursary for a singing student, the Committee had a change of heart and felt it would be preferable to retain the money 'in the area' to benefit local aspirant singers.

Accordingly they asked the Governors of the Huddersfield Technical School if they would be prepared to organise a contest for vocalists from the West Riding, up to 25 years of age, Sopranos and Contraltos to alternate, annually, with Tenors and Basses. A silver medal and a prize of five guineas was offered. The Governors agreed willingly to take on this responsibility, and initiated another contest, for pianists alternating with violinists, with a prize of three guineas. Mrs Sunderland gave the project her blessing, and pre-

sented the prizes at the first contest, which took-place on Friday evening and Saturday afternoon, 12th and 13th April 1889. There were 37 competitors – 27 sopranos and contraltos and 10 pianists. The adjudicators were John North (Conductor of the Huddersfield Choral Society), James Sykes (Huddersfield Borough Organist) and D W Evans, Singing Teacher at the Huddersfield Technical School.

Widowed in 1893 (having borne 6 children) Mrs Sunderland died on 7th May 1905. It was a remarkable life, for a person of very humble origin and who remained domiciled in Brighouse all her 86 years and very attached to her Huddersfield connections, to achieve the country-wide acclaim

Concert party with Mrs Sunderland far left

that she undoubtedly did. It comes over that she was a well-liked woman, not only among local musicians but admired by fellow artistes. Our loss is that she retired from the concert platform 13 years before the phonograph was invented.

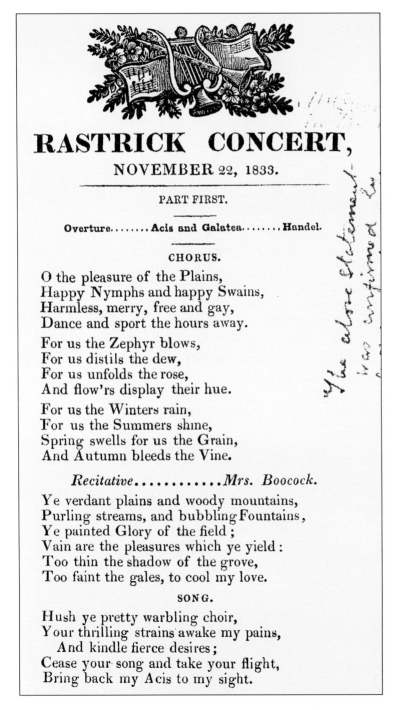

In 1889 unlike many newer competitive festivals, the MSMC began in a comparatively small way, but had a steady growth. Modern festival organisers will be bemused by the fact that in the first few years, competitors were allowed to perform only under pseudonyms (though obviously if they won prizes their names would have to be revealed!). By 1893, when there were 61 competitors, each appeared in the programme only with a number (despair for the historian!). We get to identify the winners because they were listed in the following year's programme. Classes for 'Large Choirs' and 'Small Choirs' were introduced in 1894; and as time went on (but slowly) further contests, reflecting the current need, were added. In 1916, in response to an offer of funding, a Composition Class was introduced, and for many years the distinguished adjudicators of this included Granville Bantock, Edward Bairstow, Julius Harrison and Herbert Howells. 1921 saw the introduction of a few 'Elocution' classes; while during the 20s, following a national trend, there were classes in country dancing (for schoolchildren), and ear-tests and (piano) sightreading.

The first World War seems not to have affected the course of the festival, but at the outbreak of the second World War, it was decided that the festival should be discontinued throughout its duration. Thus there was no MSMC in 1940; but all the children's classes (piano, violin, singing, choirs and elocution) were reintroduced in 1941. The immediate post-war period saw the re-introduction of the previously abandoned adult or senior classes; while the growth of instrumental teaching, promoted by the local authority, plus a surge of interest in Oratorio and Operatic classes during the 50s led to entries peaking, for the time being, to between 800 and 900 each year. During the 60s those numbers were not for one reason and another kept up (though among performers and the public the MSMC never seems to have lost its respect and reputation); but from the 70s onwards the festival committee has continually looked around for new departures which will be indicative of the aims of the competitive festival movement.

So the scope of classes has expanded where there appears to be a demand; so, for a long time now, specialist adjudicators have consistently been engaged, and, to underline the educational/ teaching function of a competitions festival, master classes and/or workshops have been made available. Creativity is catered for in both the music performance and the spoken word sections; thus the MSMC has, for many years, had a poetry-

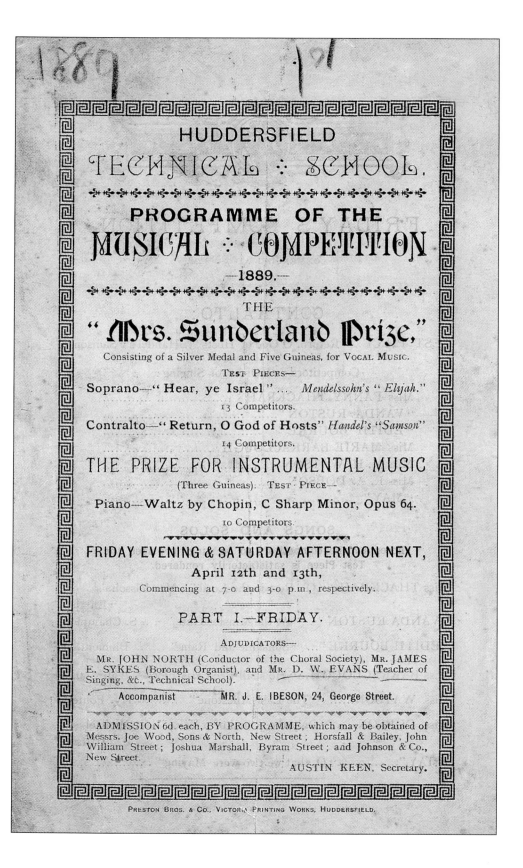

1889

HUDDERSFIELD
TECHNICAL ∴ SCHOOL.

PROGRAMME OF THE
MUSICAL ∴ COMPETITION
—1889.—

THE
" Mrs. Sunderland Prize,"

Consisting of a Silver Medal and Five Guineas, for VOCAL MUSIC.

TEST PIECES—

Soprano—"Hear, ye Israel" ... *Mendelssohn's "Elijah."*

13 Competitors.

Contralto—"Return, O God of Hosts" *Handel's "Samson"*

14 Competitors.

THE PRIZE FOR INSTRUMENTAL MUSIC

(Three Guineas). TEST PIECE—

Piano—Waltz by Chopin, C Sharp Minor, Opus 64.

10 Competitors.

FRIDAY EVENING & SATURDAY AFTERNOON NEXT,

April 12th and 13th,

Commencing at 7-0 and 3-0 p.m., respectively.

PART I.—FRIDAY.

ADJUDICATORS—

MR. JOHN NORTH (Conductor of the Choral Society), MR. JAMES E. SYKES (Borough Organist), and MR. D. W. EVANS (Teacher of Singing, &c., Technical School).

Accompanist   MR. J. E. IBESON, 24, George Street.

ADMISSION 6d. each, BY PROGRAMME, which may be obtained of Messrs. Joe Wood, Sons & North, New Street; Horsfall & Bailey, John William Street; Joshua Marshall, Byram Street; and Johnson & Co., New Street.

AUSTIN KEEN, Secretary.

PRESTON BROS. & CO., VICTORIA PRINTING WORKS, HUDDERSFIELD.

LEFT *the programme for the first Mrs Sunderland competition*

OPPOSITE *almost certainly the programme for the first public appearance of Mrs Sunderland*

writing section, with each year the production of a book containing all the entries.

Most of the MSMC takes place in Huddersfield Town Hall and in St Paul's Concert Hall, both of which contribute to a sense of occasion and importance for performers. At present, with something like 1000 to 2000 entries annually, and taking ninedays in at least two halls, it really is a festival of the performing arts which it hopes inspires participants to strive for excellence, enjoyably; and audiences to encourage them.

Most competitive festivals are proud to cite participants who have distinguished themselves

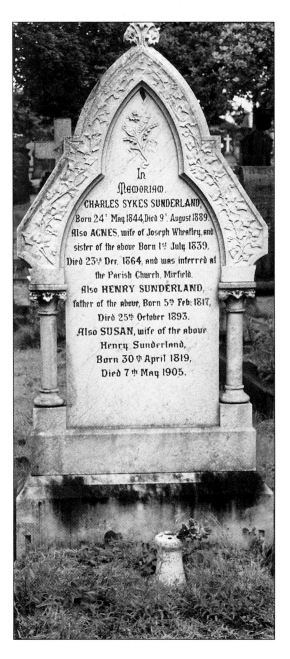

Mrs Sunderland's grave as it is today in Brighouse Cemetery

In
Memoriam.
CHARLES SYKES SUNDERLAND,
Born 24ᵗ May 1844, Died 9ᵗ August 1889.
Also AGNES, wife of Joseph Wheatley, and
sister of the above Born 1ˢᵗ July 1839.
Died 23ʳᵈ Dec. 1864, and was interred at
the Parish Church, Mirfield.
Also HENRY SUNDERLAND,
father of the above, Born 5ᵗ Feb. 1817,
Died 25ᵗ October 1893.
Also SUSAN, wife of the above
Henry Sunderland,
Born 30ᵗ April 1819,
Died 7ᵗ May 1905.

after they have taken part in their festivals. The MSMC can mention several to whom, while their professional success may not be entirely due to taking part in the festival, it did at least provide useful experience of performing in public with, we hope, encouraging guidance:

1917 'The promising young tenor from Halifax' (to quote the local Press) **Mr W Widdop** won the Tenor Solo class. **Walter Widdop**, at the time a textile mill hand, went on to become, internationally, a leading Wagnerian tenor of the period.

1924 Senior Elocution solo – won by **Wilfred Pickles** (also, strangely, of Halifax)

At present, probably the most notable MSMC contenders include:

Thelma Barlow, who for many years was in Granada TV's *Coronation Street*, and is now in demand on the theatrical stage. As Thelma Pigott, she came first in the 'Senior Elocution' class in 1949.

Paul Nilon from Keighley – first in the Boy's Treble Solo class in 1975, and in the Baritone Solo class in 1979. Paul now appears regularly to considerable national critical acclaim with Opera North, Welsh National Opera, and in European opera houses and concert halls.

David Bintley who came first in Piano classes in the 1940s. For some years he has been the highly regarded Artistic Director of the Birmingham Royal Ballet.

Lesley Hatfield (violin) won the 'Kirklees Young Musician of the Year' prize in 1986, having previously competed in 'young' Piano and Violin classes in the '70s. Now she is Leader of the BBC Ulster Orchestra, and a sought-after soloist and chamber-music artist.

In 1949, 12 year old Bradford boy **Malcolm Binns** won his 'age' Piano solo class, as he did again in 1952. For many years he has been a busy piano recitalist and concerto performer.

In the 1970s, local girl **Edwina Wolstencroft** achieved success in Piano solo and duet classes. We hear her name now, quite regularly – not as a pianist but as a producer of programmes of musical interest on Radio 3 and Radio 4. Her programme on Sir Peter Maxwell Davies notably earned a Sony award.

In 1951 **Rodney Friend** won the Violin Solo, 11-14 years class. He was to become the Leader of the BBC Symphony Orchestra.

In 1978 baritone **Mark Wildman**, after winning the Baritone Solo class in 1975, won the

KYMY prize. Now Mark is Head of Vocal Studies at the RAM, an appointment which he combines with a performing career – and he has returned to Huddersfield twice as an adjudicator at the MSMC.

Pianist **Keith Swallow** won the class for 15-16 year olds in 1946, and the J W Pearce Prize in 1950. As well as being a much sought-after piano recitalist, concerto performer and accompanist, Keith has preserved his connections with the MSMC for which he continues to accompany KYMY competitors; while he provided a house-full, Piano Master Class a few years ago.

The Contest for the Kirklees Young Musician of the Year (KYMY) Prize

During the 1940s, local Musician Mr J W Pearce discussed with Mr Harry Armitage, the then Chairman of the MSMC, the practicalities and terms under which an annual contest could be set up, each year, with a prize of £50, to assist young musicians from the Huddersfield area aiming at professional careers in music. The financial administration of the Award was to be in the hands of a Committee of Trustees; but the Committee of the MSMC agreed to stage the contest which would be for singers and pianists in alterante years, ostensibly as part of the MSMC. The first contest (for pianists) held in 1948 was won by Phillip Challis. In 1949 it was won by contralto Peggy Castle who became well-known as a performer in opera and oratorio, and later was sought to take on a teaching post as Professor of Voice at Cincinnati University in America.

Approximately 20 years later, by judicious management of the late Mr Pearce's fund, new trustees were able to increase the annual award to £100; and it was opened to other instrumentalists as well as singers and pianists. Then, following the absorption of the Huddersfield Authority into Kirklees MC in 1974, the latter offered to contribute to the value of the prize, adding a trophy and the promise of lunchtime recital engagements in Huddersfield and Dewsbury. At the same time, contestants from the whole of Kirklees (either to have been born in this area, or to have lived in Kirklees for at least five years) were to be eligible for the award. At present the total cash prize from the J W Pearce Prize Fund and Kirklees Cultural Services is £700. The contest, which calls for a short recital, is a highlight of the final day of the annual MSMC programme.

JUDITH SHERRATT

Judith Sherratt

It is with great sadness that we have to report that within only a few weeks of writing this piece especially for this book, Miss Judith Sherratt died without recovering from a stroke she had a few days before. The piece that Judith has written therefore becomes a very fitting and eloquent testimonial to the work she undertook for many years for The Mrs Sunderland Music Competition. She worked hard against ill-health to produce this piece on time. What a tragedy that she never saw it in print.

Local Authority Involvement

INTRODUCTION

I came to Kirklees knowing that music was a hugely important part of local life, and knowing that Huddersfield Town Hall had (to quote the Bournemouth Symphony Orchestra who were one of my grant aid clients in Southampton) 'the best acoustic for choral and orchestral music in the UK'. What I quickly came to realise, in addition, was how deep and how wide was local people's involvement in music, and the sheer quality of the orchestras, brass bands and the singing here.

That was the background in which I had to find ways to release resources to ensure the arts and the town halls served more of our communities, without sacrificing the strengths and enthusiasms of traditional orchestral concerts.

Working closely with the Hallé, we negotiated a new contract, so that our favourite orchestra became a partner with a clear incentive to develop and sell the series of concerts to the public. Although the Hallé's financial crisis in 1998 meant that the new arrangements got off to a very difficult start and we lost audiences, we are now back to the levels of before, with the same number of concerts costing the local taxpayers substantially less.

What's really important is that we've also been able to focus our joint efforts on audience development – something that's vital if orchestral concerts are to survive. With the Hallé we sought the views of over 500 concert-goers, and we're using their responses to shape the programme to appeal to first-time attenders while maintaining the appeal to more experienced audiences.

We have made a particular effort to bring in children, the audiences of the future: over the past three season around 600 primary school pupils have attended concerts for the first time as part of a package which gives them seats in the Mayor's box, a teachers' pack to help preparation in the classroom, and a pre-concert meeting with members of the orchestra. In addition to these one-off visits a programme of longer-term projects has seen members of the Hallé, English Northern Philharmonia and Manchester Camerata and various others working in local schools.

Though people understandably regret the passing of the days of big orchestras and expensive soloists, musical quality has been sustained. Highlights include:

November 97 BBC Philharmonic Orchestra with Joanna McGregor in a Contemporary Music Festival concert, of music by Ives, Harrison, Grisey and Xenakis. A capacity audience for a concert which featured two UK premières and was broadcast as part of Radio 3's Millennium celebrations *Sounding the Century*.

May 2000 English Northern Philharmonia and Huddersfield Choral Society in the Society's Millennium concert featuring the première of a special commission by Colin Matthews: *Aftertones – Three Landscapes of Edward Blunden*.

November 2000 Hallé Orchestra with Mark Elder CBE – the Hallé's new Music Director making in Huddersfield one of his first few appearances with the orchestra. An all-Elgar programme: *Introduction and Allegro*, *Sea Pictures*, Symphony No 1.

JONATHAN DRAKE
Head of Kirklees Cultural Services

The Huddersfield Town Hall Orchestral Concerts

'The casual visitor to Huddersfield would hardly imagine that he was amongst some of the greatest music lovers in the country. There is no festival here, no Hallé orchestra, and no Richter or Henry Wood. But, in an unpretentious way, the people of Huddersfield give probably more time to music than do those of any town of a similar size in England.'

Thus wrote an un-named commentator in the *Musical Home Journal* in March 1908. But years later there were to be plenty of Hallé and other prestigious orchestral concerts with conductors no less renowned than Richter or Henry Wood – not to mention one of the most important contemporary music festivals anywhere in the world.

Concert series involving major professional orchestras came rather later to Huddersfield than to other West Yorkshire centres. When the seven-year-old Hallé Orchestra inaugurated Bradford's subscription series in 1865, Huddersfield's music-making was fully formed but expressed itself mainly in choral singing and the burgeoning brass band movement. Such was the strength of the town's music-making that by the beginning of the twentieth century Huddersfield supported fourteen musical instrument and sheet music dealers.

Orchestral music was less well developed: until the formation in 1862 of 'Mr Thomas's Band' – the forerunner of the Huddersfield Philharmonic Orchestra; the only orchestral body of any significance was the Choral Society's band (an integral part of that Society from its inception in 1836). In due course other orchestras emerged – notably the

Artur Rubinstein who appeared in Huddersfield Town Hall in 1968

187

LOCAL AUTHORITY INVOLVEMENT

Longwood and Slaithwaite Philharmonics (the latter achieving fame in the great competitive music festivals on the eve of World War 1).

After the First World War, in Huddersfield and throughout West Yorkshire, amateur music-making of all kinds began to lose its central position in society as other leisure activities, particularly cinema, emerged. However, it was about this time that Huddersfield Corporation began to promote its own concerts.

Since 1881 the Corporation had had a magnificent Town Hall. Architecturally it was a mixture of styles and ideas brought together to express the growing aspirations and pride of Huddersfield. Because of its – roughly – shoebox shape and because of the materials used in its construction and decoration musicians soon recognised that it offered an acoustic of distinction. Years later Sir John Barbirolli described it as 'one of the finest acoustics in the country'; Andreas Seidel, Leader of the Leipzig Gewandhaus and Leipzig Chamber Orchestras, told this writer that there were other acoustics for chamber orchestra in the world as good as Huddersfield Town Hall's but none better. It offers fidelity to the timbre of almost any sound source – be it a small ensemble or a complex choral and orchestral gathering – with even balance from the highest to the lowest notes and as close as you can get to nil distortion. It is a remarkable instrument in its own right, and it contains another remarkable instrument – the 'Father Willis' organ. Henry Willis (1821-1901), arguably England's greatest nineteenth century organ builder, had been commissioned in the 1860s to build an organ for the Albert Hall in Newport. But by 1880 Newport could not maintain the instrument and Walter Parratt, organist of Oxford's Magdalen College, urged Huddersfield Corporation to buy it for their new Town Hall. Parratt was the son of a former Huddersfield Parish Church organist, and had been born and brought up in the town. As organist at Magdalen he was recognised as a considerable authority: the Corporation took his advice and snapped up the 'Father Willis' for £1,500. (Parratt was later to become Master of the Queen's Musick and earned a knighthood).

A hundred years later this unsigned description in the leaflet for the 1989-90 season of organ recitals captures its significance:

'Huddersfield's 'Father Willis' organ is a unique instrument. It was made by the firm

which also built the organs in St Paul's, Liverpool, Canterbury, Westminster and St Giles (Edinburgh) Cathedrals. A firm at the top of their profession, and one which saw the organ not just as a musical instrument, but also a spectacular centre-piece to a concert hall. The Town Hall organ was originally constructed for the people of Newport, but their loss became Huddersfield's unequalled gain when it was sold in 1880. The Town Hall's concert chamber was then designed specially to accommodate it. And what a magnificent sight it makes

Queuing for the best seats at the Town Hall – all night on some occasions. This also became a regular feature of the Huddersfield Choral Society's Public Messiah bookings

too. The fabulous pipework reaching a splendid summit in a star-burst of gilded pipes and ornate cherubs, that only hint at the rich romantic sound that bursts from its reeds. The organ can truly be described as one of the finest in the country, and it is helped by the superb acoustic in the Hall itself.

An organ concert at Huddersfield Town Hall is an occasion providing a visual thrill and an aural treat'.

By the early 1920s Huddersfield Corporation had launched a series of Municipal Concerts. These were built round the magnificent Town Hall organ and featured a guest player, usually the organist of one of the great English Cathedrals, appearing with a small instrumental ensemble or choir plus a vocal soloist. The concerts started at 6 30 pm and provided a full two hours of music without an interval. There were usually six Saturday concerts between September and March each season and the formula continued more or less unchanged until Huddersfield Corporation

was replaced by Kirklees Metropolitan Council in 1974. In all that time the cheapest seats, in the gallery, were priced at one (old) penny and the Concerts came to be known as 'the Penny Pops'. Many musicians started their careers with a 'Penny Pops' engagement including, post Second World War, Rodney Friend and Keith Swallow. Post war guest organists included Dr Francis Jackson of York Minster, Eric Chadwick of Hallé Choir fame and William Lloyd Webber.

One evening Lloyd Webber and 'Penny Pops' organiser Ron Morton were exchanging notes about the progress of their respective children. 'Julian is all right on the cello', said Lloyd Webber, 'but Andrew is beggaring about writing some music.'

For forty years from 1946 the story of Local

Authority concert provision in Huddersfield is the story of Ron Morton. He had joined the Borough Engineer's Department as an administrative assistant in 1937 and served in the Royal Navy during the war. On returning to his old job he was asked if he would help manage the Council's concerts. His immediate superior in Borough Engineer's Department was Lionel Taylor, Assistant Secretary of Huddersfield Choral Society, who had now been appointed Honorary Secretary, Huddersfield Corporation Arts (Concerts) Sub-Committee. Taylor had started a series of free lunch-time recitals in 1943, and in 1947 he and Ron Morton set about expanding the 'Penny Pops' and lunch-time recital operation by adding an orchestral series.

This was the year of the launch of the Yorkshire Symphony Orchestra. Leeds City Council was the prime mover in the venture with Huddersfield as the second biggest backer. In the late 40s and early 50s the YSO received more public subsidy than any other British orchestra. In 1947-48 it received £35.000. This compares with £20,000 for the London Philharmonic, £17,000 for the City of Birmingham and – to put it in an international context – £40,000 for the Amsterdam Concertgebouw. From the start it gave some 30 concerts a year in Leeds and 15 in Huddersfield – a huge number for the town's first-ever concert series from a professional orchestra – and Ron Morton recalls that in the eight years before its collapse its fee was never more than £400 and the cheapest seat price at Huddersfield was held at 5/- (25p). Maurice Miles was Principal Conductor followed briefly by Nicolai Malko. Between them they provided a broad span of repertoire but mostly on the popular side. There was a three-day festival of British music, which did not appeal to the public, and a three-day Beethoven festival, which did. For the Beethoven festival Denis Matthews played all five Piano Concertos. The most successful YSO concerts in Huddersfield were the 'Industrials', pot-boiler programmes for which Ron Morton sold party bookings at knock-down prices to textile and engineering company social secretaries. Although warmly received in Huddersfield, the YSO failed to capture public imagination elsewhere in Yorkshire or nationally, and with Leeds and Huddersfield bearing an unsustainable financial burden it was disbanded in 1955 (from the start, neither Bradford nor Sheffield, with their long Hallé associations, supported the enterprise). These were indeed parlous times for Britain's orchestras – as Michael Kennedy pointed out in *The Hallé Tradition*, 'The Yorkshire Symphony Orchestra, the most heavily subsidised orchestra in the country, was abolished because it failed to win public support. The Hallé, the most popular and the least subsidised, lived perilously from hand to mouth'.

Although maintenance of the YSO proved to be too much for Huddersfield Corporation it had, now, an orchestral budget and was prepared to spend on concerts. Ron Morton and Lionel Taylor lost no time in engaging the Hallé, Royal Liverpool Philharmonic and City of Birmingham Orchestras for a 1955-56 season of five concerts – so the YSO had blazed a trail for orchestral concerts in Huddersfield and, ironically, through its demise had provided other British orchestras with much-needed engagement opportunities. This first series was a resounding success at the box office and within two years Morton and Taylor were attracting other orchestras, and had added a celebrity recital. The 1957-58 season had a recital on 1 November in which Claudio Arrau played Sonatas by Mozart and Beethoven, Schumann's *Carnaval*, Debussy's *Pour le Piano* and Liszt's *Gnomenreizen* and *Mephisto Waltz*. What a concert! – on the Huddersfield Corporation file copy of the concert programme someone wrote, 'a very fine pianist; old style'! The season then continued with concerts from the BBC Symphony Orchestra and Rudolf Schwarz, the Hallé and Barbirolli, the Royal Liverpool Philharmonic and Sargent, the London Symphony Orchestra and Horenstein and the Royal Philharmonic Orchestra.

Ron Morton recalls:

> 'In the next few years all the five London orchestras visited Huddersfield, some on two or three occasions. Leading overseas orchestras such as the Moscow Philharmonic and the Czech Philharmonic and orchestras from Hungary, Bulgaria and Poland gave concerts at the Town Hall on a regular basis. These were marvellous years. We sold out at nearly every concert. We sold season tickets on a Saturday morning a month or two before the first concert, and patrons used to queue outside the Town Hall all through Friday night to get the best seats. Many famous conductors and soloists appeared at these concerts: Sir Thomas Beecham – one concert only, not long before he died – Sir Malcolm Sargent, Sir John

LEFT *Sir John Barbirolli – a regular visitor with the Hallé in the 60s and 70s*

Barbirolli, Sir Adrian Boult, Artur Rubinstein, Vladimir Ashkenazy, Yehudi Menuhin, Victoria de los Angeles, Dame Janet Baker, Jacqueline du Pre, Daniel Barenboim and Segovia.'

Beecham's sole Huddersfield appearance was on 26 November 1959 when he conducted the Royal Philharmonic in Schubert's Third Symphony, Mozart's Jupiter, Bizet's Symphony in C and Saint-Saens' Ballet Music *Samson and Delilah*. Lionel Taylor retired in 1961 and Ron Morton took over as Huddersfield Corporation's Honorary Concerts Secretary – organising, managing and marketing a complex network of concerts more or less in his spare time, for an 'honorarium', while discharging his clerical duties for Borough Engineer's Department. It is worth taking a detailed look at some of these concerts. They drew such consistently large audiences to Huddersfield Town Hall that Morton found no need for overt populism.

On 21 October 1961 Rudolf Schwarz conducted the Bamberg Symphony Orchestra in Haydn's Symphony No 97, Hindemith's *Metamorphoses on themes by Weber* (Hindemith was still alive at this time) and Brahms Symphony no 1. On 1 April 1963 Witold Rowicki conducted the Warsaw National Philharmonic in the Overture *Flis* by Stanislaw Moniuszko (1819-1872), Liszt's *Les Préludes*, and then two pieces by composers very much alive at that time – Britten's *Les Illuminations* and Shostakovich's Fifth Symphony. The concert was broadcast live by the BBC Third Programme, and little wonder! Ron Morton's concert programme says of Rowicki: 'it is largely due to his efforts that the difficult task of restoring Poland's musical life after the destruction caused by the last war was successful.' Two weeks later on 17 April Sir Adrian Boult conducted the Philharmonia Orchestra in a concert that began with Lennox Berkeley's Divertimento in B flat, followed with Symphonies by Mozart and Brahms and ended with a repeat performance of the Berkeley.

The 1965-66 season had single concert tickets on offer for 3/6d (on the risers behind the orchestra) to 9/- with a concert programme for 6d. And for that outlay concert-goers could buy into:

19 October: **English Chamber Orchestra** with Emanuel Hurwitz leading, Colin Davis conducting and Michael Roll as soloist –

Mozart and Haydn Symphonies, Mozart's E flat K449 Piano Concerto and the *Little Music for Strings* by contemporary composer Alexander Goehr.

8 November: **Leipzig Gewandhaus Orchestra** under its Music Director Vaclav Neumann – the UK premiere of the Overture *Enoch Arden* by the German contemporary composer Ottmar Gerster, Schubert's *Unfinished* and Bruckner's Third Symphonies.

29 November: **Czech Philharmonic Orchestra** under its Chief Conductor Karel Ancerl – Mozart's *Don Giovanni* Overture, *Mystery of Time* by Czech contemporary composer Miloslav Kabelac, Smetana's *Sarka* and Dvorak's *New World* Symphony.

12 January: **BBC Symphony Orchestra** led by Hugh Maguire and conducted by Jean Fournet – Beethoven's *Leonora no 3* Overture, Roussel's Symphony no 3 and Tchaikovsky's *Pathétique* Symphony; the concert broadcast live on the BBC Home Service.

11 February: **Wiener Solisten**, an ensemble of twelve strings with the American soprano Helen Donath – *Mozart's Eine kleine Nachtmusik*, a Haydn Divertimento, Hindemith's Opus 44 Pieces for Strings and arias from Mozart's operas *Lucio Silla* and *La Finta Giardiniera* and *Ascanio in Alba*.

23 February: A recital of songs by Mozart, Schubert, Schumann and Wolf by the fabulous **Irmgard Seefried**.

14 April: **Royal Liverpool Philharmonic Orchestra** with Charles Groves and Raphael Sommer – Mendelssohn's *Ruy Blas* Overture, Dvorak's Cello Concerto and Beethoven's *Eroica* Symphony.

27 April: **City of Birmingham Orchestra** with Hugo Rignold and Philip Challis – Wolf-Ferrari's Overture *Susannah's Secret*, Rachmaninov's Second Piano Concerto, Sibelius Symphony no 6 and Debussy *La Mer*.

What a season! And quite typical of a period that Adrian Smith, *Huddersfield Daily Examiner* Music Critic and General Editor of this book, remembers: 'Those were heady days. The orchestral concerts were at their peak in the last years of Huddersfield (Corporation) and the early years of Kirklees.'

Heady days and sometimes headache days, as Ron Morton explained:

'I remember the first time the Moscow Philharmonic came. They had been playing in

Leeds the night before. Our concert was due to start at 7 30 and at 7 20 their coach had not arrived at the Town Hall. When they did arrive the Orchestra demanded irons to press their clothes. We managed that, but were twenty minutes late in starting.

'Sir John Barbirolli, my favourite conductor, used to talk to me about concert-going and at me about the merits of Lancashire and Yorkshire. He used to rest in his room at the Town Hall before concerts and would ask, "Give me a knock five minutes before I'm due to go on". One night I knocked, opened the door, switched on the light and found him curled up asleep on the floor.

'Artur Rubinstein came to Huddersfield on two occasions. The first time I went to meet him at the railway station. He had travelled alone. He was nearly eighty, and had been given the wrong travel information and had had to change trains several times. He was very tired when he arrived, but immediately asked to see the piano. I took him by taxi to the Town Hall where he sat down at the piano for less than five minutes before saying, "That's all right". He was marvellous.'

1974 brought sweeping changes to local authorities in England and Wales and Huddersfield Corporation was incorporated into Kirklees Metropolitan Council, whose area extends from Batley and Dewsbury in the north east to Marsden and the Pennines in the south west. The new authority had a Department of Leisure. Within it there was an Arts Section – the first in the country – and Brian Pearson was appointed to head it. Later a Cultural Services department, separate from Leisure, was established under Brian Pearson. From the start the Huddersfield orchestral concerts were central to Pearson's thinking and he invited Ron Morton to be full time Music Officer. 'My hobby became my job,' said Morton, 'wonderful!'

Brian Pearson recalled:

'We ran the first Kirklees orchestral series at Huddersfield Town Hall in 1974, starting with a sold-out Hallé concert. We extended the Huddersfield season and started a new orchestral series at Dewsbury Town Hall. Not only did we provide series of professional concerts but we commissioned works for the organ, for Huddersfield Choral Society and for the youth orchestras. We were innovative – the Grimethorpe Colliery Band appeared in our series doing a modern programme sponsored by Pernod. The Kirklees Youth Orchestra appeared with a professional conductor and soloist. We restored the 'Father Willis' organ and appointed a Borough Organist [Jonathan Bielby, organist of Wakefield Cathedral, later succeeded by the present incumbent, Gordon Stewart] and ran lunch-time recitals. We ran Contemporary Music Network concerts and eventually became co-founders of the now world-famous Huddersfield Contemporary Music Festival.'

In 1980 Huddersfield and Dewsbury acquired an orchestra of their own – the Kirklees Concert Orchestra. Huddersfield-based freelance violinist Anthony Moran thought there was a need for a light classical orchestra in the area, and recruited members of other orchestras plus freelances from all over the north of England under his baton. Kirklees Council agreed to support the venture and until 1991 the Orchestra was a regular fixture in both the Huddersfield and Dewsbury seasons. Its concert at Huddersfield on 2 December 1985 was typical. Moran conducted, the Hallé's Martin Milner was guest leader and the orchestra list named other Hallé, Royal Liverpool Philharmonic, BBC Philharmonic, Manchester Camerata and English Northern Philharmonia players – including the ENP's Orchestra and Concerts Director among the violas! The programme was Suppé's Overture *Tantalusqualen*, Godard's *Berceuse de Jocelyn*, *Sweet Nutcracker* (a Tchaikovsky adaptation written and narrated by the renowned storyteller David Kossoff), Wagner's *Tannhaüser* March, Faure's *Pavane*, Karlsbader *Puppentanz* by Pleier, the *Gypsy Princess Waltz* by Kalman, 'Judex' from *Mors et Vita* by Gounod, and Sibelius's *Finlandia*. Moran's ideas of light classical repertoire were always as imaginative as this, with many delightful but less well-known works. However, like the Yorkshire Symphony Orchestra before it, the Kirklees Concert Orchestra never really established itself with the public and by the late 1980s it was drawing significantly smaller audiences than the big-name orchestras. After its Huddersfield concert on 4 February 1991 it was not assembled again.

Its December 1985 Huddersfield concert was part of a season that demonstrates one of the major innovations Brian Pearson mentioned. Along with three Hallé concerts, the Finnish National Radio Symphony and Hungarian State

Symphony Orchestras there were two special concerts for Huddersfield Contemporary Music Festival. On 24 November Luciano Berio conducted the BBC Symphony Orchestra and Singers in a concert of his own works for which tickets were free, and two days later John Lubbock conducted the Orchestra of St John's Smith Square in works by Schönberg, Maxwell Davies and Brahms plus Schnittke's Third Violin Concerto with Mark Lubotsky as soloist.

The season also included English Northern Philharmonia, billed as the Orchestra of Opera North, along with the Opera North Chorus under the baton of Elgar Howarth. Now here, at last, was a Yorkshire Orchestra that has not only survived but won an international reputation for its work in the concert hall as well as opera pit. Ron Morton and Brian Pearson introduced it to Huddersfield from its earliest days – Opera North was launched in 1978 – and although in the late 1980s and early 90s it did not appear in every Huddersfield season many in the regular audience regard ENP, along with the Hallé, as their own.

The principal significance of the 1985-86 Huddersfield season, however, lies in an event at its opening concert on 11 October. Stanislaw Skrowaczewski conducted the Hallé in Mozart, Wagner and Ravel and rising star Anne-Sophie Mutter played the Beethoven Violin Concerto. The concert programme did not mention that this was Ron Morton's last concert before retirement. A few days later a fulsome tribute to him in the *Huddersfield Daily Examiner* said, 'On Friday night he took his final bow. Or rather he would have done had he been on stage. Instead, as usual, he was hard at work behind the scenes as the Hallé Orchestra opened the new season in Kirklees.' Ron Morton had organised or helped organise some 1,500 concerts in his time with Huddersfield and Kirklees Councils and recalls that on two occasions the National Music Council commended Kirklees for its music service:

'We were fortunate in having Huddersfield Town Hall. It has been praised by many conductors, soloists and orchestras. Sir John Barbirolli always said it was a delight to come to such a wonderful hall. The lowest attendance at the Town Hall that I can remember was eight for a contemporary music ensemble. In fact there were more people on the stage than in the audience. The biggest attendances were for the two Artur Rubinstein recitals, each of which was attended by more than 1,600 people. People were crammed on to the orchestra risers and on stage surrounding the piano. Rubinstein had no objection. The highlights of my concert life at Huddersfield Town Hall are many, but the Rubinstein recitals and a performance of *The Dream of Gerontius* by Huddersfield Choral Society with Janet Baker for the centenary of the Hall rank very high in my memory'.

Ron Morton also noted that by this time finance was becoming a worry. Central government had begun to call into question the very principles of public provision, local authorities had spending restrictions placed on them, orchestral costs were escalating. But in the late 1980s and early 90s there were some magnificent seasons arranged by Morton's successor as Music Officer, Aidan Plender, who said 'there was something of a mini-boom going on, with money around for audiences to spend and sponsorship was easier to come by'. Plender's 1989-90 season at Huddersfield Town Hall was inspired and all except one of the concerts attracted a commercial sponsor:

6 October: **Royal Liverpool Philharmonic Orchestra** and Choir conducted by Libor Pesek – Gershwin's *Porgy and Bess* with a cast that included Wayne Marshall as the pianist, Jasbo Brown. [Sponsor Graham Builders Merchants[

8 November: **Hallé Orchestra** conducted by Jan Krenz with Christian Blackshaw as soloist – Szymanowski's *Masques*, Mozart's C minor Piano Concerto (K491), Schubert's Great C Major Symphony. [Sponsor Marshall, Mills and Sykes Solicitors]

26 November: A Huddersfield Contemporary Music Festival concert with the **BBC Symphony Orchestra** conducted by Pierre Boulez and with Yvonne Loriod as piano soloist – Eclats/ *Multiples* by Boulez, Stravinsky's Symphonies of Wind Instruments, the second UK performance of Messiaen's *La Ville d'en Haut*, Boulez' *Messagesquisse*, Stravinsky's *Song of the Nightingale*. [Sponsor Waterman Pens]

13 January: **Hallé Orchestra** with Sir Charles Groves and Philip Fowke – Mozart's Symphony no 32, Rachmaninov's Piano Concerto no 2, Vaughan Williams' *Job, A Masque for Dancing*. [Sponsor ICI]

8 February: **English Northern Philharmonia** with Elgar Howarth and Jean Philippe Collard

A full house with the Huddersfield Choral Society

– excerpts from Debussy's *Martyrdom of Saint Sebastian*, Ravel's Piano Concerto for Left Hand, new works performed by young composers from Kirklees schools, Harrison Birtwistle's *Secret Theatre*, Stravinsky's 1919 *Firebird* Suite. [Sponsor Hanson Transport]

10 March: **City of Birmingham Symphony Orchestra** conducted by Simon Rattle with Viktor Liberman and Peter Thomas as soloists – Bach's Concerto for Two Violins, Schönberg's *Verklärte Nacht*, Webern's Opus 10 Five Pieces, Beethoven's Seventh Symphony. [Sponsor Barclays Bank]

20 April: **Hallé Orchestra** with Stanislaw Skrowaczewski and Rudolf Buchbinder – Beethoven's Third Piano Concerto and Bruckner's Third Symphony. [Sponsor Armitage, Sykes and Hinchcliffe Solicitors]

30 April: **Kirklees Concert Orchestra** conducted by Anthony Moran with Keith Swallow

and soprano Marie Slorach – light classics beginning with Beethoven's *Egmont* Overture, ending with Suppe's *Pique Dame* Overture and including suites by Bizet and Eric Coates, Elgar's *Mina* Entracte and two groups of songs.

18 May: **Royal Liverpool Philharmonic Orchestra** conducted by Libor Pesek with Huddersfield Choral Society and Jane Eaglen (soprano), Ameral Gunson (mezzo), John Mitchinson (tenor), Michael George (bass), and Ian Tracey (organ) – Smetana's *Bartered Bride* Overture, Dvorak's Eighth Symphony, Janacek's *Glagolitic Mass*. [Sponsor Ivy Coaches (Linthwaite) Ltd]

Compare the 1989-90 season with the 1965-66. They both have their own character and they are both outstanding – as good as anything going on anywhere else in the country. But orchestral

LOCAL AUTHORITY INVOLVEMENT

and artists' costs had escalated by a fair bit more than the rate of inflation between 1965 and 1989 and, even with sponsorship, Aidan Plender had to work his programming magic with only one London orchestra, no overseas orchestras and no celebrity recital.

In the last ten years there have been some magnificent programmes in the Huddersfield seasons but there have also been some gargantuan efforts to wrestle with the problems of finance, central government attitude to local authority service provision and shifting patterns of audience response. Adrian Smith has voiced his concern in his *Huddersfield Daily Examiner* reviews and elsewhere about the effects of these problems. In recognising the growing financial constraints he observes:

'Not surprisingly there has been a relentless descent from those heights – though some outstanding individual concerts have certainly taken place: among them, one given by English Northern Philharmonia playing Prokofiev's *Romeo and Juliet* and Ravel's *Daphnis and Chloe*; a visit by the Finnish Radio Orchestra under Jukka-Pekka Saraste (with a riveting Sibelius Fifth); the veteran Soviet pianist Tatiana Nikolaeva in the Schumann Concerto; Tasmin Little in a wonderful account of the Elgar Violin Concerto; the Bournemouth Symphony Orchestra and Kreizberg who introduced us to Markevich's *Rebus*. Nevertheless the repertoire has shrunk alarmingly. 'Viennese nights', Vivaldi's *Four Seasons*, Rachmaninov's Second Piano Concerto and Elgar's Cello Concerto turn up with monotonous regularity.'

This writer would add to Adrian Smith's list of 1990s outstanding individual concerts: the visit of the Leipzig Chamber Orchestra and Michael Collins; the English Northern Philharmonia with Matthias Bamert and Robert Hayward in Mahler's *Lieder eines fahrenden Gesellen* and Bruckner's Seventh Symphony – both these concerts from the 1993-94 season and my own period as Kirklees Music Officer. From the 1994-95 season: English Northern Philharmonia, Huddersfield Choral Society with Jane Glover conducting and Jean Rigby, Neil Mackie and Stephen Roberts in Mozart's *Vesperae Solennes de Confessore*, Elgar's *Sea Pictures* and the world premiere of David Matthews' *Vespers* which was commissioned by Kirklees Cultural Services and the Choral Society

to mark the centenary of Sir Malcolm Sargent's birth.

The Hallé with Tadaaki Otaka and Bruno Leonardo Gelber in Stravinsky's *Fireworks*, Rachmaninov's Third Piano Concerto and Walton's First Symphony – from the 1995-96 season. The Swedish Radio Symphony Orchestra with Okko Kamu, Anna Lawson and Peter Mattei in Sibelius' *Karelia Suite*, Mahler's *Des Knaben Wunderhorn* and Tchaikovsky's Symphony no 5 – from the 1996-97 season. And, of course, all the concerts jointly promoted in the 1990s by Kirklees and Huddersfield Contemporary Music Festival – such as the BBC Philharmonic and Luciano Berio, and several English Northern Philharmonia concerts conducted by Paul Daniel and Elgar Howarth with works from composers such as Tippett, Ben Mason, Ligeti and Mark Anthony Turnage.

For all sorts of reasons – cultural, political and financial – 'public' provision of traditional orchestral concerts is in a critical (indeed some would say 'terminal') condition There is no doubt that future Huddersfield Town Hall orchestral concert seasons will be different in character and appeal to what has gone before – but that does not mean they will not be as excellent. Nothing remains the same, and in a financial climate so much more restricted than Ron Morton's mid-1960s or even Aidan Plender's mini-boom of the late 80s there has been a real possibility that the concerts at Huddersfield Town Hall would be abandoned. The Hallé Orchestra has traditionally been more committed to local authority concert series than other orchestras and is deeply concerned about the problem, for Huddersfield and elsewhere.

With the appointment of Mark Elder as Hallé Music Director and John Summers as Chief Executive – formerly Chief Executive of Northern Sinfonia who has a clear and experienced understanding of Yorkshire's concert series – a new chapter in the story of Huddersfield Town Hall concerts is about to begin.

CHRIS ROBINS

The writer gratefully acknowledges the assistance he has received from Brian Haigh, Brian Pearson, Aidan Plender, Adrian Smith and, above all, from Ron Morton.

Music Businesses

Banks of York

1756 was an important year in musical history, for it saw the birth of W A Mozart – and Banks Music...

In York, John Camidge returned to his home city, allegedly having been taught music by Dr Maurice Greene and Handel at the Chapel Royal. He immediately took over as organist at the Minster, the first of three famous generations of Camidges in that post. Also on 29 June of that year, the York Courant printed an announcement which heralded the beginning of a new era in the city's music: the shop which was to become Banks Music. It was to be the start of a line of music publishing in the city which continues to this day. Musician, instrument maker and businessman, Thomas Haxby was a man of many talents – today you can see one of his harpsichords in the replica of the original shop that is part of the York Castle Museum.

Thomas Haxby's premises can still be easily identified if one looks up at the 18th century rainheads topping the fall pipes from the roof-gutters in Blake Street: the relevant ones are initialled 'T H' and dated 1773. Haxby built up an impressive retail business whilst developing a more important musical factory. Eventually his attention to the manufacture and repair of keyboard instruments became the priority, and he sought a purchaser of the retail side of the trade. In due course, one Samuel Knapton, a hairdresser born in 1756, bought the business in 1788 and transferred it to other premises in Blake Street. Samuel Knapton was a 'cellist and was highly respected in York musical circles; he became known as 'the father' of the York Musical Society, of which he was for some time president. When his son, Philip, came of age he joined his father in the business. He too

was a hairdresser – indeed a 'barber surgeon', whose work encompassed much more than mere 'hair care'. He played the organ at St Sampson's Church and composed music which was published nationally. A number of his songs achieved widespread popularity, including *Caller Herring*, *Clan McGregor* and the ballad, *Ah Country*. His book of psalm and hymn tunes went into several editions, sold not only in York but also in London by major music publishers such as Chappell's and D'Almaine's.

In 1803 the Knaptons relocated the shop in Coney Street, where it was to stay until the Banks era began in 1855. It was they who developed the publishing side of the music business in which the firm of Banks has since specialised. Examples of their sheet music can be seen in York City Library

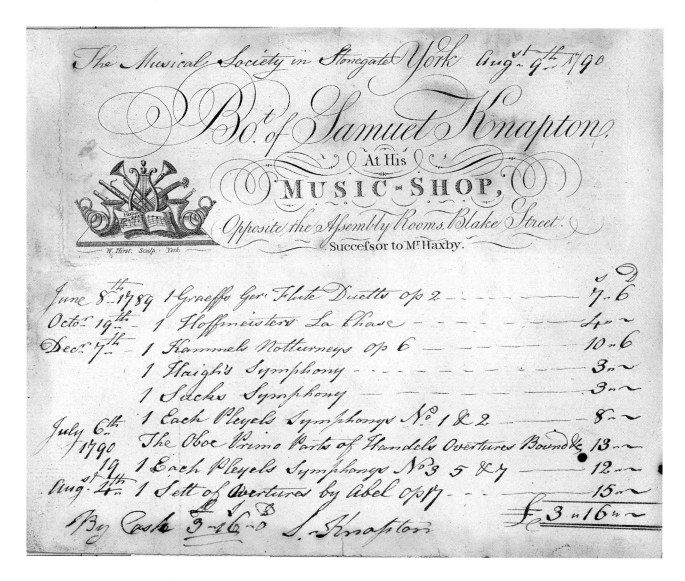

and they also occasionally turn up in antiquarian bookshops. Samuel Knapton, having sold the business in 1829, died two years later at the age of 74. Philip Knapton continued his career as a professional musician, but his energetic life undermined his health and he died in 1833 at the age of only 44. Portraits of both Knaptons (Samuel with his 'cello) hang in the 'camera cantorum' at York Minster Choir School

From a surviving inventory taken at the time of the sale of the firm, we have a clear idea of the nature and extent of its trade. The total stock was valued at £1,764/5/8d and included a wide variety of keyboard, string and wind instruments and also harps. Most of these instruments are familiar today, but others have long been obsolete – flageolets, flageolet flutes, keyed bugles and barrel organs. The shop also stocked printed music,

ruled paper, reeds and strings, all very much as can be found in Banks Music today.

The next family to take on this singular York music trade was the Hardmans, who like the Knaptons had begun their careers as hairdressers (and periwig makers). They lived in Blake Street, where they also ran tea and oyster-rooms. William was the eldest of the four sons of Edmund Hardman (a peruke maker) all of whom played stringed instruments: William himself played viola, John and James, the violin and Daniel, cello and bass – a veritable family string quartet. Both John and Daniel were 'city waits' (musicians by appointment to the Lord Mayor); with the trumpeter James Walker, Daniel laid the foundations of the modern brass band in 1833. William was indeed an accomplished musician and contributed to music-making in the city throughout his life.

He played in orchestras at Selby Abbey, Westminster Abbey and in the Great Yorkshire Festival orchestra of 1823, alongside his brother, John, and Philip Knapton. He directed the small orchestra in the church of St Martin le Grand and contributed to race-day entertainments at the Assembly Rooms with his Quadrille Band accompanying the dancing. In 1838, his own set of quadrilles was performed by his band in the Egyptian room at the Assembly Rooms on the occasion of the coronation of Queen Victoria. He also produced a piano reduction of these, which still exists.

William Hardman died in 1855 and the firm was purchased by Henry Banks, the first of five generations to develop it. Born on Christmas Day

Banks Music in Stonegate

1821, Henry was probably the son of Christopher Banks, a bookseller and stationer. He became an employee in the Hardman business in 1840. Having purchased the stock, he almost immediately transferred the firm to 3, Stonegate. Some time after 1904, the firm moved to 2, Stonegate – a most advantageous corner-site, looking directly on to St Helen's Square: this was to remain the Banks address until 1985. Henry is reputed to have put all his energy into the music-selling profession, building his shop into the finest in the north of England. In his capacity as concert organiser for the city he came into contact with all the great musicians of his time. Like his predecessor Philip Knapton he was a church organist, at

BELOW Judith Thorpe, Banks' present proprietor
RIGHT Aunt 'Jan' outside Banks in Stonegate

COMPANY TREE

Thomas Haxby (1730-1796)
started the firm in 1756

Samuel Knapton (1756-1831)
took over in 1788

William Hardman (1792-1855)
took over in 1829

Henry Banks (1821-1881)
took over in 1856

Louis Henry Banks (1849-1934)
took over in 1881

Cecil Golightly Banks (1880-1960)
took over in 1934

Peter Dresser Banks (1909-1977)
took over in 1945

Janet Marie Banks (1907-1980)
took over in 1945

Judith Thorpe (1936-)
took over in 1986

various times holding appointments at Anglican, Methodist and Roman Catholic churches.

He married a Miss Theresa Golightly (whence came the unusual middle name of his grandson) and they had two sons, both musical. The elder, William, received his tuition in York until the local teachers could do no more. He was sent off to the conservatoire in Leipzig for a thorough musical education so that when he returned to York, he was able to pursue a successful career as music teacher and composer. Louis Henry Banks, born in 1849, was a boy chorister at the Minster and learned piano and organ. When his father died in 1881, Louis took over the business and continued to run it until his death in 1934. It was he and his son, Cecil Golightly, who really made something of the publishing side of the business, building up stocks of sheet music which gave Banks of York a world-wide reputation. From 1945 the firm was in the hands of Peter Dresser Banks (who looked after the publishing side) and his sister, the redoubtable Janet (known affectionately as Aunty Jan), who was in charge of the retailing operation. The current owner, Mrs Judith Thorpe, a niece of Peter and Janet, took over in 1986. By this time, former employees had become directors, and in a move to keep pace with modern developments, the firm left Stonegate and occupied larger premises at 18, Lendal, York, which offered improved public facilities while retaining the homely approach so valued by its regular customers.

In September 2000, Banks Music completed the refurbishment of the first floor Sheet Music department. It now has a revolutionised and modern look, together with a unique design. Tucked away in the corner of its first floor department, you will find a family-run coffee lounge where you can sit down to a fresh cup of coffee or tea, and a slice of freshly-baked cake and browse through the Groves and text books at you leisure. According to customers, it is well worth a visit!

Today Banks' interests extend through all aspects of music. As one of the largest 'collecting houses' in Britain, it stocks the imprints of almost every music publisher, compact discs and tapes, and string, wind and keyboard instruments. Its world-wide mail-order department supplies customers as far away as America, Africa, Australia and most of Europe – and just about every corner in Great Britain. The firm also services and supplies most of the education authorities and colleges in the north of England, many other parts of the country, and international schools. As 'industrial' members of the Schools Music Association, Banks arranges music courses and other musical events all over England and provides displays at a number of important festivals for the benefit of concert-goers who wish to follow the scores of the music being performed.

In 1994 a new Hi-Tech department was created to serve the needs of the modern musician and composer of every kind, providing music software for computers and electronic instruments.

A large staff possessing a wide range of specialist knowledge is on hand to meet the needs of anyone interested any aspect of music, and customers can be assured of a helpful and friendly welcome. A day spent browsing in the Lendal premises of this old-established firm is like having a personal introduction to the York of some 200 years ago, a York in which then, as now, it played a most important part.

To Miss Banks Sincerely yours
Henry J. Wood
Queen's Hall, May – 1936!

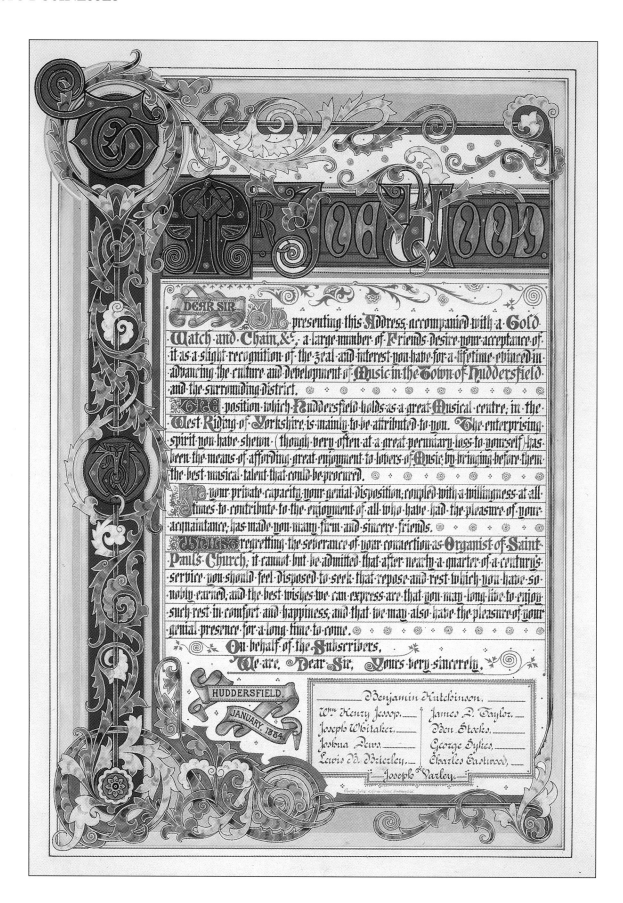

J Wood and Sons Ltd (Bradford)

'…The position which Huddersfield holds as a great Musical centre, in the West Riding of Yorkshire, is mainly to be attributed to you. The enterprising spirit you have shewn (though very often at a great pecuniary loss to yourself) has been the means of affording great enjoyment to lovers of Music, by bringing before them the best musical talent that could be procured…'

So runs, in part, an illuminated address which was presented, together with a gold watch to Joe Wood in January, 1884, on the occasion of his retirement as organist and choirmaster of St Paul's, Huddersfield, a position he had held since 1861. His work as a church organist was, however, as the address made clear, merely one aspect of a lifetime's devotion to music.

Born in Halifax in 1826, Joe was the son of a former army bandsman, whose wife inherited some property in Huddersfield. They proceeded to rebuild the property, and the large music room which he added soon became a prominent feature of the Huddersfield concert scene.

Music was thus part of Joe's life from his birth. He was something of a musical prodigy: by the age of seven he had learned to play french horn, trumpet and piano, played percussion in the Huddersfield Old Band and later took up the organ, his first church appointment on this instrument coming at the age of 13. (In this respect, however, he was to be eclipsed by Albert Lister

Joseph Wood, the firm's founder. OPPOSITE *the illuminated address presented to him in 1884*

PIANO Warehouse, JOE WOOD & SONS BEETHOVEN HOUSE 39, New St., Huddersfield.

J. WOOD & SONS,
Piano Makers, Importers and Dealers,

Offer the most favourable terms for Cash or by Instalments. They have now a BEAUTIFUL SELECTION OF PIANOS, in all the newest designs.

Instruments Tuned, Repaired, Polished, Packed, Removed or Warehoused ON MOST REASONABLE TERMS.

SOLE AGENTS FOR THE FAMOUS BECHSTEIN PIANOS.

TELEPHONE 156. And at BRADFORD. ESTABLISHED 1850.

also manufactured pianos, bringing over German technicians to train his own workforce. Despite the success of this venture (in eight years or so it is estimated that the firm produced over 4,000 instruments), he abandoned it in the face of the rising demand for more elaborate pianos (though tuning and repairs were to remain a major aspect of the business). He also went into the publication of original sheet music: the firm was to remain active in the field for over 40 years (see Judith Blezzard's article elsewhere on this). Ever quick to spot new potential markets, he was an early promoter of the phonograph (gramophone), which Thomas Edison had invented in 1877. In that year Wood extended his empire to Bradford, sending his son William to take over a music business already established there (d'Estes).

Through all this time, following his father's example, Wood became a leading concert impresario in both Huddersfield and Bradford (where in 1865 he played a major role in launching Charles Hallé's famous Subscription Concerts in the city's new St George's Hall). He was always ready to incur losses when engaging distinguished soloists who were not always 'crowd-pullers' (shortly

Peace – later to become a nationally renowned organist – who in 1853 was appointed organist at Holmfirth Parish Church when only nine).

By 1850 Joe had established himself as a teacher of piano and singing and had become a leading figure in the musical life of the town. In that year he founded his music business and quickly showed that he possessed notable entrepreneurial skills Initially selling pianos, other musical instruments and sheet music, for a time he

A concert party with Joe Wood seated far right and Mrs Sunderland seated left

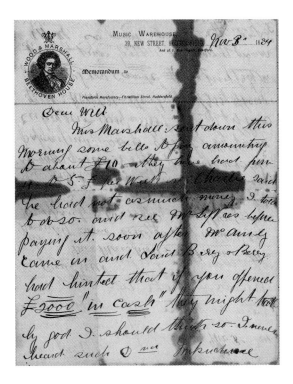

LEFT *letter from Wood to John North.* BELOW *Joshua Marshall* BOTTOM *John North*

before his death he brought the celebrated Russian pianist Pachmann to Huddersfield: there was a disappointing audience, but Wood bore the financial loss with equanimity). He was also a noted performer in his own right – as pianist, organist and singer and, indeed, comic (an enormous *Examiner* obituary notice running to many thousands of words included a reference to his 'irresistibly amusing burlesqueing of the extravagances of the Italian melodramatic operas.')

Wood's career epitomises a fascinating socio-musical phenomenon, particularly evident in Huddersfield – how a town's thriving musical life revolved around a tightly-connected handful of people. Wood's organ teacher was Henry Horn (first conductor of the Choral Society). Wood's own pupils included both Joshua Marshall and John North (two later conductors of the Choral), and both these gentlemen were to become partners in Wood's music business (it was not until 1902 that the firm reverted entirely to his sons). Wood also had strong connections himself with the Choral Society (he sometimes played violin in its 'band'), and with Ben

Stocks, a leading campaigner for the building of the Town Hall in 1881. His successor as organist of St Paul's (and possibly a pupil of either Joe Wood or John North) was Arthur Pearson, himself an important teacher of the next generation of Huddersfield organist/conductors.

These interlocking relationships were not always harmonious. Joshua Marshall, as well as being a musical and business colleague of Joe Wood, had also married one of the latter's daughters. Shortly after Joe Wood's death Marshall fell ill (the nature of his illness is not altogether clear, but there is evidence to suggest that it was mental rather than physical), and in 1885 he had to relinquish the conductorship of the Choral Society (John North succeeded him). Even more seriously, Joe's sons made an attempt to oust Marshall from the music business. Marshall's wife was prepared to accept this, but on condition that she be paid £2,000 in cash. Wood's letter to John North (reproduced above) expressed in no uncertain terms his angry reaction to this demand. Hoping to find support in the law he sought an opinion from a leading London lawyer: the response (also pre-

ABOVE the Piano Factory staff c1895

that he remained a partner in the firm until his death (probably in 1902). Political machinations of this kind - by no means rare in family businesses - were to recur in later years.

Succeeding generations of the Wood family have sustained the business to this day, adding, as each has emerged, radio, television, electronic instruments and so forth to their wares, whilst remaining faithful to the core provision of piano tuning and restoration, and the sale of sheet music. In the process, the firm has sometimes expanded, sometimes contracted: at various times there have been shops in Halifax, Leeds and Skipton. It has also survived three disastrous fires – two in Bradford (1905 and 1977), the other in Huddersfield.

This occurred on Friday 17 January, 1964, when the New Street premises were completely gutted with the loss of tens of thousands of pounds in instruments, records and sheet music. Remarkably, despite the speed with which the building was engulfed by flames, no lives were lost. Equally remarkably, the next day's *Examiner*

served in the Wood archives) made it clear to the Wood brothers that they had in fact attempted to do something which was legally quite indefensible. How the matter was resolved is not clear, though it is known that Marshall recovered his health and

carried the headline 'Woods to Reopen on Monday': the owners of a nearby vacant building had offered the premises for temporary use, and Midland Bank had provided £100.00 to ease cash-flow problems. Mr C R Wood, the managing director, assured the staff that their jobs would be safe: meeting them in a nearby café he told them that 'you will be required to turn up on Monday morning, and you will be recompensed for any loss of belongings and wages' His son, Richard, recalls being summoned from the Bradford shop to come to Huddersfield as quickly as possible, and finding a smouldering wreck on his arrival. He was able the next day to recover many of the firm's records and the firm's ledgers which had survived the blaze.

MUSIC BUSINESSES

Much the most significant developments in recent years have taken place in the firm's Bradford arm. In 1968, Richard Wood, the founder's great-great-grandson, saw the great commercial potential of the burgeoning 'Early Music' movement: since then, the Bradford Early Music Shop (now with a branch in London) has developed into the country's leading supplier, now known the world over, of every conceivable 'period' instrument (recorders, viols and spinets, theorbos and citterns – the list is endless).

Another coming trend spotted by Richard Wood was the emergence of the computer-based organ. In conjunction with the University of Bradford Wood's have made the 'Bradford Computer Organ' with its remarkably faithful reproduction of the sounds of the pipe organ a leader in this field also. Five English cathedrals have now installed these instruments

In 1995, the firm was demerged into two separate companies. The original J Wood & Sons Ltd, now in its 150th year, operates in Bradford (with Gough and Davy's, its Hull branch); the other in Huddersfield with its Wakefield branch. More recently J Wood & Sons Ltd has merged with G A Williams of Darlington and Newcastle, together forming one of the strongest musical businesses in the country.

It is a sad fact of 'progress' that virtually all the independent music businesses which flourished at the end of the 19th century (Bradford, for instance, had no fewer than 46, Halifax, 18, and Huddersfield, 14) have long since disappeared. One can only speculate as to why J Wood & Sons Ltd has proved to be a rare survivor: could the simple reason be that the firm originated in Huddersfield?

BELOW the fire of 1964. Photo HUDDERSFIELD EXAMINER

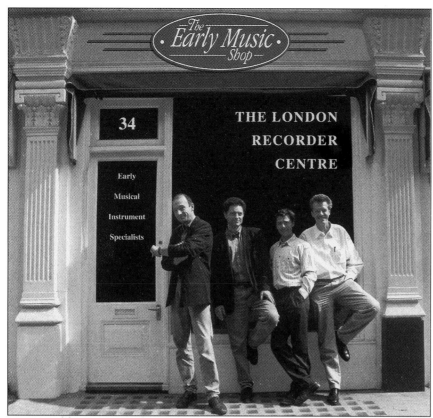

BELOW *staff outing in Whitby to mark the firm's 100th anniversary and* LEFT *the Early Music Shop, London*

Banks Music Publications

Banks Music Publications was established by Ramsay Silver (1931-1996). He worked for Oxford University Press for several years as publishing manager and in 1972 was offered and bought the publishing side of Banks Music, York. Shortly afterwards he made the decision to specialise in choral music, including archive work for Oxford University Press.

Banks Music Publications is now regarded as the most comprehensive service available for the supply of choral items. Since Ramsay's death in 1996 the company has remained within the Silver family and is managed by his wife Margaret.

Banks has a thriving publishing programme: the Eboracum Choral Series is a successor to the original York Series, and contains music mainly by modem composers and arrangers and now numbers over 400 titles. Dr Francis Jackson, the highly respected Yorkshire composer and organist, has been the series' general editor for many years. In addition to choral music, Banks publish a select number of pieces for organ, piano, voice and other solo instruments.

Their office and showroom is situated in Sand Hutton, a small village situated amidst idyllic surroundings in the North Yorkshire countryside. They have a unique choral centre, where customers are encouraged to browse through thousands of choral titles. There is a piano and a two-manual organ available to assist them in their task of choosing repertoire. The Banks staff are friendly, knowledgeable and dedicated and are happy to advise on the selection of pieces.

The firm have specialised in choral music for many years and are now able to offer the most comprehensive service available for the supply of choral items. The appreciation shown by so many of their customers prompted them to build on their reputation, and they have created the first Choral Centre in Britain. They have copies of most choral leaflets currently in print in this country, along with thousands of titles that have been out of print for years, and which they have made available again. They provide Archive works for Oxford University Press, IMP and smaller publishers.

Organs & Organ Builders

INTRODUCTION

An important amount of music-making, mostly amateur, goes on in church and chapel. There are probably more non-professionals playing the organ in public than any other instrument except the piano. According to the National Pipe Organ Register (which is not yet complete), there are at least 560 organs in the West Riding today. Nor is this a recent phenomenon; it is recorded that, as far back as the 1550s, there were 19 organs in parish churches in the East Riding.

Nevertheless, a large proportion of the organs in West Yorkshire were constructed for the many nonconformist chapels which sprang up in the prosperous nineteenth century, often with the benefit of patronage from the mill-owners. initially some chapel congregations regarded organs as too redolent of the established church, but the practical considerations of leading a large body of hymn-singing overcame their reluctance. By contrast, once the non-conformists had reconciled themselves to the use of organs in worship, they tended to purchase instruments which were considerably more ambitions that those in the established church. An organ originally built in 1880 for a Baptist chapel in Shipley now graces Guildford Cathedral, in Surrey.

Although most organs installed before 1800 had been made in London, organ-building workshops were established in Manchester and York in the eighteenth century and, in 1824, Joseph Booth founded his business in Wakefield, building large organs for Brunswick Chapel (1828) and St Peter's Chapel (1838), both in Leeds. These two instruments were considered very advanced for their date and were of a size surpassing most cathedral organs of the time. By 1870, over twenty firms trading as organ-builders were listed in West Riding trade directories. As in most areas of endeavour, initial expansion was followed by consolidation. This was accelerated, in the case of organ-building, by the introduction of steam-powered woodworking machinery. If a firm was not big enough to afford a steam engine it could not compete, one London organ-builder going bankrupt in 1885 as a direct consequence.

One external event had a profound influence on Yorkshire organ-building, giving locally-made organs a distinct difference in sound from those made further south. In 1862 Doncaster Parish Church made the daring decision to buy an organ from Edmund Schulze, of Paulinzelle in Thuringia, Germany. His father had exhibited an organ at the Great Exhibition of 1851 (at the invitation of Prince Albert) which had been widely admired. Edmund Schulze later went on to build the organ now in St Bartholomew's Church, Armley, Leeds, which retains a national reputation to this day. After the Doncaster organ was completed, Schulze's 'voicer' (the craftsman who gives an organ its final sound) decided to stay on in England and joined the East Riding organ-building form of Forster & Andrews, bringing

Wood of Huddersfield organ, St Paul's, Armitage Bridge

Schulze's forthright voicing style with him. With their overhanging galleries, nonconformist chapels soak up sound so a slightly smaller (and therefore more economical) instrument that, boldly-voiced, could nevertheless fill the chapel with sound was highly popular with the money-conscious mill-owners who often provided the finance. As a result this voicing style was copied by other successful organ-builders in Yorkshire and was characteristic of the work of Peter Conacher of Huddersfield, of

Abbott (later Abbott & Smith) of Leeds, Wordsworth & Maskell of Leeds, Laycock & Bannister of Keighley, Brindley & Foster of Sheffield and, in the twentieth century, J J Binns of Leeds.

Some of these firms attained a considerable size, Forster & Andrews making an average of twenty-five organs a year between 1865 and 1900, and requiring a work-force of well over 100 men. The most successful Yorkshire organ-builders gained reputations and customers which were much more than purely local. J J Binns' best-known organ is in the Albert Hall, Nottingham, Forster & Andrews sent organs to South Africa, Australia and South America and their instrument in Ter Aar Church, Amsterdam is still highly prized. Some years ago, when in Vancouver Island, in Canada, this writer came across a Peter Conacher organ of about 1880, still in original condition.

An organ-builder has to be multi-talented. He needs musical skills, abilities with mechanism and woodworking, plus the necessity entrepreneurial energy to make the business flourish. It is thus inevitable that organ-building firms rise and fall as peoples' careers mature. In some cases the sons of the founders were able to make a contribution but often, after the retirement of their principals, organ-building firms either changed hands or went into decline.

The story of the Conacher firm illustrates this well. Founded by Peter Conacher in 1854, the firm prospered, moving to larger workshops in 1859, 1873 and 1910. Peter Conacher's brother split off in 1879 to form a rival concern but Peter's son continued the company until his death in 1913. The third generation was not very interested and the management passed to James Stott who, in the 1920s, took up the manufacture of organs for the silent cinemas, becoming number three in the UK and the only maker outside London.

What of organ-building in the West Riding today? The chapel and church building boom, characteristic of the years before 1914, no longer exists, so the demand for new instruments is much smaller than it was a hundred years ago. Technological changes have meant that the economies of scale are also much less than they were; portable electric tools obviate the need for steam engines! The result is that there are probably just as many firms of organ-builders in the area

today as one hundred years ago but that they are all relatively small concerns. Probably the largest is the firm of Wood of Huddersfield, founded in 1966 when Philip Wood broke away from Conacher's, and now run by his son David. This company regularly manufactures new instruments, its most recent being for a school chapel in London. Others in the area include John Clough of Bradford (who has a national reputation for the leather parts of organ mechanisms), and Peter Wood, formerly of Wood Wordsworth (successors to Wordsworth & Maskell of Leeds) and now based near Harrogate, as well as Andrew Carter in Wakefield and Malcolm Spink in Leeds. The most unusual firm is that of David Leach, housed in part of the 1910 Conacher factory at Springwood, Huddersfield, who makes small exquisitely-finished self-playing mechanical organs with the music stored on floppy disk instead of perforated paper rolls. The original Conacher firm, now owned by John Sinclair Willis, today specialises in providing internet facilities for musicians and musical instrument makers.

But it doesn't end there! Organ-building is mostly a woodworking craft and the manufacture of metal pipes (mostly of tin/lead alloy) is a separate trade. There are also three companies in the Leeds area who specialise in making metal organ pipes which they supply to organ-builders for use in new instruments. F J Rogers Ltd, established in 1897 and now owned by the Buckle family, is a considerable enterprise. Organ pipes made in Bramley can be found in new instruments as far away as Japan and the United States of America as well as in the new organ in the crypt chapel of the Houses of Parliament in London.

Although not as well known as the brass bands and choirs of the area, organ-building developed a distinctive voice in the West Riding and one which, under very different conditions, still survives today.

John Norman

John Norman studied organ under H A Roberts and acoustics under Dr W B Stephens. He worked on seven cathedral organs before leaving full-time organ-building and has been a professional organ consultant since 1978. He is a member of the Cathedrals' Fabric Commission for England.

John Clough

John Clough's organ-building career started after leaving school when he was apprenticed to the well-known firm of Driver & Haigh in Bradford. He worked there as a junior for three years until he was called up for National Service in 1955. He spent his National Service career in the band of the 5th Royal Inniskillen Dragoon Guards but on de-mob he joined the well known Huddersfield firm of Peter Conacher as an organ builder. It was there that he learned the craft that was to stand him in good stead in future years in bellows-making. In 1965 he was invited to join the firm of J W Walker & Sons of London as their Yorkshire representative. He covered the county as Walker's representative and supervised all the work that was done on the York Minster organ during its major restoration in the years 1967-74.

In 1975, ten years after he had joined J W Walkers, the entire external staff was made redundant to make way for a new regime, and this was the point that John chose to form his own firm. He was joined later by his two sons, Richard and David. The firm of John Clough has a reputation for quality work largely in restorations and rebuilds and now looks after several important organs in the region, particularly Bradford

RIGHT Bandsman John Clough sitting at the console of the Royal Albert Hall organ

FAR RIGHT in Bradford Cathedral

Cathedral, Halifax Parish Church and others. In addition to his noted reputation for excellence in leather work John carries out restorations of bellows, feeders &c for the trade, which form a major input into the restoration of important organs amongst them the famous Willis organ in Huddersfield Town Hall.

John has a lifetime interest in brass banding. He spent 28 years playing the euphonium and baritone in Black Dyke and later with the Sellers band. A photograph showing John in banding uniform and sitting at the organ console of the Royal Albert Hall illustrates his interest in both fields.

Peter Wood & Son (Harrogate)

The proprietors of the firm are Peter Wood, the third generation with his son Mark, the fourth generation of this Leeds Organ Building family.

Peter Wood's grandfather John Wood, joined the company of Wordsworth & Maskell, established in 1866, as foreman progressing to become a partner with the creation of Wood Wordsworth & Co. Ltd. Many organs were constructed up to the outbreak of World War I. On average one organ a week was being manufactured for the home market and export all over the world by a workforce of over one hundred men.

Two of the most notable early achievements were the four-manual instrument in Epping Parish Church and St Margaret's Church. Kings Lynn, rebuilding the famous Snetzlcr organ. Many of the ease designs were created from an association with the Reverend F H Sutton and the architects Bodley & Garner. The most technically advanced was a four-manual organ built in 1889 for Rudston Parish Church near Bridlington, combining a detached console with the first completely electric-action instrument outside London and now recently rebuilt by his descendants.

The tonal style of these organs in the Victorian and Edwardian periods followed the trend of

By Appointment
to The 11th Duke of Marlborough

The largest house organ in Europe

ABOVE *the console of the famous Willis Organ in Blenheim*

OPPOSITE *the restored 1884 Abbott organ by Principal Pipe Organs in St Michael's Church, Barton-le-Street, nr Malton. Photo KEN SHELTON*

English organ building, but changed with some continental influence, to the characteristic style that the company became noted for.

John Wood's youngest son, John William, continued the partnership after the First War so surviving one of the most difficult periods in organ-building, utilising his skills and adapting pneumatic action to his many creations, the most notable of which was the three-manual organ at St George's Crypt in Leeds. The rebuild of the Leeds Town Hall organ at this time was amongst the firm's most notable achievements.

Wood Wordsworth ceased trading in March 1981 but, with his son Mark, Peter Wood created the current business in Harrogate, converting an old flax farm with its many barns and outhouses into workshops, surrounded by an idyllic habitat. Trading has flourished here for nearly twenty years, concentrating mainly on classical and his-

toric restorations and major rebuilds, including an instrument for the new Leeds Grammar School, a large concert organ reconstructed from an original 1912 J J Binns.

An interesting new market has been developed in Japan where English-style weddings are now the fashion. This requires the building of pseudo-English bridal churches all over Japan, complemented with artefacts from the UK such as pews, altars, pulpits, stained glass windows and of course the pipe organ. Redundant organs are acquired, completely restored and refurbished and installed in these churches.

Peter Wood & Son has been associated with Blenheim Palace and its organs for over twenty years. He is restoring in stages the famous 1898 Willis organ in the Long Library – a schedule of work which is likely to last a further five years.

Principal Pipe Organs

Geoffrey Coffin's career as an organ builder sprang from his background as a musician and organist.

He was organ scholar at Emmanuel College Cambridge, then became Administrator of The National Youth Orchestra of Great Britain before being appointed assistant organist to Dr Francis Jackson at York Minster in 1971.

During this time he also worked for J W Walker and Sons Ltd, as a tuner and organ builder and subsequently represented the firm as Northern Manager and later as Contracts Manager at their Suffolk factory.

An opportunity arose in 1983 to establish Principal Pipe Organs. Early expansion has continued steadily and the firm currently has six full-time and other part-time workshop staff, many of whom are active musicians. Restoration of mainly mechanical action instruments forms the nucleus of the firm's work together with the production of new organs with mechanical key action.

In only seventeen years it has gained an enviable reputation for musical integrity and the highest standards of craftsmanship and is in wide demand.

In 1992-93 an enlarged PPO team undertook the complete restoration of the 1903 Walker organ in York Minster (four manuals and 69 speaking stops), including additional new slider soundboards and speaking stops. The completed scheme extends to 81 speaking stops (5,282 pipes) and continues to receive high critical acclaim.

Other work of particular interest in recent years has included new two manual and pedal organs for St Johns Church, Baildon, the mediaeval church of All Saints' North Street, York and the newly built Church of the Ascension, Middlesbrough.

The PPO team has also undertaken the historic restoration of other important instruments, including an early (c.1850) Father Willis originally made for Apsley House, the Duke of Wellington's London home. It has also recently restored the same builder's 1890 three-manual and pedal organ made for St Martin's Church, Scarborough.

The PPO workshops are situated on a trading estate just outside the York city walls.

new instrument in 1968, and a series of practice/chamber organs soon followed. The firm's first major new contract was for the Huddersfield Polytechnic (now University) music department – a three-manual and pedal organ of 40 stops. This significant instrument (built 1976/77) established the reputation of the growing firm.

Since that installation the company has worked on many important organs in cathedrals, churches, chapels and educational establishments all over the country. Rebuilds have included St Asaph Cathedral in North Wales and the famous Snetzler/Hill organ in Beverley Minster.

The firm has also established a reputation for fine new mechanical action instruments, the most recent being at Forest School, North-East London.

In 1976 Philip's younger son David joined the firm. Having been brought up through the workshop he has been involved in all aspects of organbuilding, and for many years he has been responsible for the voicing of all the firm's new pipework. In 1999 David became the firm's Managing Director.

Wood of Huddersfield

Philip Wood was born and educated in Huddersfield, where as a boy he began organ studies with Winifred Smith FRCO. At the age of 17 he was apprenticed to the well-established Huddersfield firm of organ-builders, Peter Conacher & Co Ltd. In 1954 he was appointed representative for Northern Ireland and subsequently became the area manager for the whole of Ireland.

In 1964 he was recalled to Huddersfield to take up the position of the company's General Manager.

In 1966 Philip Wood established Wood of Huddersfield (organ builders). He built his first

LEFT *Forest School*
Chapel, NE
London 1999.
OPPOSITE TOP *a*
rebuild of the Hill
organ in St Asaph
Cathedral with its
new organ case,
1998
OPPOSITE BOTTOM *a*
new organ in
St Cross Clayton
1995, Manchester
Photo Greaves of
HUDDERSFIELD

INDEX/GAZETTEER

INDEX/GAZETTEER

INDEX/GAZETTEER